BE MY WITNESSES

THE CHURCH'S MISSION,
MESSAGE, AND MESSENGERS

Darrell L. Guder

WILLIAM B. EERDMANS PUBLISHING COMPANY
GRAND RAPIDS, MICHIGAN

FOR JUDY

Copyright © 1985 by William B. Eerdmans Publishing Company
255 Jefferson Ave. S.E., Grand Rapids, MI 49503

Library of Congress Cataloging in Publication Data

Guder, Darrell L., 1939-
Be my witnesses.

Bibliography: p.
1. Church. 2. Mission of the church. 3. Evangelistic work. I. Title.
BV600.2.G83   1985   262   85-10129

ISBN 0-8028-0051-3

CONTENTS

72330

PREFACE

This is a book about the church and its mission. I might as well have said, "This is *another* book about the church and its mission." It has been a long time in coming, because I have been wary about adding more paper and print to the already vast discussion of the church "out there." In the last few years, however, I have sensed that perhaps my own experience in the church (better, the churches) and my own pilgrimage in ministry might become a helpful contribution to the discussion of the church. My intention, then, is to contribute to the church's continuing study of its mission, with the hope that, if there is any discussion of what I am advancing here, my approach will be helpful.

Although the study of dogmatics, and especially the theology of the church (ecclesiology), is my particular field of interest, I suspect that this book is more a work of "irregular dogmatics" than "regular dogmatics." Karl Barth defines "irregular dogmatics" as the kind of theology done outside of a particular theological school, and without any intent to cover the discipline exhaustively (see *Church Dogmatics,* I/1, pp. 275ff.). He also says that "irregular dogmatics" "nearly always tend to be strongly influenced by the person and biography of their authors" (ibid., p. 279). Certainly that is true in this instance.

This book is a summary of my "biography with the church" until now. Since much of my work has been with Christian men and women who are deeply involved in ministry but who are not ordained, I have written with them in mind. I hope that this "irregular" book will stand the test of strict dogmatic and scholarly review, but I have chosen to do without the more obvious marks of such scholarship. There are no footnotes, very few citations, and an absolute minimum of non-English terminology. To say that this is a book for "the educated laity" (however we define them) should not render it uninteresting to the members of the theological guild. But I strongly feel that responsible theology must be written for use in the church at large, and so that desire has guided me in the style and methods I have chosen here.

If "person and biography" are so important to works of this kind (and I think that these categories are more powerful in regular dogmatics than Barth was prepared to admit), then I should preface the book with a little personal background. My only purpose in doing so is to help the reader understand why I am taking this approach, and what kinds of experience have led to it.

My background as a Christian is in a large, conservative Presbyterian church, the First Presbyterian Church of Hollywood. My parents were deeply involved in the life and ministry of the church, and I grew up in its Sunday School; and so our family was very much an extension of that parish. The educational vision and ministry of Henrietta Mears and her associate, Ethel May Baldwin, had a strong impact on me. From early on, I learned that the service of Christ was the most exciting thing there was, and that every Christian should seek to find out God's will and follow it with total commitment.

Until the end of my third year in college, I had experienced very little of the rest of the Body of Christ, but I sensed that what I had experienced was definitive: it was what the church ought to be. When I turned nineteen, however, I had the opportunity to enlarge my experience: I went abroad to study. I originally intended to stay for a year in Germany, in order to learn the language, and then to travel to Scotland, where all good Presbyterians go. But Germany prevailed, and that first visit lasted eight years.

At the University of Hamburg, I entered into the world of Lutheran thought and life, particularly accented by the horrendous struggles of the Third Reich and its aftermath in the German church. At the same time, I began my own journey of discovery into the world of theological scholarship. It was my good fortune to be taught by scholars whose own theological work was marked by personal Christian conviction and a strong commitment to ministry. I am particularly grateful for what I learned from Leonhard Goppelt, Hans-Joachim Kraus, and Helmut Thielicke, in the classroom as well as in personal relationships.

The study of theology in an academic setting had an evangelistic effect upon me: it awakened me to dimensions of the gospel I had not yet grasped. My Lutheran friends and teachers gently taught me the meaning of grace. My Reformed mentor, Professor Kraus, helped me to appreciate the wealth of insight and enrichment of faith that applying critical tools to biblical study provides. The Lutheran church in which I lived and worked taught me much about the sacraments and ministry.

While at Hamburg I had the opportunity to do doctoral research on the question of the secularization of originally Christian American colleges (I examined Princeton as a case study). I was permitted to combine the study of theology, American language and literature, and the history of education in a very exciting and stimulating way. During that research, I began to wonder at the effects of narrow and restrictive Christian thought upon the church's mission. I observed how the so-called Princeton theology of the nineteenth century actually contributed to the secularization of that college. I found myself questioning parts of my own tradition as I discovered the evangel in other traditions, speaking freely and calling forth both faith and commitment.

At the conclusion of my doctoral program I was given an opportunity to serve in the Lutheran church of Schleswig-Holstein as the first upper-school pastor in the district of Blankenese-Pinneberg. Without ever intending it, I was entering upon a new chapter of "practical ecclesiology" and "experiential ecumenics"! My ordination by the Presbytery of Los Angeles was to a call issued by the bishop of South Holstein. My examinations were written under the supervision of the provost of Blankenese-Pinneberg, who also heard and evaluted my ordination sermon. All this was then evaluted and approved by my home church, and the final step was my oral examination before the presbytery in Los Angeles. Obviously, the constitutional issues were difficult. They had never ordained anyone to a Lutheran call, and I had never been to a Presbyterian seminary! But it was all finally approved, and I continued to work in the Lutheran church, discovering as I did how Reformed I was.

Just before embarking upon that first ministry, I asked Hendrikus Berkhof for some guidance (I was clerking for him at the General Council of the World Alliance of Reformed Churches in Frankfurt). Could I function in good conscience as a Reformed minister in a Lutheran church? Could I face an altar with a cross (perhaps even a crucifix!) on it, chant liturgies, and distribute the Lord's Supper to men and women kneeling at an altar rail? Professor Berkhof first had to stifle his astonishment that the Church of Schleswig-Holstein had actually called a Reformed minister into its service (I think there were some in the church headquarters in Kiel who were also trying to figure out how that had happened). Then he said that as a Reformed theologian, I had the freedom to minister in whatever situation God had called me.

During my stay in Germany many strands of the Christian church's diverse traditions began to weave together in my life. I often worshiped in Anglican churches throughout my years as a student—they are frequently the only English-speaking church in a European city. For one year I worshiped in a German Methodist church in Hamburg and discovered much of that tradition I had not known. In a variety of ways, I was involved in both Reformed and Lutheran churches in Germany. I became a volunteer interpreter for the World Alliance of Reformed Churches, thus entering into the marvelous and fascinating worldwide family of the Reformed faith. And while ministering in northern Germany, I also worked with the Roman Catholic agencies for youth ministry and found there partners in faith and in ministry. All of these experiences, combined with my years of ministry with German young people in the upper division of the *Gymnasium* served to help me discover that freedom about which Professor Berkhof spoke.

After three years in Schleswig-Holstein, I spent four years on the staff of my home congregation, the First Presbyterian Church of Hollywood, as minister of Christian Education. Under the gracious leadership of Raymond Lindquist, I was permitted to rediscover my own roots and engraft into my ministry the experiences I had had during the previous eight years in Germany. At Hollywood, many people in leadership positions shared a concern for the theological education of the laity. But this concern was linked with an equally great desire for the evangelistic outreach of the church. Those years, the late sixties, were marked by our encounters with the youth culture and rebellion that literally surged up and down Hollywood Boulevard, a few yards from the church.

This was a period of extreme, often puzzling contrasts in my ministry. I was going back and forth between Southern California and East Germany, where I had marvelous opportunities to meet Christians in every area of ministry, from the local parish to the bishops of the church. The questions of the "cultural bondage" of the church, which are a theme of this book, began to concern me. In many discussions, primarily with laypeople, I began to wonder about our definitions of the church's mission, its place within a culture, and its compromises with that culture. In addition, I had a growing conviction that we were not providing our membership with the kind of biblical and theological equipping they both needed and wanted in order to carry out their Christian commitments outside the congregation's organized life.

Another series of surprises led me back to Germany. I was asked to join the faculty of the diaconic college of the Church of Württemberg (in southwest Germany), preparing men and women for professional ministry in the diaconate. I did not even know what the Protestant diaconate in central Europe really was, although it has been a major force in the church there for 150 years. In the Karlshöhe College in Ludwigsburg, I taught theology and education and helped to redesign their curriculum. That experience opened many more doors of encounter with the diversity of the church. I came to know Swabian Pietism, post-Vatican II Catholic renewal, the diaconic communities of the church, and the various ministries of the ecumenical agencies in Geneva, especially the Lutheran World Federation and the World Alliance of Reformed Churches. There were even some limited opportunities to learn about the church in the Third World, especially Africa, through my work with the World Alliance.

At every turn, I found that my definitions of the church and its mission were not broad enough to include the authentic ministries and impressive Christians I was encountering. Of course, living in a foreign culture made me all the more aware of the cultural limitations of my own American Christianity. It also made me grateful for what I had experienced growing up at the Hollywood church. Gradually I began to realize that I was not going to be able to arrive at some simple synthesis.

When I finally learned that the German church was not a "state church" but an "established church," and that the very different forms of church life there were not necessarily less Christian than the voluntaristic form of church life in which I had grown up, I began to appreciate the rich diversity of Christ's body. I remember the surge of excitement I felt when I discovered that the Eucharist at an altar expresses our being Christ's guests at his table, at which he is the host, while the table fellowship of my tradition expresses the community he calls together. Both forms of celebration are valid and complementary. I needed (and still need) that diversity within my experience of worship.

Those four years at the Karlshöhe, where I was surrounded by expressions of Christian commitment to diaconic labor (homes for the handicapped, the elderly, abused youth, asocial men), taught me that evangelism cannot be merely verbal. The doing of the gospel must necessarily surround the saying of it. At the Karlshöhe College I began to teach courses on the mission and ministry of the church. I am grateful to the students there who were willing to share their visions and frustrations as we worked together to find a responsible theological foundation for the living of our lives as ministers of this church.

The final surprise in my pilgrimage in the church was the call to Young Life. I had no past experience with this mission, and I really did not know anything about the problem of so-called parachurch organizations. But the organization wanted me to come in and work on the theological education of its staff. In the process, I also was made responsible for teaching the systematic course that deals with the theology of the church. Thus, over the years I have worked with the Young Life staff to clarify their concept of the church and the churches. At the same time, these men and women, who are seeking to reach teenagers outside the faith, are looking for a theologically responsible definition of their own ministry and its relationship to the rest of the church.

Thus, as we have sought together to develop responsibly our own theological education, I have been forced to "do ecclesiology" constantly: to relate to each other the concepts of evangelism, diaconics, formal and informal ministry, community, Christian nurture, and even the sacraments in a mission that is evangelical, ecumenical, interconfessional, and yet united around the calling to present Christ to young people. The result is the Institute of Youth Ministries of Fuller Theological Seminary and Young Life.

We have had frequent opportunities to probe our understandings of the church and its ministry. In theological dialogues with the German church, we have carefully analyzed Young Life's concepts of incarnational witness and ministry. We have met with many groups of pastors and church leaders, not only to discuss the tensions between an organization like Young Life and the traditional churches, but more to talk about the evangelistic mission of the church and its theological undergirding. The Episcopal Diocese of Colorado, through its bishops, William Frey and William Wolfrum, has given me valuable opportunities to think out loud about the church and its mission. In a sense, they are the direct stimuli for this book, and I am grateful to them for their encouragement and many expressions of interest.

The network of dialogue about the church and its mission has constantly broadened. I am deeply grateful for the opportunities given to me by Young Life to serve in such a way that I could learn more from the process than I could possibly ever teach anyone else! That encouragement led to the sabbatical during which I wrote this book.

Through writing it, I have discovered again how many threads of theology and tradition have been woven together in my experience. Theologians like Barth, Thielicke, Kraus, Goppelt, Berkhof, Blauw, and Newbigin have been nurturing me since I began to discover the world of theology. Otto Weber became something of a theological mentor as I labored through the translation of his *Foundations of Dogmatics,* an experience close to going through seminary again. Robert Paul has become a friend and theological mentor through his excellent books and his interpretation to me of the complex situation of the church today.

But primarily it has been my students, mostly in the Institute of Youth Ministries but also in various adult classes at the First Presbyterian Church of Colorado Springs, who have challenged me with the need to grasp the mission of the church both in its centrality—to be Christ's witnesses—and in its complexity—to understand how vast the task of witness is. My hope is that this book will help them both to learn and to do their ministry more effectively.

At the same time, I hope that this book will contribute to the worldwide discussion of the church's mission today, especially within the Reformed family, as it pursues a crucial discussion of the theme "Called to Witness to the Gospel Today" under the auspices of the World Alliance of Reformed Churches.

Finally, I am deeply grateful to those who have provided support and encouragement during the writing of this book. I want to thank my colleagues in Young Life, especially those in my own Department of Ministry Resources, but also many others throughout the country whose questions and experiences have stimulated my thinking. Mr. Norris Aldeen, a life-member of the Young Life Board, has been a source of strong support and encouragement. Four friends, Lester Comee, James Edwards, Robert MacLennan, and Terence McGonigal, have read the manuscript and provided valuable suggestions. My mother, Eileen Guder Triplett, in my opinion one of the ablest lay theologians I know, helped me greatly by reading and critiquing the manuscript.

My final thanks goes to God's greatest and most wonderful surprise for me, my wife, Judy. She has been a constant encouragement, a source of good-humored and insightful criticism, and in every sense a partner without whom I would not and could not attempt a project of this kind. It is to her that I dedicate this book.

Karl Barth wrote, "We have seen that it is the promise and task of this proclamation to be God's Word to men" (*Church Dogmatics,* I/1,

p. 288). My prayer is that this discussion of the church's mission will lead us to consider what that verb "to be" really means—so that together all Christians, in all parts of the church around the globe, might "be his witnesses."

—Darrell L. Guder

Colorado Springs
Easter 1984

Part One

TOWARD A THEOLOGY OF THE CHURCH'S MISSION

"But you are a chosen race, a royal priesthood, a holy nation, God's own people, that you may declare the wonderful deeds of him who called you out of darkness into his marvelous light. Once you were no people but now you are God's people; once you had not received mercy but now you have received mercy."

—1 PETER 2:9–10

One

THE CHURCH'S PLACE
AND PURPOSE
IN SALVATION HISTORY

1.1 THE POWER OF THE PRESUPPOSITIONS

The God of the Bible and of biblical faith is a God who makes himself knowable. This is the central assertion of both Jewish and Christian faith, and it is my presupposition in this book. God has acted and spoken, and he has enabled people both to hear and to respond to his action and his word. Christian theology speaks of this basic fact as "revelation." God pulls aside the curtain so that those whom he has chosen to hear and to respond may recognize his action and his word as genuinely his. This entire event is called "faith"—the God-enabled hearing and responding to God's self-disclosure within our human experience, resulting in the special relationship with God for which he created us. What is for the outside observer a mere fact of history becomes for the enabled hearer the self-disclosure of God, God making himself knowable in our human experience.

For some Christians, those statements may appear to be self-evident. They might even be regarded as so obvious as not to merit mention. For other Christians, these statements may have already set off alarm signals, so that the reader is thinking, "This is clearly going to be a hopelessly conservative book with which I do not need to waste my time." The fact is that those who call themselves Christians cannot universally subscribe to even the most basic statements about the nature of the Christian faith. If this book is going to stimulate any kind of helpful discussion about the church's calling, it will be necessary first to clarify these differences and to define where I stand within the entire spectrum of Christian thought. At the very beginning, then,

I would like to describe how I perceive the situation with regard to our basic presuppositions for Christian thought, and then I would like to insure that my own approach is as clear as possible. To do this, we need to look backward in Christian history just a few centuries.

There is a kind of great divide in Christian thought about this central emphasis upon God's self-disclosure that I emphasized in the first paragraph above. Whereas it is quite clear from the long course of Christian history that God's self-revelation has been the point of departure for Christian thinking, since the onset of modern critical thought (for simplicity's sake, let us say since the eighteenth-century Enlightenment) even those in Christian circles have questioned this assumption. Part of the effect of the secularization and modernization of Western civilization has been to question the idea that God may be understood as the one who acts and speaks first. Many Christian thinkers have been unable to accept anymore the assertion that God is personally involved in history and in human experience, and that he can be known personally. Without rejecting the basic concept of God, they have drastically reworked the Christian faith, based upon the assumption that God, understood as a principle or concept, does not intrude in human affairs. They do not see him as a God who is personal, who speaks and can be heard. The general thrust of Christian faith and thought among these thinkers has tended to begin with the understanding of the human person, and then to "work upward" toward the concept of God.

The reaction to this shift in Christian thought is varied and often passionate. Losing a personal God, questioning the possibility of knowing God in a personal relationship, setting aside the possibility that God could directly intervene in human affairs—these are the results of modern critical thought that have led many parts of the church to a wholesale rejection of critical methodology. For many Christians today, the essence of orthodoxy is resistance to and rejection of the course of modern thinking. The struggles that characterize much of the church cluster around these issues of God's nature and work, and thus give rise to questions on the reliability of the biblical record as a witness to a history initiated by God and really experienced by those whose faith stories are recorded in Scripture.

However, the development of modern Christian thought, and especially of the critical theological disciplines, is not really uniform and cannot be totally confined to one particular approach. There have been and there are today many articulate intepreters of Christian thought who have not joined the mass exodus from the classical understandings of the faith, who have not concluded that modern scientific insight must mean rejecting all that is divine, personal, and transcendant in the biblical record. At the same time, many of these thinkers have found that much of the work done with the tools of critical research has been helpful in grasping more clearly the authentic meaning of the biblical witness. We can be grateful today that we have so many more resources available to us for the careful study of God's word and the accurate interpretation of its meaning for our pilgrimage.

The real issue, then, is always the presuppositions with which we are working. Although there is a danger of oversimplification here, we may make this valid distinction: If one presupposes that God cannot be properly understood as personal, that is, cannot be known in a personal relationship, as the One who has initiated and continues to initiate history for the accomplishment of his purposes, then obviously one will have to rewrite most of the major chapters of Christian theology. Such a prospect is frightening to many Christians and certainly is a threat to the great traditions of Christian interpretation summarized in our creeds and confessions. But this presupposition is a decision that some people make, which they bring to the Bible and to Christian faith and practice. However, it need not be the only presupposition with which we must work. The course of modern thinking does not force us to arrive at such conclusions . . . and certainly there are many witnesses to that fact in the Christian church today.

It is extremely important to recognize the power of such presuppositions. My students hear from me, very early on in any class I teach, that one of the most important tasks in theological study is to recognize the writer's presuppositions. They are not always clearly stated, and it may take some mental detective work to find them. But until one knows what a writer is assuming as he or she approaches the theological task, one can easily misunderstand or fail to grasp the real message being advanced by that writer. I trust that my presuppositions are clear—and based upon a response to God's self-disclosure, which is subservient to his Spirit and in substantial agreement with the "majority view" of the Christian church through the ages and around the world today.

Thus, to restate them: God is knowable and acts to make himself knowable; he is purposeful, and his purpose is to restore his sinful creation to himself; Scripture is the written witness to God's actions in history to bring about that restoration, leading toward its ultimate completion. The gospel, then, is the good news of a loving God's desire that his rebellious creation be reconciled with him, and of the action that he has taken and is carrying out now to accomplish that reconciliation. (This is the first of many attempts to define the gospel; see also Chap. 5.)

These are the basic presuppositions that the reader should understand in order to grasp why and how I am dealing with the mission of the church as I do. On the basis of these presuppositions, I am working from the persuasion that the church of Jesus Christ continues today to be the result of God's sovereign action in history, that its existence and purpose are to be understood within the context of God's purposes, and that his action is moving ahead through history toward the certain completion of what he has begun.

I am further presupposing that the biblical record authorizes us to understand God's history in the Old Covenant (or Old Testament) as an earlier part of the same history that is continued in the New Covenant (although there is much in that initial history with God's chosen people, the Jews, which is as yet not complete and is for us an open chapter, veiled in mystery). It is, therefore, both necessary and helpful to look at the Old Covenant as our history, and to understand our own place in God's action as a continuation of what God was doing then. We need to discover in the experience of Israel parallels and precedents of our experience. We may, in fact, read the faith stories of the Old Testament as experiences of the reality of God that are by no means foreign to us. We should come to know the believers in that history as people like us, as ancestors in the same historical pilgrimage, from whom we learn and gain encouragement. The use of the fruitful results of critical biblical research makes that all the more possible for us today.

This perspective on the whole sweep of salvation history from the Old Covenant to the New is needed, I think, for a very simple reason. It is not always easy to maintain "the long view" of God's purpose and work in human history. In the dailiness of our lives, the routine and mundane character of human existence as we experience it, we find ourselves losing sight of the overarching purpose and challenge of God's history with us. I have sought to imagine what it was like to be a citizen of Israel centuries before Christ. We can assume, I think, that the normal man or woman then did not move from day to day with some spiritual sense of "being chosen" and "being led by God." The routine of life jeopardized a vibrant faith as much then as it does today. The Jew living under Solomon or one of the many kings in either the

Northern or Southern Kingdom would easily find his or her faith flagging, would be more preoccupied with survival or the quality of life or with the small but real challenges of family and friends than with the great scope of Israel's call and purpose in God's salvation history.

The central events of worship and celebration in Israel were intended to refocus the entire people upon that call and purpose. The worship traditions, the writings of the nation, the people's customs and celebrations—all were part of a vast structure of memory and promise that would inspire and revive faith. But even these resources, given (as I believe) for the purpose of creating and sustaining a vibrant faith, could be diluted and distorted. Worship could become routine in the temple in Jerusalem just as easily as in the local church today. Faith as life's focus could become just as marginal in Israel as it is in the Christian church today. We are the same basic humans, with the same sinfulness and spiritual weakness now as then. Thus, we read the prophets in the Old Testament as powerful critics of *our* reality, although they are directly addressing the shortcomings of Israel in another time and in very different circumstances.

After twenty centuries of pilgrimage through time, the Christian community necessarily struggles with the same problem: keeping our eyes focused upon our purpose in God's salvation history. It is realistic comfort to see that the New Testament church already addressed this issue. We see in the Catholic Epistles (1, 2, and 3 John, 1 and 2 Peter, James, and Jude) as well as in the letters to the seven churches in St. John's Revelation, that the early Christian congregations faced very similar problems as soon as they moved on to their own second generation. When the generation of those who converted to Christianity from paganism became the older generation, and began raising their children in this new faith, the threatening power of routine, dailiness, and the dilution of commitment began to be felt in the church. This is not surprising; it is, in fact, an essential aspect of the way in which God works in history—through the human, the normal, and the routine. A great part of the challenge of the church is to understand properly our calling: to see it as a calling to obedience in the mundane historical situations in which we spend most of our lives.

And yet, we are intended to know and to be gripped by the awareness that all that is happening in our world is under God's sovereign rule and is being drawn by him to his certain conclusion. The mission of the church is being carried out in a world in which appearances will always be deceiving. The church itself, as God's instrument, can be recognized as such only through the gift of faith. The ancient church taught us to confess that we "believe (in) the church." In the older language of Western faith, the church said *"Credo ecclesiam"*—I believe that the church is God's "chosen race, a royal priesthood, a holy nation." And we believe this over against the out-wardly visible—yet hardly persuasive—evidence. With regard to the mission and work of the church, the nature of faith remains the same— it is faith, not sight. But it is to be *informed* faith, faith that is truly a response to God's actions and words, and not a conviction we have conjured up in ourselves to meet our needs.

Therefore, as we seek to work out our understanding of the mission of the church today, we want to be careful to work from the scriptural witness, under its tutelage and control.

It will not help to discuss the church, after these twenty centuries, and yet ignore the contradictions, the weaknesses, and the disappoint-ments that the church presents to us. Our grasp of the church's mission must deal honestly with this "scornful wonder" (to use Leslie Glenn's fine phrase). What we will discover is that the humanity and the frailty of the church are genuinely a part of its divine-human nature. Properly understood, the "fleshly" aspect of the church is an essential aspect of the way it continues the meaning and reality of incarnation.

1.2 CALLED TO SERVE

The call of Abraham in Genesis 12 is usually regarded as the beginning of salvation history, understood as God's actions in human history to bring about his intended reconciliation of his creation to himself. But the background to that major event is found in the first eleven chapters of the Bible, the "prehistory." The best place to begin our study of the church's mission is at the beginning, with the founda-tions of the biblical witness found in the first chapters of the Bible.

For our purposes here, we want to address one major theme from these basic accounts in Genesis 1-11. These records were passed on, as we know, as Israel's confession of faith about God's initiation of all human history. And yet, Israel does not play a major role in this prehistory. The early Genesis accounts are "universal" in scope—that is, they deal with God's foundational purposes for all creation, for all humanity, for all history. Adam ("man" in Hebrew) is the figure of all humanity, not just of Jewish or Christian humanity. All of God's human creatures are made "in his image." All receive the great creation com-mand to tend and order and subdue this marvelous creation in obedience to God's good purposes. And yet, all of this creation has rebelled and finds itself in opposition to its Creator.

For our grasp of the church's mission, it is important to begin with the fact that God's purposes in creation and in salvation are universal: God has the whole world in view, even as he carries out his work through those few (the patriarchs, a people, a remnant) whom he chooses. This universal scope of Genesis 1-11 is carried through in the New Testament with its frequent reference to "the world"—"God so loved the world that he gave his only Son"; "in Christ God was reconciling the world to himself" (John 3:16; 2 Cor. 5:19). When we approach the task of understanding the mission of the church, we do so from the perspective of a whole creation separated from its Creator and yet loved and sought out by that same Creator. The course of salvation history is God's action to reconcile this creation to himself.

Thus, when God calls Abraham to make of him and his descendants a blessing, the universal scope of God's action is emphasized: "By you all the families of the earth will bless themselves" (Gen. 12:3; cf. 22:15-18; 26:3-5). The call of Abraham and the setting apart of the nation that he founded, Israel, is dealt with in Christian thought under the topic "Election." The term refers to the fact that God's actions in salvation history include his choosing some people to carry out his purposes—for the benefit of all. Election, understood biblically, is God's purposeful action within the total scope of his gracious desire to save his erring creation. Thus, Israel is not called, or elected, for its own benefit, to be a special religious culture that is to enjoy privileges not given to anyone else. Rather, Israel's election is functional to God's universal saving purposes.

Election is a calling to service. God calls, and enables the response to his call, not solely for the benefit of the one called, but for a greater purpose, for which the called-out ones are now enlisted and enabled. Certainly, those who experience this call encounter God in a relationship filled with blessing and enrichment. They are "blessed in order to be a blessing." Their knowledge of God sets them apart from the rest of the creation. Their insight into God's purposes, as he has disclosed them, gives them a unique serenity and peace. Their portion of blessing includes the gift of God's guidance for the structuring of their entire lives, so that they already experience the firstfruits of that restoration and salvation which is God's purpose for all. The chosen people receive the Ten Commandments as a restatement of God's creation purposes for the world. And in Israel, these commandments can become a reality, making of Israel a beacon light of justice and goodness for the world—now as well as then.

Yet the blessing experienced by the called must never be emphasized at the cost of the reason for the calling. The blessing received is a form of divine equipping for the task, the service to which Israel, and later the church, is called. We pervert election whenever we separate the blessing from its function as a way in which God enables the called to serve. The result is spiritual arrogance, a sense of religious specialness that leads the called to raise even higher the walls of separation from the rest of the "uncalled world," to protect themselves from profanation, and to avoid the very service to which they have been called. Ultimately, this one-sided emphasis must result in a preoccupation with one's own salvation, or one's fitness for salvation.

When the called-out ones lose sight of the purpose for their calling, they begin to think that the calling was given so that they might be saved. They lose the universal view of God's purposes, and make of God a provincial deity whose major occupation is saving these chosen ones. They begin to struggle with the logic of God's decisions, trying to work out a rationale for all those who are not called and thus not saved. They assume a rigorous division in God's purposes, in which he directs his love to some and his wrath to all the rest. They even begin to work out the evidences that they are saved, and they become obsessed with their own spirituality or lack of it.

It is this perversion of the understanding of calling against which our Lord is speaking in his polemic addresses directed to the "Pharisees." He is not denouncing all Jewish devotion, nor all of the entirely admirable and imitable aspects of the learned piety of the Pharisees. But he is radically rejecting the idea that God's election is to the privileged enjoyment of God's blessing, separate from God's purpose to save his entire creation. Jesus is addressing the misunderstanding of election in his day, which has emerged constantly in the history of the church.

Another way to speak of this is in terms of the "benefits" and the "mission" of God's calling. Those whom God calls experience the benefits of that call, that is, the goodness and the spiritual excitement of knowing God and sharing in his love and grace (which is really what "blessing" means). But these benefits are integrally connected to the mission for which they are given. "Mission" has to do with "the purpose for being sent out." Ultimately, God called Abraham so that a people could be set apart and then sent out to be God's agents to accomplish his saving purposes. The Old Covenant believer was characterized by being set apart, in anticipation of that next chapter of divine initiative. In the New Covenant, as we shall discuss below, the believer is characterized by "being sent." Both receive benefits in order to be used in this mission.

Failure to grasp this essential link between benefit and mission results in the one-sided evangelistic preaching so characteristic of today's Christian church. We tend to present the gospel as God's way of getting the individual saved. We call upon people to come to Christ to be saved, as though that were the ultimate purpose of our proclamation. As I shall emphasize throughout this book, that is only half of the message. We are the elect, those who are already receiving the blessing of our salvation, because God has enabled us to respond, has given us the foretaste of the blessing, so that he might enlist us in his service as he completes the work of salvation that he has begun. Our savedness is not our privilege but our responsibility. To reduce the scope of the saving work of God, to say that Christ died "to save me," is to say far too little, and thus to distort the gospel. We must learn that the church's calling, or its election, is properly understood as a continuation of what God was doing in Israel. We must see both the purpose in God's call and the many ways in which that call was misunderstood and abused in the Old Covenant—for the same kind of sinful distortion of our gospel calling takes place in the church today.

We might ask how this separation of benefit from mission comes about. The answer is undoubtedly more complex than we can address in this study. The sinful and self-centered nature of rebellious humanity is certainly the root cause. Our rejection of God is so pervasive that we can individually and even corporately distort his love and grace so that we reduce his Good News to a program that helps me (and it certainly does!) but does not require of me that I become an obedient servant of the Lord within salvation history. Diluting the biblical message in this way does not render us "unsaved." I do not believe that God's grace is to be measured so narrowly. But it does mean that those who profess to be his people can hinder God's work in history as much as they can further it.

In the course of Christian history, this separation of benefits from mission can be seen in a number of major developments, each of which would merit a great deal of discussion. For instance, we observe that the sacraments, instituted by our Lord as supreme forms of equipping for ministry, have evolved into "salvation rites," seen primarily in their function of conveying and affirming our savedness. They tend to degenerate into "salvation things" under the control of the church, which then becomes the semidivine administrator of grace through these events. The power of the medieval church was closely related to the concept that the main goal of the church's calling is to save souls, and the authority to exclude people from that salvation is also within the church's powers.

Modern society experiences a gospel proclamation that focuses, as we said, entirely on personal salvation as an end in itself. The gospel is presented with no emphasis at all upon God's all-embracing purposes for his creation. Even Christian obedience is reduced to the realm of the private and personal. For example, the view that the Christian church should not be involved in politics is a typical result of the failure to grasp the fact that election to faith is election to service, that the benefits of the call may not be separated from the mission. We do in fact tend to preach the New Testament gospel as though our Lord said to Nicodemus, "God so loved the Christians (or better, those Christians with whom I agree and identify) that he gave his only Son." And so if we go to the world, we go with a gospel of personal salvation, rather than with a summons to the adventure and risk of discipleship and obedience.

Yet God called Abraham and promised to bless him so that he and his offspring would be a channel of blessing to the entire world—to "the nations." That is the sense of election for the church, and the only appropriate backdrop for our concept of the church's mission. To concentrate on the benefits apart from the mission is to reduce and dilute the whole meaning of election. To refocus election on the question of who is saved (or who is not saved) is to distort the very meaning of the event. Salvation, as we shall discuss later, is an ongoing event in the Bible, based upon the unquestionable certainty of what God has done, what is going on now in the life of the church and in the individual Christian, and yet also looking forward to its consummation in God's drawing together of all history into the completion of his purposes (see 5.2, pp. 78-88). The abuse of the concept of election is almost always linked with an erroneous preoccupation with one's personal salvation, and a failure to see the biblical emphasis upon the future tense of salvation.

1.3 CHRIST IN SALVATION HISTORY

As the course of salvation history in the Old Covenant moves from the universal to the particular, from the broad sweep of Genesis 1-11 to the narrowing focus of Genesis 12ff., there is a dominant note of future expectation. Israel looks forward to what God will do in the future. This expectation takes a variety of forms, and one cannot orchestrate a unified theme for Israel's view of what the future will bring. But Israel's past history with God is an ongoing affirmation that God will continue to act and will complete his saving purposes. Of this the prophets are sure. But speculation about the precise shape of the future leads nowhere.

The Old Testament prophets announce God's word to a specific situation, calling upon their hearers to respond with obedience, faith, and endurance. They reaffirm God's promises and faithfulness and look toward the future when God will complete all that he has started. But the prophetic message in the Old Testament does not give Israel an infallible blueprint that will permit the nation to recognize the Messiah or any other detail of the historical consummation of God's purposes. If that were so, then the scholars at Herod's court at the time of Jesus' birth would have done a better job of interpreting the signs of their times than they did.

Salvation history moves toward its culmination, contrary to all the human ways of thinking that surround Old Testament expectation. God's certain completion of his saving work cannot be stopped by Israel's disobedience. Even if only a remnant of the called people will serve as the channel for the continuing mystery of salvation history, that suffices for the completion of God's work. It was never characteristic of God's work that the events should be overwhelming demonstrations of divine power. Faith always remains faith, which means that only those eyes and ears that God enables to see and hear what he is doing will recognize his work. God chooses the unlikely ones, the unexpected, to be the agents for his work. It must be known that God's work is the result of *his* power and grace, not the combined product of divine initiation and human implementation. Even in the Old Covenant, we must see that we are "saved by grace," that our experience of God's goodness is itself an enabled response.

Just as God chose the Jewish nation, a minor force in the sweep of human history, the youngest son of Jesse to be the founder of the dynasty that will serve God's purposes, and only two tribes of the original twelve for the final stage of preparation—just as God always worked through the unlikely, he now brings salvation history to a head through a peasant girl and her puzzled husband, a birth in Bethlehem, and a boy growing up in Nazareth. Jesus enters the world of his day proclaiming that "the time is fulfilled, and the kingdom of God is at hand" (Mark 1:14). But outwardly, there is little trace of any fulfillment in Israel, and certainly the kingdom is not overtaking Rome and restoring Israel to its proper glory.

The incarnation, death, resurrection, and ascension of our Lord are the central events of salvation history. They are the content of the gospel. This life, this person, his actions and words and everything that happened to him in the last week of his human existence are the climax, the mid-point of salvation history, as Oscar Cullmann has taught us. The mission of the church is the proclamation of that event and its meaning: " . . . that you may declare the wonderful deeds of him who called you out of darkness into his marvelous light" (1 Pet. 2:9).

In order to understand the mission of the church as it emerges out of the salvation event of Christ, we need, however, to see just what God has done in this "incarnation." The term itself is another way of saying "the Word became flesh." It is the technical term for the amazing fact that God personally entered our history and our experience as the man Jesus, that Jesus "did not count equality with God a thing to be grasped, but emptied himself . . . " (Phil. 2:6-7). It is the culmination of a long history, itself characterized by God's "incarnational" action on our behalf. The entire Old Testament record testifies to the many ways in which God allows his word to "become flesh." The direction of divine action is always from God's majesty and sovereign transcendence to his experienceable and historical immanence—that is, God always moves into our realm of experience and makes himself knowable on human (and thus sinful) terms. It is the very nature of God's grace that it "condescends." Calvin spoke of the way in which God "accommodates" himself to our reality, for our sakes.

The incarnation of Jesus Christ is the ultimate and unrepeatable accommodation of God to our reality and to our need. "For our sake he made him to be sin who knew no sin, so that in him we might become the righteousness of God" (2 Cor. 5:21). But as that unique and unrepeatable event, it stands in a long sequence of God's gracious condescensions for us. God let his word become flesh in the call to Abraham, in the exodus and the giving of the Ten Commandments, in the ordering of Israel's existence, in the judges and the kings, and in the prophets and the temple community. Israel could never climb a holy mountain in order to become more godlike and more god-pleasing. God always came to his people and built the bridges of reconciliation and fellowship, whether they were bridges of sacrifice, worship, or wisdom.

In Christ, God built the final, decisive, and unique bridge. In this incarnation God decisively and finally enabled the reconciliation of creation, which climaxed in the death and resurrection of Jesus Christ and his enthronement as Lord. The long and often disparate lines of Israel's expectation found their fulfillment in Christ. Beyond Christ, there would be no other event needed for reconciliation to take place. And the entire event was a disclosure on human terms of the self-giving love and sovereign grace of the God who seeks to restore his creation to himself.

The church's mission is based upon who Jesus Christ is and what God has accomplished through him. These events, to which the New Testament testifies, are the foundation of the church's existence. "By [God's] great mercy we have been born anew to a living hope through the resurrection of Jesus Christ from the dead" (1 Pet. 1:3)—that has happened; it is unshakeable fact and granite foundation.

In seeking to understand the church's mission, we will always return to this foundational event of the gospel. But we need to see this event as it follows after what God had already been doing through the centuries of preparation and expectation that we call the Old Covenant. We need to recognize that the incarnation of Christ was the climax of God's incarnational activity on behalf of his creation, from creation onward. God expressed his grace to sinful Adam and Eve by making them clothes to wear. His love was "enfleshed" in that mundane act. He demonstrated his incarnational care for his people by prescribing the orders and regulations of society as we find them in the Pentateuch (the first five books of the Bible). Those long and often obscure passages detailing how Israel is to organize its life are, taken together, an impressive testimony to the "enfleshed" compassion of God toward his people. Thus, without in any way diminishing the uniqueness and mystery of the Word becoming flesh, we recognize that in Jesus Christ God's way of working throughout history reached its apex. From that middle point we date our time, we derive our certainty, and we receive the content of our message. In the next chapter we shall return to the significance of the incarnation for our theology of the church.

1.4 THE CHURCH AS PART OF THE GOSPEL

If the salvation events had concluded with Easter, ultimately there would have been no effect upon the course of human history. The experience of those who knew Jesus before and after his death and resurrection would have remained a closed chapter to the world. The gospel does not reach its conclusion on Easter morning; there is more, necessarily more. The liturgies of the church have preserved this important insight in their celebration of Eastertide. After several Sundays of exploring what this great good news means (*Quasimodogeniti,* the possibility of new birth; *Misericordias Dei,* the dimensions of God's mercy; *Jubilate, Cantate, Rogate, Exaudi,* the great reasons to rejoice, sing, pray, and look forward expectantly), the church in these great traditions celebrates Ascension Day, the enthronement of our Lord, and Pentecost, the enabling of the church to carry out its mission.

The church is an essential part of the gospel, a necessary development within salvation history. Without the giving of the Spirit and the enabling of the Christian community's proclamation, the good news of what God has done on the cross and at the empty tomb would never be heard. "How are they to hear without a preacher? And how can men preach unless they are sent?" (Rom. 10:14-15). Just as God called and set apart the nation of Israel to be blessed and become a channel of blessing to all nations, he now calls and sets apart a people, the "new Israel," to proclaim what he has done. Preparation in the Old Covenant has been followed by fulfillment, and the time has come to cross the borders and bring the new reality of God's saving action to all of his rebellious creation.

The place and purpose of the church within this grand sweep of salvation history, then, is to be the agency by which the message of God's reconciling actions will be made known. The church is "God's own people, that [it] may declare the wonderful deeds of him who called [it] out of darkness into his marvelous light" (1 Pet. 2:9). As we shall explore further below, the church is the result of God's action, another expression of God's gracious willingness to disclose himself within human history on our terms, understandably—and thus within the ambiguity of human experience. We cannot address the *what* and the *how* of the church's mission if we do not grasp its essential place in salvation history. It is neither a footnote nor a marginal event. It is not a later distortion of the simple message of the great teacher Jesus. Rather, it is the necessary work of God for the implementation of the witness to the gospel.

Jesus prepared his disciples to become the apostolic college upon which the church was to be built. He passed on to them the task of carrying on, even "completing" his work (Paul says that his sufferings "complete what is lacking in Christ's afflictions for the sake of his body, that is, the church"; Col. 1:24). He promised them the needed teacher and comforter to equip them for this work. He "sent them out," gave them this mission, and, after Easter, completed the task of preparation before his ascension. There can be no question that the New Testament church understood itself as the direct result of God's action and Christ's preparation and empowerment. Further, as we read the New Testament carefully and see how the witnesses wrote their varying instructions for the early church, which have together become our New Testament canon, we note in their use of the Old Testament their overpowering conviction that God had drawn all of salvation history together in Christ, and now a new and final chapter was commencing: the epoch of the church, of the witness to the good news that reconciliation has been made possible in Christ.

The church was blessed with faith in Christ in order to become a blessing to the world, as the herald and witness to the Good News. Its message is the message of Christ: "Repent, and believe in the gospel!" (Mark 1:15). And, with the power of the Holy Spirit, it is now to "be Christ's witness."

Two

THE INCARNATION:
THE WHAT AND THE HOW
OF GOD'S ACTION

2.1 GOD'S WAY OF DISCLOSING HIMSELF

Not only does God disclose himself to us so that we may know him and respond, but he does so in an amazing way. He comes into our experience on our terms. We have referred to this basic fact of revelation by using the term *incarnational* when we spoke of Christ in salvation history (1.3, pp. 12-15). We now will examine more closely the significance of this biblical assertion. As stated above, the incarnation of Jesus Christ is the unique and unrepeatable event of God's entry in his Son into history, for the purpose of completing the saving work of reconciliation that took place on the cross. However, this unique incarnation is at the same time the epitome of God's way of making himself knowable and experienceable in human history. It is the way of "condescension," of "accommodation"—it is "incarnational."

There is a long history of tension within the Christian community on this point. Very early in our history, a view of the Christian church and Christian behavior emerged that could also be called "incarnational." It was associated with the idea that the church was the "prolongation of Christ" in the world (the *Christus prolongatus*). Gradually this became the idea that the church, as the Body of Christ, could share in the perfection of Christ. And through very special representatives of that church, those who were called saints, much of the perfection of Christ was carried forward and realized within human experience. The incarnation was rightly seen as the way in which God worked and intended to continue to work through the Christian church. However, this interpretation erred at a significant point. It shared the one-sided emphasis upon the benefits of the gospel, the experience and certainty of personal salvation, and further concluded that this salvation could be perfectly realized in at least some believers (the saints).

As a result of this view of grace and salvation, the church became the administrator of God's grace through its rites and disciplines. The incarnation had become the possible form of saved existence. The mission of the church as a witness to Christ the Lord who was sending his church into the world to serve him underwent a subtle change: personal blessedness was emphasized, with the incarnational possibility as the highest form of spiritual attainment; grace became a "thing" managed and distributed by the church; the specific task of witness was reserved for the spiritually select (which resulted in the division of the church into clergy and laity); the focus of Christian existence became preoccupation with one's own salvation and the works needed to maintain that blessed state; and Christian obedience was seen almost exclusively in terms of personal piety and participation in the churchly celebrations and rituals of faith (see also 1.2, pp. 8-12).

The Reformers objected to that concept of spiritual perfectability and that interpretation of the incarnation, which viewed the church as a "salvation agency." Luther banished from church structure the religious orders with their systems of spiritual discipline and their vision of attainable perfection. The Reformers were united in their emphasis that we are saved by God's action, justified by his grace, reconciled to the relationship of children under our heavenly Father—and that we can do nothing either to contribute to or cooperate with that process. "We are beggars, that is true" was the summary of Luther's profound grasp of the gospel of grace. Justification by grace alone became the battle cry of the Reformation, and it has continued to mark the major distinction between Roman and Reformation Christianity. (In all fairness, we should note that the great disparity in the views of the gospel held by the contesting parties 450 years ago has been considerably reduced in the continuing process of theological discussion and reformulation.)

The church's emphasis upon the incarnation was suspect. Reformation Christianity (at times to a fault) rejected any concern for the "doing of the word" and placed all the emphasis upon the preaching and hearing of the word. The fear of works righteousness led many to an inappropriate one-sidedness in which Christian piety was primarily a passive spirituality, a confession of our total reliance on God, which was, however, often accompanied by a theological reserve when it

came to translating the concrete effects of the gospel in our lives into
actions that might have an impact on our world.

Of course, this was not true of all currents of the Reformation.
There was also considerable concern expressed for the practical outworking of the gospel. Luther himself emphasized that the gospel,
properly understood, must produce good works—which is no more
than a restatement of Paul's summary in Ephesians, where he begins by
stating that " . . . by grace you have been saved through faith; and this
is not your own doing, it is the gift of God"—and then continues with
a statement that relates God's grace and our work in a way that has
often been forgotten in many Reformation circles: "For we are his
workmanship, created in Christ Jesus for good works, which God
prepared beforehand, that we should walk in them" (Eph. 2:8-10).

Often the concern for the outworking of the gospel took the form
of legalism, a rigorous imposition of disciplines construed as the necessary expression of a life saved by grace. The reactions to such
extremes came immediately, so that the history of Protestant Christianity appears very much like a pendulum swinging back and forth between an emphasis upon grace alone to a concern for the actions that
express that grace.

The major streams of Reformation Christianity, both Lutheran and
Reformed, have stressed the centrality of grace and our dependence
upon God's action to justify us, that is, to make us right with God. But
there has been a tendency to neglect a necessary link. The biblical
record teaches us that *what* God has done for us (reconciliation,
justification, ultimately salvation) is ultimately intimately connected to
how God has done it. God has entered into history, "enfleshed" his
actions, and become incarnate, in order to accomplish his reconciling
and saving purposes. He has overcome our rebellion by becoming part
of our history, finally and conclusively in the incarnation of Christ. And
the continuation of that work, which is the witness to what God has
done, is to be "incarnational," is to continue to link the *what* and the
how of God's action. The witness to the unique salvation events of
Christ's incarnation is itself to be incarnational. Justification by grace
is communicated through incarnational witness.

At this point, the Reformation needs to continue (we do espouse,
after all, the concept of the "church always in the process of reforming": *Ecclesia semper reformanda!*), and to examine what it set aside
when it rejected the centuries-old concern for the incarnational
expression of the gospel in the life of the Christian individual and
community. This reexamination is taking place today, as we discover

more and more of the valid spiritual insight contained in the Roman Catholic tradition of spiritual formation and direction. The challenge in today's discussion is to relate the "benefits" of spiritual formation to the "task" or "mission" of the church, so that we do not again find ourselves emphasizing personal spirituality and neglecting the reason that the Spirit does equip us so effectively.

Part of our problem may be linked to the fact that the Reformation did not move significantly far in its correction of the "benefits"/ "mission" dichotomy. The Reformers were mostly concerned with the needed revision of the church's erroneous theology of salvation and with the one very important side of the gospel, the "benefits" aspect. Luther, after all, was driven to his spiritual insights through his struggle with the question of whether he could personally be certain of his salvation. Melanchthon, Luther's colleague and systematizer, actually spoke of the heart of the gospel as being the reception of "the benefits of Christ." This was a true statement, but it still fell short of the biblical concept of being called to service, of being blessed to be a blessing, of benefits for the purpose of equipping for service.

Put very simply, the Reformation concern with regard to the mission of the church was with the proper preaching of the doctrine of the gospel and its proper interpretation in the sacramental practice of the church—and with other corrections that radiated out from this central thrust. The Reformation did not, as such, deal with the mission of the church to a world outside of Christ, because the world was still basically a Christian world that needed a reformulation of its understanding of the faith and a reforming of the church. Secularization had not yet become the central challenge to the church, as it has in the twentieth century.

In the sixteenth century the church had little evangelistic concern for the nonbelieving world. Luther regarded the Turks at the eastern gates of Europe as "infidels," revealing that he was still part of the medieval structure that divided the world into Christian and non-Christian in such a way that the "infidel" margins of civilization could be battled but seldom evangelized. It would take the emergence of the modern age with the expansion of the known world to include vast regions dominated by other religions before the mission of the church would begin to be refocused in terms of evangelization. It is difficult for Western churches to build on Reformation roots in developing a theology of the church's mission, since those roots are clearly inadequate as they derive from medieval "Christian society." Today, much of our thinking about the mission of the church is stimulated by the

questions and answers put forward by the so-called Third World
churches (see the lifelong work of Lesslie Newbigin and E. Stanley
Jones, for example).

Thus, part of the task we face today is to correct the neglect of
the incarnation in many Protestant circles, being careful not to fall into
the trap of medieval spiritual perfectionism, which was, as we have
seen, a possible but incorrect application of incarnation to Christian
reality. Rather, our understanding of incarnation and incarnational
activity is to be rooted in the fact that it is—and always has been—
God's way of acting. To say that God has acted incarnationally is to say
that God has made his word become fleshly from the very outset, so
that we might hear and respond to it. Perhaps the greatest wonder in
the biblical teaching on revelation is the amazing willingness of God
to let his self-communication be so cloaked by and intermingled with
human frailty.

Much to the discomfort of all thinkers who would prefer God's
actions to be chemically transcendent and untouched by human reality,
the Bible portrays God as active in human events and working through
human instruments who are neither perfect nor outwardly suited for
this high honor. The qualifications of those whom he chooses seem to
have little importance. Abraham, for example, is honored by the entire
community of faith as being a paradigm of true faith in his willingness
to follow God's command to rise up and go. But *why* God chose him
we do not know. Nor, incidentally, do we know how God addressed
him. But we can be certain that God made himself hearable and
knowable on Abraham's terms.

All through the Old Testament, we observe God's actions enmeshed with an often puzzling human element. We struggle with God's
leadership of Israel in the period of the conquest. It is hard to maintain
a propositionally pure concept of God and yet deal with the God of
Joshua and Judges who apparently accomplishes his purposes through
the cruel instrument of war. We approach biblical history from the
framework of eternally true propositions and logical formulations.
Thus, the realities of a God who functions in a fleshly way, who works
in and through his creatures and in his sovereignty even turns their
sins and rebellion to his purposes, burst apart all our neat, closed
systems. We cannot fathom how God could "get his hands dirty" in
such a human way. We have found it offensive to talk about God
anthropomorphically, that is, to describe God in human terms, ascribing to him human emotions and reactions. For centuries, the Christian
church sought to avoid the embarrassment of a God who acted incar-

nationally throughout the Old Covenant. It did so by interpreting these Scriptures allegorically, that is, by looking for subtle spiritual principles and truths behind the mere literal accounts. In other words, to solve the problem of a God who acts incarnationally in our history, the church simply refused to deal with that history in a straightforward fashion.

But the glory of biblical revelation is the very fact that God does continually intervene in our history in such a way that the Word becomes flesh. And it is part of what we must mean by "inspiration" that his Holy Spirit helps us to perceive the presence and work of God in otherwise human events, distinguishing the necessary humanness in the divine encounter, and yet realizing that to separate the human and the divine is to make God an untouchable idea rather than a personal God who can be known and loved and served. Just as the Christian church struggled for centuries to define the two natures of Christ, human and divine, and ultimately got no further than to state clearly all the things that this "doctrine of the two natures" could *not* mean, we must ultimately admit that God's self-disclosure in human experience presents us with a revelatory fact that cannot be disentangled into its divine and human components, but is rather at the very heart of the wonder of God's coming to us. He comes to us only in the human forms of his self-humiliation. He does not come as propositional truth or logical syllogism, but as a loving and acting God who encounters us, confronts us with his real and mighty presence in our experience, challenges us with his purpose, and enables us to respond.

If we dilute the mystery of God's incarnational action, we fall into one of several traps that the church has often fallen into throughout its history. We might tend to read the Bible as an ahistorical record, a collection of lessons, morals, and wise teachings from which we can learn much by dint of our application (a form of self-salvation through mental activity). If we do, we will miss the amazing fact that God, the personal and majestic Creator and Lord, is really a God of action and involvement, of encounter and exchange, who can be known personally and is not to be conceived of merely as a moral idea. We might, alternatively, make him into an abstract principle, the utmost attainment of our human intellect, ascribing to him the highest and profoundest predicates of knowledge, power, presence, and majesty. Or, in a related fashion, we might accept the biblical record but posit a rational necessity about the person and work of God that must explain away the humanness of the record (its so-called contradictions) and, in effect, enforce a standard of reason to which God must subscribe.

But at best all such definitions are a subtle violation of the second commandment, because we are in fact creating a god after our own image.

Incarnation is the astounding fact of God's gracious entry into our lives and history, with the ambiguity that must attend it. We encounter God in holy history, speaking our language, working within the givens of Jewish culture, disclosing himself with images and experiences that "make sense" to the people in that time and place, just as they are. Before the incarnation of Christ, God was enfleshing his word, his gracious purposes, in the whole course of salvation history. He permitted his will to be advanced by David, who at best was a highly self-contradictory servant; by a Solomon who ultimately let his frailty overpower his wisdom; by an Israelite nation that was marked more by disobedience than by faithfulness to its calling. We do not experience God outside of history, but always in it. Even the direct appearances of the transcendent, the so-called theophanies, bear the marks of the specific time, place, and culture in which they happened. They were experienced as encounters with the majestic God; and yet, even on Sinai, God comes to man in ways man can grasp and respond to.

We are, then, contesting the rejection of the incarnation as a central part of our ongoing obedience to the gospel mandate. God's incarnational acts in the Old Covenant prepared the way for the gospel. The task now is to see how the church is to continue that incarnational obedience.

2.2 THE INCARNATION OF CHRIST AND THE CONTINUING ENFLESHMENT OF THE GOSPEL

The incarnation of Jesus Christ, the Son of God who became man for our sake, is the central event and fact of salvation history, and the central content of the Christian message. Looking back upon the whole course of holy history in the Old Covenant, we recognize that the enfleshment of the Word is the climax of a long, incarnational process in which God had been entering into the experience and history of his creation in many ways, to disclose himself, his purposes, and his will, to guide as well as to reprove his people. But in the incarnation of Jesus Christ, something absolutely new and unique took place. The Word became flesh; the humanly impossible happened. God accepted the limitations of his own creation, and through his Son accomplished the reconciliation that humanity needed in order to be restored to the relationship with God for which we were designed. Because it is humanly impossible for any one of us to build that bridge back to God, God built it to us. Built around this wonderful and mysterious fact is the entire Christian faith.

But, as we have said, incarnation is both the event of salvation and the way in which God accomplishes his saving purposes. Without diminishing the uniqueness of the historical events of the first three decades of the first century, we must see that God's incarnational action, especially in its epitome in Christ, must continue—and it must do so incarnationally. To understand this is to grasp the thrust of much of Jesus' own preparation of the disciples for the mission that lay before them. Jesus was, in fact, preparing the disciples for the incarnational ministry that would result from the saving events of his own incarnation, life, suffering, death, and resurrection.

When we read the gospel accounts attentively, it is difficult to maintain the church's old distinction between the benefits and the mission of salvation. Jesus calls the disciples to be "fishers of men," and then equips them for both the agony and the glory of that task. As we see most particularly in the parables that deal with the kingdom of God, Jesus challenges his disciples with the mystery of this mission. They must understand that the kingdom of God, which is near, of which they will experience a foretaste, a "down payment," is not under their control. They will sow and experience a great variety of responses, including rejection. But they will also reap and experience a great harvest. And yet, they are not to be surprised when the wheat fields of the kingdom are filled with weeds that look like wheat, but ultimately will have to be burned. They must accept the fact that they cannot control the time or the size of the harvest. But nothing is so certain as that the harvest will come in, and it will be overwhelming. God will complete the bringing in of the kingdom—and in that confidence they are to go about their mission.

The disciples and all who follow after them will experience this mission as a tension between confidence in God and rejection by much of the world. Their "salvation benefits" are the source of great peace; they can trust God to provide for them in any circumstances. But their salvation has a strong and mysterious future tense. Jesus cannot tell them when the kingdom will be ushered in with its universal finality. There is a battle to be fought, and they will need to endure. At times, the gospel will mean not peace, but a sword. To obey Christ will mean to depart from the accepted channels of behavior in the social orders in which the church lives in the world. Disciples of Christ will not fit neatly into the world into which they are sent. They will discover that there are crosses to be taken up, if they will follow Jesus.

Jesus sends them out to proclaim his message and to continue the work he had begun and was doing during his earthly ministry. They will find themselves going into all the world, making the nations into Christ's disciples, baptizing them, and teaching them to be obedient to Jesus' teaching (Matt. 28:19-20). They have joined Jesus in a three-year pilgrimage that has led to the cross, and, under his tutelage, they have begun gradually to see that all of the expectation of the Old Covenant has converged surprisingly and mysteriously in him. They will understand, as his promised Spirit teaches them, that this tragic death on the cross was the final and necessary event that now makes it possible to preach to all nations repentance and forgiveness in his name. They will discover that all power in heaven and on earth has indeed been given to Jesus Christ, and thus they are empowered to go and disciple. Of all this, they are witnesses—and that means that they now have a task to do because of their unique experience with Christ (Luke 24:44-48).

In the great Final Discourse and High Priestly Prayer recorded in John's gospel (John 13-17), Jesus develops in a number of directions this necessary link between the benefit of knowing and following him and the mission on which the disciples are being sent. The disciples are instructed to follow Christ's servant example, to become a community whose love will be its most compelling message to the world. They are assured of the continuing presence of Christ in their lives. But they are promised more than they already have: the gift of the Counselor, the Holy Spirit, who will enable them to understand and to do more than they have already done. They will confront a world that will harshly rebuff them, beginning with their own nation. But they will be the channels through which many will come to know God's love and be drawn into his service. In an astonishing parallel to the action of God in sending Christ, he now sends out his disciples: "As thou didst send me into the world, so I have sent them into thy world" (John 17:18). God's incarnational way of working is to continue in those who carry on his work: the disciples and the church.

The overall thrust of the teaching in this great passage, in harmony with the preparation of the disciples in the Synoptic accounts, could be described in this way:

Because of what has taken place in the incarnation of Christ, its meaning and possibility are now to be made known to the entire world by a community that is powerfully being called into existence, and will continue to incarnate the presence, the message, and the reality of

God in Christ. This ongoing incarnational ministry is to be the continuation of Christ's work, not to do what he did not do, but to carry out the meaning of what was accomplished through him. The love he revealed to his disciples in their intense community, to the people of his day as they sought his help while not understanding his message, and to the world in his self-sacrifice on the cross is now to be the powerful medium of communication through his community, as it obediently carries out his mission. They are sent out to be witnesses (John 15:25-26), to be evidence within the world that the Good News has happened and is available to all who will respond.

Our Lord intended, in preparing his disciples for their ministry, that they proclaim the message so that people might hear, and that they incarnate the reality and meaning of that message in their lives individually and corporately, so that their message will be visible and audible. Just as Jesus both said and did the Good News, his followers, as witnesses, are to be messengers whose message cannot be separated from their persons and their lives. Jesus did not equip the disciples, and the church that was to form out of them, merely to be good communicators. Rather, he equipped them to be credible witnesses, people whose whole lives make their communication authentic and powerful. Whenever the Christian church has failed to grasp this incarnational necessity, that the message and the messengers cannot be divided in our understanding nor in our practice, a diluted gospel has resulted.

We are saying, then, that our concept of message, communication, proclamation, and preaching must be developed incarnationally—in relationship to the enfleshment of the gospel in the life of the proclaiming community. This concept is perhaps most compellingly developed in the apostolic literature that describes the church as "the Body of Christ."

2.3 THE CHURCH AS THE BODY OF CHRIST

Of the many images used for the church in the New Testament, the concept of "the Body of Christ" is certainly one of the most incarnational. Admittedly, it incorporates a number of themes into itself. It emphasizes the intimate relationship between Christ's people and himself, and is in that sense the Pauline equivalent to John's theme of the vine and the branches. It is another way of talking about being "in Christ" and Christ being "in us." In addition to that aspect of its meaning, it also is used to emphasize the interdependence and organic nature of the church. The Body is made up of many members, all of them entirely intertwined with each other and yet distinct in function and even in appearance. The apostle Paul uses this image to combat the heretical divisiveness that is offended by the diversity of the Christian community and seeks to arrive at uniformity by dividing the Body and bringing all the like parts together.

But the term *body* has another, important nuance, which relates it to our understanding of the incarnational ministry of the church. The body is also visible: it is the means of presence. By means of our bodies, we are present in the world in space and time. The use of such an image points out that the church is a historical reality. It is present in the world; it can be seen, it has many parts, and it must function organically within the world. "Body of Christ" language militates against an overspiritualization of the church, which refuses to deal with the empirical and practical realities of historical existence.

Since the church is such a real and historical presence in the world, it is especially important for us to consider that it is the Body *of Christ*. It is the presence of Christ in the world in a very concrete and historical way. Jesus had promised his disciples that he would not forsake them, that he would be present with them "to the close of the age" (Matt. 28:20). They would continue to abide in him and he in them (John 15:4). Wherever even two or three would gather in his name, he promised to be present in their very midst (Matt. 18:20).

When we link the concept of "Body of Christ" together with the New Testament emphasis upon the church as the witnessing community, we may proceed further to another aspect of the meaning of this term. As the Body of Christ, we are the community through which Christ is present in and reaching out to the world. The witnessing role of the church is the representation to the world (and to each other in the church) of the fact and opportunity of the gospel. To be the Body of Christ, then, means to be the channels through which the work of Christ continues to be done. Christ has committed to his church the proclamation of the great event of reconciliation that he accomplished on the cross, and, in that sense, the completion of the work he both began and did: the declaration of the "wonderful deeds of him who called you out of darkness into his marvelous light" (1 Pet. 2:9). As his Body, we are to incorporate ("embody") that message as we proclaim it.

This is the reason that the example of Christ is referred to so often in the New Testament instruction of the churches. For the apostolic teachers of the church, Jesus Christ was the Savior and Lord whose life was also the textbook for the way in which the community was to function. In his teaching, Paul constantly refers to Jesus as the model for the church. We find a particularly intriguing example of this in Paul's admonitions to the Philippian church (1:27-2:11), where he summons them to a corporate life worthy of their common calling, and then addresses the problems in that community. These problems—pride, self-interest, ego, and rivalry—are very human frailties that are weakening and even threatening to divide the Christian community in Philippi. Paul emphasizes strongly that such behavior is not an option for a Christian community. Believers are to be united, to think alike, to have the same love for each other, and to develop an attitude of self-giving for the sake of each other. And then he cites his example: "Have this mind among yourselves, which you have in Christ Jesus . . . " (Phil. 2:5). The so-called Christ Song, which he then quotes, is one of the major statements in the New Testament on the person of Christ and his relationship to the Father. It is of great significance dogmatically and has been the staging ground for debates spanning the centuries. But here, in the epistle, this great statement serves as an example for the attitude that should prevail among Christians. Paul makes no distinction between the sublime theology of the nature of Christ and the significance of the incarnational example of Christ for the church. These are diverse dimensions of the same great fact: In the incarnation, God accomplished his work of salvation and at the same time defined the way by which that work is to be carried out through history until "the close of the age."

To grasp the fact that Jesus continues to be the teacher of the church as he is worshiped and acknowledged as our Savior and Lord means that we discover anew the great importance of the New Testament accounts of the life and ministry of Jesus for our Christian obedience. The incarnation, as a once-and-for-all event, continues to be a contemporary reality for us as we discover that Jesus came to show us how to be obedient, how to translate the message into our relationships and action, and how to be a discipling community constantly being discipled by its Master. Many Christians have a regrettable tendency to relegate the Gospels to the children in Sunday School, and to concentrate on the Epistles for adult Christian study. But if we study the Epistles carefully, we will see how dependent they are upon the earthly ministry of Christ. Thus, we deprive the adult Christian community of a major source of instruction and guidance if we ignore the model for incarnational ministry that our Lord himself provided for us.

When the early Christian church was facing the problem of its continuation in time, which meant that new generations of believers were growing up in the church and no longer could go to the first apostles to be instructed in the faith, the leaders began the process of drawing together those written records that were generally acknowledged to be useful in teaching the faith and discipling the converts. The Gospels were an essential part of that collection. By examining those records we can determine something about why the early Christians selected those portions that ended up in the canon of the New Testament (since we know that Jesus said and did much, much more than is recorded in our Bible). In general, we see that the early church saw in Jesus the revelation of God's divine design for obedient human living, for faithfulness to God and his calling, and for the ministry of one person to another as representatives of God's gracious care and presence. So, the study of the life encounters and teachings of Jesus has become a central part of our learning process as we seek to discover what it means to be Christian. The post-Easter perspective on the life and ministry of Jesus is really a discovery of our Lord as both the model and enabler of the discipleship to which we are called.

We cannot divide Jesus' earthly ministry into a benefits versus mission compartmentalization. He integrated within his person, both in his actions and his words, the total meaning of salvation. How easily that is forgotten in the Christian church! When we present the gospel history as though it began on Good Friday, we greatly restrict both the content and the meaning of the gospel. And we deprive ourselves of fundamental resources and understandings for the church's mission. Jesus proclaimed blessing, good news, a coming kingdom, a new relationship with the Father, and justice to the oppressed and the poor as evidence that God was truly at work in the world. This means that he proclaimed wholeness and reconciliation for God's erring creation. These belong together for him. In this, he is a spokesman for the Hebraic concept of salvation, which is best understood as restored wholeness, as healing, as reconciliation in those relationships that are broken, and as restoration to the purposes for which we were made. A narrow view of salvation as "getting one's eternal life in order" will not be found in the preaching and teaching of Jesus. And it should not be a part of the incarnational ministry of the church, if it is faithful to its Lord.

The intensive encounter with the person and work of Jesus leads not only to the experience of saving grace that God desires for us but also to an ever-growing comprehension of the task for which Jesus has set us free and then sent us out. As the ongoing enfleshment of his Good News, of him as the Lord whose Body we are, we are to seek to be totally obedient, responding to the total gospel, and proclaiming the entire counsel of God. We are an amputated Body of Christ if we neglect or intentionally set aside any part of the proclamation and the model of Christ. *He* is the Word: his words alone are not our message, it is his entire person—his actions, his purposes, his freedom, and his vision. He is "the way, and the truth, and the life" (John 14:6).

As the Body of Christ, we are called and enabled to embody him as his ambassadors to the world. But this incarnational understanding of our being his Body must not be misunderstood as though we could also achieve his perfection. That is the error I mentioned earlier (2.1), which has played a major role in the history of the church. The difference between Jesus Christ and his Body, the church, is that he is the Lord and Savior who died for the world, and for this Body. The Body must, however, be cleansed, be made pure and holy by the action of its Lord. It will be presentable in its perfection only when the process of salvation is complete, which will be in the future tense of our faith, at "the day of the Lord" (see the discussion of the bride of Christ in Eph. 4:21ff.). The incarnational understanding of the Body of Christ comprehends within itself this emphasis upon our dependence on God's gracious love extended to us through Christ. The first form of incarnational witness of the church is its constant testimony to its forgivenness, and its need for continuing forgiveness. In our incarnational calling, we enflesh both the need for God's grace and the reception and reality of God's grace at work in our members.

There is a very real danger that this incarnational understanding of the church could lead to a revival of the "holier than thou" attitude among Christians. To say that we are the Body of Christ and thus that we enflesh him and his message could be misunderstood to mean that we bear in ourselves the spiritual perfection of Christ. We must, at all costs, avoid this ancient error in our concept of incarnational Christianity. Because Christ is "in us," because we "abide in Christ," we live in the realm of a new hope, a new certainty directed toward God and his faithfulness, a new knowledge of God and of his purposes. But we also live with the tension of our old and new creation still struggling with each other. We live with the reality of sin in our midst, in ourselves. Our incarnational identity struggles with the fact of our rebellion and our sin. But the way in which this struggle is carried out is significant for our proclamatory task.

D. T. Niles defined the church as one beggar saying to another beggar, "I know where bread is." Our incarnational life is a possibility given to us by God's grace, not something we have earned. It is the

result of our "putting on Christ" (Rom. 13:14), which happens because Christ enters into our lives, accepts us as we accept him, and
begins the work of new creation in us. Our witness is the witness of
"Christians in process." We are admonished by the apostles to give
close attention to the credibility of our witness as Christian individuals
and as a community. But the apostle Paul is remarkably candid about
his own shortcomings and confesses his dependence upon Christ in
the midst of that internal struggle (Rom. 7:21ff.). Incarnational ministry, as we shall discuss in greater detail below (Chap. 11), does not
draw attention to itself, but points to Christ. Just as Jesus directed the
attention of his hearers to the Father, we as his witnesses are to point
people toward him. And we must be sure that they are encountering
the total Jesus, the Jesus who proclaimed both salvation and mission,
who spoke of grace and justice, who revealed the total reality of God's
love as a love that redeems but also rejects when rejected.

Understanding the church incarnationally, as the Body of Christ,
and thus as his continuing presence and ministry in the world, we can
then deal honestly with its imperfection and its holiness. We recognize
that it is a human body, part and parcel of the humanity for which
Christ died. It is not a stranger to sin, but knows its sin far more clearly
than do those who have not experienced the wonder of forgiveness.
Its holiness is found in its calling: it is set aside (the basic meaning of
"holy") for God's purposes. That action of God will have its effects in
every area of the church's life—this is what "enfleshment of the gospel"
means. But the church will never move beyond its posture of dependence upon God's forgiving grace. The ancient liturgical practice of
beginning every service of prayer and worship with the confession of
sins and assurance of pardon demonstrates a profound insight into this
tension in the church. Christians begin each day at the foot of the
cross, as penitents, who receive grace for healing and for empowerment to serve. Thus, incarnational ministry is a continuing testimony
to the ongoing work of God, which makes whole and makes useful.
The Body of Christ is the forgiven Body, the struggling Body, the Body
that needs constantly to hear the gospel that called it forth, and to be
reevangelized, so that it can carry out the mission to which it has been
called.

Part Two

THE CHURCH'S MANDATE: BE MY WITNESSES

"But you shall receive power when the Holy Spirit has come upon you; and you shall be my witnesses in Jerusalem and in all Judea and Samaria and to the end of the earth."

—*Acts 1:8*

Three

THE VISION
OF THE CHURCH IN ACTS

3.1 FROM JERUSALEM TO THE END OF THE EARTH

The story of the church in the Book of Acts is not only a narrative of what happened in the first and decisive chapters of church history; it is also a theological interpretation of the church's mission, expounded in the form of plot and story. As such, it is typically Hebrew in spirit and form (even though Luke was writing to a Greek reader). Hebrew theology is a theology conveyed by events and their interpretation more than through propositional statements and abstract essays.

To say, though, that the Book of Acts has such a theological purpose is by no means to lessen its historical significance or reliability. It has been fashionable to be radically critical of the historicity of Acts, at least in some scholarly circles. That trend is turning around, however. Peter Stuhlmacher, professor of New Testament at the University of Tübingen in Germany, pointed out at a theological discussion several years ago that the way the story is told in Acts is by far the most plausible account of the events that took place when the church began. If, in fact, the foundational events of the church were God's actions initiating this new movement, then we should expect that the history would also be theology. That is the very nature of the incarnational understanding of God's self-disclosure: history is theological; that is, this particular history can and must be interpreted theologically.

The Book of Acts begins with its own "table of contents." In verse 8 of the first chapter, our Lord tells the disciples that his mandate will be carried out "in Jerusalem and in all Judea and Samaria and to the end of the earth." The rest of the book then relates how that did, in fact, happen: in Jerusalem first, then in the surroundings of Jerusalem, Judea, followed by the breakthrough of the mission in Samaria, and culminating in the ministry of the apostle Paul, who took the gospel to the then-known "end of the earth." This universal scope of the mandate is picked up again at the begining of chapter two, where the list of places from which the festival visitors in Jerusalem came (2:9-11) systematically portrays a sweep of the world (as it was then known) from east to west. The Good News is to be proclaimed to the entire world. For that purpose, God will give his Spirit to empower this witness.

We have spoken above of the fact that the church is essential to the gospel (1.4, pp. 15-17). The founding of the church as described in Acts emphasizes that fact. In the final post-Easter appearance to the disciples, our Lord gives them a charge that he directs to the future, and the angel follows the charge with a promise: Christ will return just as he has left. Thus, at his ascension, the focus is upon the carrying on of Christ's mission. God does not intend for the disciples to continue only to enjoy the benefits of their faith in the risen Lord; rather, they have experienced his victory because God has called them to carry on the work of declaration. To do so, they must now face and overcome enormous barriers.

First, they are not able to do this task in their own strength. After three years of instruction as the students of a rabbi, living with him day and night, memorizing his sayings and actions, and being saturated with his person and work, they would appear to be uniquely qualified to carry on his work. But that preparation is not enough. Nor is the sequence of amazing encounters with the risen Lord all that they need. They are persuaded now that he is alive, that far more has happened through this life and death than they had ever dreamed. They undoubtedly have begun to glimpse the overwhelming meaning of these events. The two disciples on the road to Emmaus (Luke 24:13-35) have learned from Jesus himself how the Old Covenant has now been drawn to its fulfillment in Christ, and how the events of his death and resurrection are the marvelous and necessary climax of the divine work of salvation. What they learned during that remarkable walk, while their hearts burned within them, they certainly by now had shared and discussed with the other disciples.

But understanding and knowledge are not enough; more is needed. These events and their meaning, the message of the gospel, must now be declared, and that declaration is to be a uniquely empowered event that actually calls forth the response of faith. The announcement of what has happened is going to be such a radical message, such a challenge to the world (both Jewish and Gentile), and the implications of a faith response to it are so life-changing, that it cannot be attempted as a purely human undertaking. The promise of the Holy Spirit (Acts 1:5, 8) points forward to what must still happen: the God who has acted in raising Christ from the dead will now act in an equally powerful way, giving his Spirit so that this church will be enabled and empowered to carry out its assigned mission. The work of the church will clearly be the result of God's action and not the humanly developed strategy of a new cult.

Thus, the task of the church cannot be assumed with human strength. That problem is resolved at Pentecost. As we shall see, the Holy Spirit comes in power and baptizes with a special power that makes persuasive witness possible. From the outset, the emphasis of the church's pilgrimage will be upon the fact that the work of Christ in and through the church is always *his* work, and not merely an example of human religious achievement. The first Christians experienced their faith as a God-given gift, one that surprised and challenged them at every level of their being, "turning the world upside down" (Acts 17:6).

Another problem confronting this small community is the issue of Israel's expectations and the radical correction of those expectations as a result of Christ's life, death, and resurrection. A great arc is drawn from the first chapters of the Bible (see 1.2, pp. 8-12) to the events of Pentecost, a link between the universal purposes of God for his creation and the election of Israel to serve God's saving purpose on the one hand, and the present call and enablement of the new Christian community on the other hand. The event is marked by promise and fulfillment. God's creative purposes in Genesis 1-11 were for all people, and Abraham's call was to become a blessing to all the nations. God elected Abraham and Israel to serve his purposes for all people. But that universal scope of election and service was to remain a future theme of the Old Covenant. At the same time, it was a mysterious aspect of Israel's calling, usually obscured in the twisting path of Israel's resistance to God's call and insistence upon understanding its election as privilege.

Ultimately, Israel's sense of its mission was summed up in the nation's separation from all other nations and cultures and its concentration upon the holy city, the holy building, and, within that temple, the holy room, the Holy of Holies. Johannes Blauw has spoken of this thrust of Old Covenant movement as "centripetal"—all movement is toward the center. There is very little concept of God's action moving beyond these boundaries. In fact, the faithful Jew must come from the farthest reaches of the world to experience the festivals of faith and share fully in his nation's religion. Pentecost was such a festival, and the people had gathered from all the then-known world.

Now, however, Jesus promises that the disciples will lead a mission that will go out from Jerusalem to the end of the earth. The direction will be changed. The walls of separation will have to be taken down. The man-made boundaries that can become insurmountable will now be breached by a people with a message that can no longer be contained within any particular culture. The gospel is to go not only to the Jews but to the Samaritans, which was shock enough. But more than that, it is to be taken out to the Gentiles, to the vast population that, according to the generally held view of that day in Israel, was rejected because it was not elect.

The disciples were Jews. They derived their identity from the great tradition of their people's faith, and their sensibilities and attitudes had been molded by that tradition. They could not easily move outside of that vast and pervasive conditioning. They could not truly have understood what "the end of the earth" meant when Jesus made that promise on the Mount of the Ascension. They were going to experience some traumatic challenges to their own sense of identity. In effect, in a revolutionary step forward in salvation history, the centripetal direction of salvation history was now being turned around into a centrifugal movement outward into all the world (Johannes Blauw). Jesus emphasized "all the world" in the Great Commission at the end of Matthew's gospel, and Luke underlines that same point with his program for the geographic spread of the gospel in Acts 1:8. This radical discontinuity is essential to the beginning of what we call the era of the church.

Certainly, there is also continuity from the Old Covenant to the New. Salvation history has been proceeding for centuries through the presence and adventure of Israel. God has been leading history forward to its climax in Christ. Now "the time is fulfilled," and the gospel is to be proclaimed. It is a message of fulfilled promise, of a history emerging from history, of a process of faith that goes back to Abraham. The election of the church can be understood properly only as a calling and setting apart for service that follows after and builds upon the call of Abraham and the setting apart of Israel. We must understand the church to be rooted in the ancient call to Israel, moving further ahead in salvation history but not ultimately displacing Israel (Rom. 11:28ff.).

As salvation history progresses, change, newness, and discontinuity move together with the continuation of what God began in creation and the election of Israel.

Let me add here that when we speak of "Old" and "New" Covenants, we should under no circumstances understand the "New" to be a negation of the "Old," or as a value judgment that overlooks how God was already working out his saving purposes in the Old Covenant and is mysteriously continuing to do so in the New. Some today would rather speak of the "First" and the "Second" Covenants, in order to emphasize the unique significance of God's faithful promises to Israel. Although I have not adopted this usage, I have found it to be a helpful reminder that God's history with Israel is not yet finished; therefore, the Christian church must carefully avoid any taint of superiority or pride over against Israel. The "engrafted branch" of the Gentile church (Rom. 11:17ff.) has not replaced the ancient tree, and God's faithful promises will be fulfilled. While we must speak of discontinuity in order to understand the newness of the gospel, ultimately, in a mysterious and larger sense, God will reveal a continuity for Israel about which we cannot even speculate.

The discontinuity between the Old and New Covenants, seen from the perspective of the Old Covenant, is geographical, cultural, and theological—and so, obviously, is traumatic. The promise of Jesus now becomes the plot of Luke: what is given in the promise will now have to be discovered by the early Christian community. It is often a painful discovery. The Spirit's leading of the church into the fullness of "all the world," that is, into "Judea, Samaria, and the end of the earth," causes the people to struggle. In fact, only through its pilgrimage through time can the church discover the vast dimensions of the meaning and application of the gospel. The early Christian community, although evangelized and instructed by the apostles themselves, did not fully grasp what the gospel meant. In fact, the church has not yet grasped the full meaning of the gospel. But at Pentecost, as a result of our Lord's promise, the church began a process of discovery that is linked with its obedience as it enters into the world. (A very important part of the theological task is to explore the dimensions of the gospel that have not yet been fully grasped by the church; see Chap. 5.)

For our understanding of the church today, it is of the greatest importance that we grasp these events described in the first chapters of Acts as our own history, the first chapters of our pilgrimage; they must be definitive for us. The Spirit entered the church at Pentecost, starting a movement that continues in and through us, the church of today. Like the generations of Israel that preceded Christ, we live between two great facts: our calling and equipping at Pentecost, and the expectation of what God will do to complete his work of salvation in the future. And during that period of time between our initial calling and the ultimate consummation of God's salvation history, we are called to be witnesses who go out to the end of the earth. God has given us his Spirit to enable us to obey that command.

Although the direction of our movement has changed from a focus on one land, one city, one temple, and one holy room, the basic fact that we are called by God for his purposes, that our election is to service, and that we share in the calling of Israel (while God continues and will complete his special history with that people) makes us the heirs of the Old Covenant as well as the firstfruits of the New.

3.2 "BE MY WITNESSES"

The central idea in the mission promise of our Lord at the beginning of Acts is his prophetic promise that the disciples will be his witnesses. When the Spirit comes to them and gives them the gift of power, their very identity will be transformed into that of witnesses. As such, they will carry out the ministry of that witness throughout the world. Thus, Jesus has established that the task of the Christian church, as it is first given to the disciples in the Book of Acts, is to be his witnesses. This fundamental understanding transforms the disciples into apostles, and they, in turn, convey it to the church throughout time.

The task committed to the church by Christ transforms its bearers. They do not merely become people who do or say a particular thing. They are to become a different kind of person: a witness. The origin of this word is particularly important for our understanding of the church's mission as incarnational ministry. The basic term applies to the person: the *martys* (witness) is a person. Closely linked with that term, however, is the further concept, predominantly found in John's writings, of *martyria*, the content of the witness, or the testimony that is given by the witness. The *martys* communicates the *martyrion:* the person who is a witness gives a witness or testimony. We have difficulty with these distinctions in English because we use the same word for both the person and the content of that person's testimony. The witness bears witness. But that ambiguity in English is also theologi-cally instructive because it emphasizes the basic thrust of the definitive statement "You shall be my witnesses." It is impossible to separate the meaning of the witness as person from the content of the witness borne by that person. The witness "incarnates," as it were, his or her witness.

From the outset of Acts, the concept of witness has a two-pronged meaning (found also in other literary traditions in the New Testament). The root meaning of *witness* refers to a person who can give a firsthand report of the facts of an occurrence because he or she was there. In secular usage, the witness is one whose report is reliably based upon personal experience. This element of experience is important. The witness does not report hearsay but what he or she has seen and heard in a direct encounter. The reliability of the witness's message is then a question of that person's integrity and accuracy in reporting. The early church emphasized the special importance of the eyewitnesses to Jesus, those who had been with him and taught by him before his death and resurrection. They form the original apostolic college upon which the church was founded. Eventually, through God's leading, others joined the original group: in particular the apostle Paul, but also the deacon Stephen.

In the New Testament, however, and especially in Luke-Acts, the witness is more than a reliable reporter of what happened. Here, the events witnessed to control the concept of *witness*. The salvation events of the life, death, and resurrection of Jesus Christ are events of a very special kind, beyond the analysis and categories of ordinary historical reporting. As such, they are no less factual—they really happened. It is, however, both impossible and inappropriate to evaluate their facticity and their historicity on the basis of our normal standards for historical analysis. These events reveal the nature and purpose of God; they are events God is carrying out within our human history, in which he is the subject, the initiator and doer of that which happens. While such events defy customary analysis, they can be witnessed. There were eyewitnesses present. Jesus did appear after his resurrection, and those who encountered him became very special witnesses.

Now, however, we can experience these events, these self-disclosures of God, only through faith. That is the other level of meaning for *witness*. The witnesses, the people, bear a witness; they proclaim a message that can be grasped only through the enabled response of faith, through the acknowledgment of who God is and what he has done in the saving history of Jesus. We can identify the witnesses as Spirit-used vessels whose own experience is integral to their message. To be credible witnesses, they must know Jesus Christ as Lord and

Savior in their own experience. They have come to that confession because God has enabled them to participate in and witness these events and recognize him and his saving purposes in them. They are eyewitnesses who cannot be merely objective reporters of what they have seen, but who have become deeply involved participants in the events, with all that they mean, in whom the events are now continuing to happen as they are empowered to bear witness to what they have seen and heard.

As witnesses, they must bear witness. They are to make known this experience, this intimate knowledge of God and his saving purposes. But the power of their testimony is not to be sought in the persuasiveness of their report, as might be the case with an effective witness in a court of law. Rather, the Spirit, working in the witness, will enable the hearer to acknowledge the truth and relevance of this testimony, and thus will draw that hearer into the witness's experience to share it, and, ultimately, to become a co-witness.

The declaration of God's wonderful deeds is thus channeled through the human experience and the human reporting of these witnesses, originally the disciples, the foundational apostolic college, and through them to the entire church. "Be my witnesses" defines the fundamental mission of the church, derived from its establishment and empowerment as described in Acts. The fundamental definition of the church, then, is not to be restricted to any of its entirely necessary activities, such as preaching, or sacraments, or service; rather, we are to define the church by the identity of its members. Being a witness is the identity out of which all of the functions of witness flow. Each Christian is to be a witness. The person as witness carries out the task of witness. The community made up of persons as witnesses carries out the common task of witness.

Thus, the mission of the church must be understood in connection with the actual experience and identity of the Christian individual and community. Admittedly, the Western world today overemphasizes the individualism of faith. We will speak about that later. But at one point this individualism is entirely appropriate, and that is where we define the person as witness in terms of his or her experience. What makes a person into a witness is the experience of Christ to which that person can testify. Apart from that experience, it is impossible to grasp properly what it means to be a witness. Of course, that is the core of the Christian faith. As Luther stated, the issue is one's personal discovery that Christ's saving death and resurrection were not only *pro nobis* (for us), but *pro me* (for me); that is, the gospel events directly concern, touch, and transform me as I respond to God's call to me. This is the process of becoming a witness, for to be a Christian must mean to be a witness. If we do not make that stipulation basic, then we fall back into the benefits/mission dichotomy. Christ died for my sins and made me a witness—those testimonies belong together. They are, in effect, two sides of the same truth. What Christ has made us, we must then become. (That will be the subject of our further discussion of the nature of witness; see esp. 6.1, pp. 91-96.)

This fundamental transformation of the person into a witness is described in many other ways in the New Testament. Jesus himself, when calling his disciples, said that they would become "fishers of men"—a change of identity. He also changed Simon's name to Peter, a sign both of his authority and of Peter's transformed identity. Paul speaks of our becoming new creatures, of putting on Christ, of leaving the old and experiencing the new. He teaches us that we must be transformed by our mind's renewal, and then we shall recognize the will of God. Christians are converted people, which means that, as changed people, they have been turned around and are now going in a different direction. They march in that new direction so that they will be witnesses in the world, authentic evidence of the truth of the gospel as the Spirit works through them to call forth faith.

The understanding of Christian identity as witness links the personal faith experience with the mission of the church and Christ's call to every Christian. But we must be very careful that we do not immediately reduce the meaning of *witness*—as often happens in evangelicalism today. The text does not say "You shall give testimonies"; it says, "You shall be my witnesses." This comprehensive definition of Christian life and work should be probed for its breadth and depth, and not limited in its scope. The mission of the church is as big as the whole gospel of Christ, whose witness the church is: "*My* witnesses"! In my critique of modern evangelism (I will turn to my criticism of the term *evangelism* later; see 8.1, pp. 133-36), I will address the too narrow understanding of witness. Witness as an activity is not simply saying certain words, or giving certain kinds of speeches. It is the whole life and work of the Christian church, encompassing the life and work of each Christian individual as a witness. If any part of the church can be defined apart from the meaning of witness, both as person and as activity, then it is questionable whether that particular aspect of the church really belongs within the community of faith (see Chap. 9).

Since it is the platform for all that follows in this study, we shall here summarize the importance of the mission promise, "You shall be my witnesses":

1. The primary definition of the church is given in the mission promise of Acts 1:8: "You shall be my witnesses."

2. This definition of the church's mission is a prophetic promise, which means that under God's power, its realization and fulfillment are certain, because God's Spirit will do it (Pentecost!).

3. This mission promise will lead the Christian community into a radically new endeavor, going out to the end of the earth.

4. To be such a witness, the Christian community has to have experienced what it is witnessing to; that is, the disciples were witnesses because of their personal experience and history with Christ, both before and after his resurrection.

5. This identity as witness is comprehensive—it defines the entire individual and the entire community. At the same time, it defines the central activity of this community, to bear witness, to make our experience of Jesus Christ known so that through this witness the Spirit may call forth faith.

6. To be a witness is to belong to the Lord to whom we witness: he says that we are *his* witnesses. Lordship is central to witness, which means acknowledging and submitting to Christ as the Lord of our lives.

3.3 THE ENABLING EVENT OF PENTECOST

In our summary above, we stated that the definition of the church in Acts 1:8 was a "prophetic promise." "You shall be my witnesses" defines what the church is going to be "when the Holy Spirit has come upon you." Like all biblical promises, its fulfillment is certain because God is going to do it. The new identity of witness, both individually and corporately, is the result of God's precedent action. We shall note, from the very outset, that this action of God works both individually and corporately—the dichotomy some so often emphasize in our Western tradition is not relevant. Individuals and their experience are part of the whole, and the whole is comprised of all its individuals, who are mutually dependent and mutually define and affect each other.

The actual fulfillment of this prophetic promise is portrayed in Acts 2, the account of Pentecost, the "birthday" of the church. It is important for our theme to see the way in which that great event did, in fact, carry out the prophetic promise of Acts 1:8. It was the unique event of enabling that called forth the church as the "witnessing community" (Suzanne deDietrich) and sent it out on its pilgrimage. As we have emphasized before, this event is an essential part of the gospel, and so the observance of Pentecost as a holy day is one of the church's major celebrations, completing the cycle initiated at Easter.

On Pentecost, while assembled in one place, the first Christian community experienced unusual events: a rushing wind, tongues of fire, the capacity to speak in the languages of all those gathered in Jerusalem from the then-known world for the Jewish festival. The rushing of the wind was not really a strange experience for a people rooted in the Old Testament experience of God, for it called to mind the fact that God had often revealed his presence in the form of a wind. Wind was a mysterious reality: its origin could not be determined, particularly in a prescientific age, nor could it be precisely defined or quantifed. Yet no one would deny its reality and presence. It was, thus, a very useful image for the mysterious reality and presence of God. And it had served as such since the creation accounts, when the "wind of God" hovered over the waters as creation was initiated. For those gathered in that place in Jerusalem, the rushing wind was a powerful sign of the presence of God, the God of the Old Covenant, continuing his work in their very midst.

The tongues of fire on their heads were significant in a similar way. Fire was also an image for the mysterious, purging, and inexplicable presence of God—we think of Moses and the burning bush, the fire that consumed Elijah's sacrifice on Mount Carmel, and the pillar of fire that led Israel through the wilderness. This fire, however, reveals itself as flames burning over each individual's head. It is no longer a fire in one particular place, a holy presence of God to which his people must come, such as the fire of sacrifice at the altar in the temple. Rather, the presence of God is distributed here throughout his people, those who are to be his witnesses. This is an important expression of the great turning point in salvation history brought about by the gospel events. Now the movement is outward to the world, whereas in the Old Covenant it was centered upon the holy place (again, the movement from centripetal to centrifugal, to use Johannes Blauw's image). These witnesses are now to be "temples of the Holy Spirit," vessels in which the Spirit powerfully resides and through which the Spirit will enter into the world.

The tongues of fire are an intensely incarnational image for our understanding of the mission of the church to be Christ's witnesses. The experience communicates the way in which the church is to carry out its mission. Christ will go out into the world, through the work of his Spirit, in the lives of Christians both individually and corporately. There is but one fire, and the entire body bears the same message and serves the same Lord. But each individual Christian, as a flame-bearer, is a witness. Thus, the relationship between the individual and corporate natures of the church is well defined in this Pentecostal image, and we must be careful to do justice to both dimensions of the church's call in our attempts to explain and to understand the church's mission.

The individual and corporate meaning of the tongues of fire is, if you will, the Lucan version of Paul's Body of Christ concept, which also relates the individually important functions of the members to the corporate unity and integrity of the entire community. It is a powerful image, seen against the backdrop of Old Testament experiences. Whereas the Holy of Holies was the only place where God could be directly encountered (at least in those theological traditions of Judaism that emphasized the temple cult), now the veil is rent, and every Christian, as an empowered witness, has become a "Holy of Holies" through whom God can be experienced in the world. Thus, the tongues of fire are an experiential statement of what it means to *be* the witness, to *be* the presence of Christ in the world. But we must remember that God gave them this possibility; it was the result of his action and was in no sense related to the prior qualifications or merit of the witnesses. They were, to be sure, assembled and waiting. They were ready to be used. It would not be undue conjecture to say that they were not placing obstacles in the way of God's work in their midst. Nonetheless, God made them into witnesses by his sovereign action.

The theological structure of the account, which has often been discussed by biblical scholars, relates centrally to our understanding of the incarnational mission of the church, as we have just seen. We have already observed that the geographical composition of the crowd in Jerusalem for the Jewish festival (Acts 2:9-11) represents the entire known world. They all hear the message in their various languages, not in the holy language of their ancient faith and community, but in the tongues they now speak in their dispersion among the cultures of the world. All the world is addressed with the message and meaning of Pentecost. The Spirit intends, with this enabling act, to send these messengers, this community, into all the world, in order to communicate effectively to that world. It is the Spirit's purpose that all nations should hear "in their own tongues." The witnesses who bear the presence of Christ into the world (the tongues of fire) as the result of God's powerful and direct intervention in history (the rushing wind) are now enabled to communicate the gospel so that all can hear, understand, and even respond to this message.

Thus, it is the work of the Spirit to make of these first Christians a community that both enfleshes the presence of Christ in the world, as the bearers of the flame, and also communicates the message. Both belong together. *Being* a witness and *saying* the witness are inseparable aspects of the one calling. One should not overstate the importance of sequence, but there does appear to be theological significance in the order of the three signs of the Spirit: the mysterious and powerful presence of God is first, to make plain that all this is God's action, a surprise for the people to whom it happens, and not the result of any action of theirs but rather God's direct intervention. Then follows the granting of the Spirit's powerful presence in each person's life, to make of each of them a witness. This is the presupposition that makes verbal communication possible. The message comes from messengers whose own identity has already been transformed by the One who is the theme of that message.

Emphasizing that sequence, and the total thrust of the Spirit's enabling and empowering action, the apostle Peter then preached the church's first sermon. He does so "standing with the eleven," Luke's way of making it clear that Peter is part of the original apostolic community to whom this ministry has been entrusted. His sermon, which we will not analyze in detail, is a powerful example of Spirit-enabled communication of the gospel message. Peter proclaims historical experience, which he must as a disciple/apostle, an eyewitness whose authority is a combination of his experience and the new empowerment of the Spirit on that signal day. He builds his sermon toward the confession of Jesus as Lord and Christ, as the awaited Messiah and Redeemer of Israel and the world, and the enthroned Lord over all creation. His proclamation is the announcement of what God has done, of the events that have now culminated in the strange and wondrous experience of Pentecost. His theme is salvation history, now at its apex, experienced and testified to by this emerging community of faith, and ready to be proclaimed to the world.

The power of his proclamation is such that his hearers are "cut to the heart" and want to know what they should do in response. This is a paradigm of Spirit-enabled proclamation: it is a presentation of God's actions in such a way that the hearer is moved to ask what his or her response can be. Peter does not manipulate his listeners, nor does he protect them from the harsh sides of the message: the human complicity in Jesus' death is bluntly stated. The sermon is a channel for the work of the Spirit, who calls forth questioning among the hearers. Peter can then respond to their questions with a direct appeal for their faith decision. They can repent, be baptized, and receive forgiveness and the promised Holy Spirit. They can become heirs of the promise that has always been theirs and is now both fulfilled and accessible to them. And many did.

The gift of the Holy Spirit on Pentecost, then, enabled the witnesses to begin incarnational ministry: to become bearers of the presence of Christ in the world, and to communicate the gospel so that all the world could hear it. With this enabling power, the Christian community is to go out across all borders, to every culture and language, and make the gospel known to all people. The geographical spread envisioned in Acts 2 is Luke's way of saying what Matthew meant when he reported the Great Commission: "go out to *all* the world." But the results of the empowering act of the Spirit include another, very significant dimension. The Spirit, while enabling incarnational witness and comprehensible communication, also creates a new community of salvation. The last verses of chapter two are a final part of the Spirit's Pentecostal work. The empowered community expands rapidly. To respond to the proclamation of the gospel must mean to become part of a radically new and different community.

The entire community described in Acts 2 is understood as an essential part of the witness—they had "favor with all the people" (v. 47). This emphasis upon the central role of the community as a witness is then carried out in far greater detail in all levels of New Testament literature. In the rest of the Book of Acts, Luke explores both the negative and positive aspects of the development of this witnessing community, ranging from their experiment with common ownership of all property (2:43-46) to the tragedy of Ananias and Sapphira's willful deception of the community. In Paul's letters and in the general Epistles, the integrity of the witnessing community is a central theme, underlining the apostolic conviction that God has called forth a people to "declare the wonderful deeds" of the gospel. We shall return, therefore, to several aspects of the community's witness as we explore our theme further.

3.4 THE COMMUNITY OF WITNESS

We have stated that the concept of witness, as both a definition of the individual and a description of his or her function, may be regarded as the operative concept in Acts for the church. "You shall be my witnesses" is what the entire book is about, and from chapter two to the end it tells the story of how this came about in the early church.

Martys and *martyria,* as two dimensions of the one calling and witness
of the church, will serve as our basic definition of the church's purpose.
Related to these two terms are three other New Testament terms, all
of which have received considerable emphasis in discussions of the
church. Our concern is to understand them in their relationship to the
central and overarching concept of witness. These terms are *kerygma*
(proclamation), *koinonia* (community), and *diakonia* (service or
ministry).

Ecclesiologies, systems of church doctrine, tend to dwell on just
one of these terms and arrange the others around them. Our intention
is to understand them all as they relate to the concept of witness,
without diminishing their own significance. Avery Dulles, a Catholic
theologian, has very helpfully introduced the concept of "models" for
the theological task of defining the church (see his excellent book,
Models of the Church). We shall return to this concept in another
context, but one could illuminate the methodological questions by
saying that some ecclesiologies use the *kerygma* model (Dulles calls
this the "herald model"), some emphasize the *koinonia* model (which
Dulles calls the "mystical communion model"), and, more recently,
some have emphasized the *diakonia* model (which Dulles deals with
as the "servant model"). Probably Dulles would ascribe what I see as
the importance of *martyria* as the operative concept to the "herald
model," but I believe that this is too narrow a view of the meaning of
witness.

The interest in the *kerygma,* the message preached or proclaimed,
has been especially strong in twentieth-century Protestant theology. In
particular, Karl Barth strongly emphasizes the proclamation of the
Word (his work has been called "kerygmatic theology" and "theology
of the Word"). Many of those who follow Barth's theology have a
marked tendency to limit biblical witness to verbal proclamation, even
to the extreme of restricting the kerygmatic reality to the preaching of
the Word in the traditional settings of Christian worship. This limitation is not fair to the whole scope of Barth's concept of ministry, and
it certainly is a questionable reduction of the church's task. It divides
the church into two groups: those who preach and those who listen.
Christianity appears to become solely the attentive response to the
preaching of the Word. The "incarnational translation" of the message
is left underemphasized (the unfairness to Barth surfaces here, because
he certainly was concerned with the translation of the Word into the
world). This emphasis is clearly a further chapter in the Reformation
emphasis upon the Word, especially the Word proclaimed, connected

with some Reformation reserve about too much emphasis upon what we do about it (the phantom fear of "works righteousness").

In our understanding of the New Testament mandate to the church, we see the *kerygma* as absolutely central, but yet linked to the broader definition of the church as a people of witness. As we have already pointed out, Peter defined the church as a race, a priesthood, a nation, a people—all corporate terms having to do with the life-encompassing identity of the church (1 Pet. 2:9-10). Elsewhere in his epistle he speaks of the Christian community as an alien people, a people on pilgrimage. He is clearly connecting the Israel of the Old Covenant to the church of the New. And this called-out people is "to declare the wonderful deeds of him who called you out of darkness into his marvelous light." A people declaring, as he expounds in this epistle with its emphasis upon obedience as the basic definition of faith, upon holiness, upon a Christian community with integrity, upon suffering for the sake of Christ, upon responsible ethical behavior in a pagan world, will be a people whose entire life is one of witness, and whose declaration will have to be in actions and in words. Too narrow a definition of declaration will not accord with the overall intention of Peter's epistle.

In Acts, the proclamation of the Word, such as Peter's sermon, comes out of and also produces an empowered community. The message is not disembodied. It is stated by Peter who is standing among the eleven. It takes place after the entire community has been made into bearers together and individually of the presence of God through his Spirit. The *kerygma* is the verbalization of the event that has called forth this community, and of its meaning for the entire world. To separate the *kerygma* from the *martyria* of the Christian church is to make the gospel into propositions to be affirmed rather than to understand it as the opportunity to know God in a personal and life-transforming relationship, called faith, and then to serve his purposes.

Thus, the basically correct emphasis upon the Word, which is so closely linked to the concept of *kerygma,* can be one-sidedly developed. The Word, in its Old Testament context, is not merely spoken words but is God's action communicating him and his purposes to those whom he enables to hear and to respond. God's Word is an event (see Gen. 1:3). Jesus Christ is God's Word as the event of the enfleshment of God in human history and experience. When we begin to treat the concept of Word as mental and propositional content alone, we lose its Hebrew wholeness. The Word is a person who can be known, and about whom we can make content statements that are true as they reflect his truth, but never exhaust the truth that is in him. We are not prevented from making propositional statements about the Word, because the Word has become audible and even doable. But our propositions will always fall short of him. Our *kerygma* does not equal the wholeness of the presence of Christ in the world (although we are to grow up toward that wholeness; see Eph. 4:12-13). What we say about him is a part of what we are and do because of him. The message is not only verbal but also visible and observable.

In a sense, this breadth of the concept of *kerygma* is implied in the Catholic and Protestant concern for the sacraments. The sacraments are events that communicate the gospel—Augustine called them "visible word." As *kerygma*, they declare the Good News, but they are also events that participate in and even convey to us God's action of grace for us. Word and sacrament, the great Reformation themes, are an expansion of the concept of *kerygma* beyond the solely verbal and mental to the visible and experiential, while simultaneously correcting the one-sided sacramental understanding that neglects the Word and makes the sacrament a salvation-producing work administered by the church.

The concept of witness includes these dimensions. The witness as a person must also convey the witness as content, both in actions and in words. Our concern must be for the integrity of both the person of the witness and the content of his or her message. The *kerygma* is the essential distinction of the witness, because the cause and motivation of the witness is made known through the declared message. Christian actions that remain wordless, that are not accompanied by *kerygma*, might well be effective witness, but they easily remain ambiguous. The gospel is to be said, but it is to be said out of the reality of the community and its action in the world, which are integral to Christian witness.

The authenticity and validity of the witness of the community is tested by its *kerygma*, its proclamation. Its message is to be Christ, and its witness as community is to demonstrate Christ. Heresy can creep in at both points: the way of being the witness can fall prey to error, and the content of the message can misrepresent or distort the apostolic proclamation. The church must be on guard against both forms of disobedience. But it is an equally pernicious distortion to separate the message from the community in witness, or to allow the community in witness to exist without proclaiming its message.

Therefore, the *martys* and his or her *martyria* are characterized by the declared *kerygma*. The message is embedded in the empowered reality of a community of witnesses that has been present in the world since Pentecost. Out of the community emerges the message, and the proclamation of the message, empowered by the Spirit, leads to the response of faith, which in turn builds up and expands the community. In that sense, there is a cyclical relationship between *koinonia* and *kerygma*, community and its proclamation.

There is a similar cyclical relationship with the concept of *koinonia* (community) as it relates to *martys* and *martyria*. Frequently used in the New Testament, this term particularly emphasizes the corporate, the "people" aspect of the church. The community is comprised of all those who have Christ in common. They are called to each other as a result of their being called to Christ. They are the presence of Christ in the world as his Body. The credibility and reliability of their witness is an essential part of the work of the gospel in the world. They exist to be witnesses and to bear witness. Thus, the concept of *koinonia* is closely linked to *martyria*. The *koinonia* is made up of *martyroi* (witnesses), and what they have in common is their *martyria*, their witness, the experience and the message of Christ.

We shall return to this central theme later, but for now it will suffice to emphasize that there is no *martyria* in the world apart from the *koinonia*, and that the reason the *koinonia* exists is to render witness in the world. The community of Christ is not an end in itself but a part of God's accomplishment of his saving purposes, as we have stated before. The *koinonia* becomes self-centered and spiritually arrogant when it forgets or underemphasizes that its purpose is *martyria*, witness. To anticipate the later discussion, the community is to *be*, to *do*, and to *say* the gospel, the Good News, the *kerygma*, and God has constituted it as a community and empowered it with the Spirit for that very task.

Diakonia, "service" or "ministry," has received more attention recently, as some ecclesiologies have reacted to secularization and urbanization by emphasizing the fact that the Christian church is to serve human need, to be salt dissolving in the world, and to render Christ's love "unto the least of these my brethren." This very important emphasis, often lacking in those traditions that emphasize the preaching of the message as the exclusive form of declaration, has taken up the New Testament emphasis upon service and servanthood and made it into the central model of the church. Certainly there is good biblical reason to emphasize this particular theme when we talk about the church. But here again, we need to see that *diakonia* is properly understood in relationship to *martyria*. *Diakonia* is the serving expression of the truth of the gospel as God's purpose and determination to make all things whole and restore his creation to himself. Thus, there is a necessary expression of the *martyria* of the church in its concern for and involvement in healing service, wherever possible and needed.

But again, as with *koinonia* and *kerygma*, the *diakonia* is to express our mandate to be "witnesses" in a whole and comprehensive sense. When the tendency is present to emphasize service at the cost of verbal declaration, then an unacceptable division of the New Testament definition of the church is creeping in. If *diakonia* is the *doing* of the gospel, then it must be linked with the identity of the witness who *is* the incarnation of this Good News, as well as with the *saying* of the witness, the content of the Good News.

Martyria, on the other hand, is a hollow reality if it does not include the doing of the gospel, the servanthood that Christ himself modeled when he washed the feet of the disciples, that he practiced throughout his earthly ministry as he dealt with the maladies and suffering of the people who surrounded him and as he addressed the hypocrisy and inequities of his day. Witness is more than a verbal concept, and the New Testament stress on servanthood ensures that we do not limit the meaning of witness to that which is only verbal. At the same time, we must see that the term *diakonia* is used in a variety of settings, even including formulations like "ministry of the Word," which indicates that we should be careful about assigning only one dimension of meaning to this term—especially when there is a suspicion that we are bringing our political and social agenda to Scripture to receive biblical certification for our programs.

The concept of *martys/martyria*, then, must find its expression in the actions of the church discussed in the New Testament under the terms *kerygma, koinonia,* and *diakonia.* Our focus may shift from time to time from one to the other of these component aspects of the church. But our goal in developing an understanding of the church, or a biblically rooted ecclesiology, will be to incorporate all of these themes in our language and imagery. This happens best, I am persuaded, when we relate them to each other around the initial mission promise to the church: "You shall be my witnesses."

The way, then, in which the incarnation of Christ continues in history is through the life and ministry of the church that he has called into being and empowered through the Holy Spirit. God is completing his work of salvation through this called-out people, the Body of Christ, and he is disclosing himself to the world he desires to restore to himself through the witness that this church is and does and says. His self-disclosure is within human history and experience, and is thus marked by the ambiguity and tension of human reality. And yet it is God's action, and he does make himself knowable in this surprising way. To speak of the church in this fashion, as the continuing incarnation of Christ, as the Body of Christ, as the empowered witness, is not to become ahistorical with regard to the church or to put it on some pedestal of perfection. Rather, it is to confront the amazing condescension of God, who out of his love for his lost creation intervenes in our history for our sakes, and works sovereignly to enable us to recognize and respond in faith to this self-revelation. As that response happens, the community of the called-out ones grows. But that growth is God's gracious work so that the ministry, the task for which the church is called and set apart, can be done more effectively, so that "all the world" might be reached. Thus, the church must understand its calling not as a privileged call to its own salvation, but rather as a call to service, an enlistment in the work of God toward his ultimate goal of saving his creation. As a servant people, the church progresses through history knowing that God's history with his creation is mysterious beyond our speculation, and yet crystal clear in its basic purpose: "In Christ, God was reconciling the world to himself, not counting their trespasses against them, and entrusting to us the message of reconciliation. So we are ambassadors for Christ, God making his appeal through us" (2 Cor. 5:19-20a).

Four

REALISM ABOUT THE CHURCH

4.1 THE DISAPPOINTMENT OF HISTORY

We have described the church's mission in very high terms: incarnation, Body of Christ, witness. We have said that the formation of the church is an essential part of the gospel, a major event in salvation history. But we have also emphasized the ambiguity and tension in such a view of the church: "It will not help to discuss the church, after these twenty centuries, and ignore the contradictions, the weaknesses, the disappointments that the church presents to us" (supra, p. 8). The more we develop an incarnational understanding of the church's mission and function, the more imperative it is that we deal candidly with the so-called disappointment of the church's history.

Critics of Christianity excel in pointing out the great credibility gaps, which are plainly seen, between what the gospel espouses and what the church has actually been and done. "Hypocrisy" is the favorite accusation these critics level at Christians and Christianity. The study of the church's history is a very sobering undertaking for any Christian, but it is especially challenging for the Christian whose faith structure does not permit much ambiguity or mystery. Contemporary evangelicalism can be greatly threatened by such a study, and often the escape route is to render a sweeping judgment over centuries of our history. Such judgments often postulate the withdrawal of the Holy Spirit until whenever this or that particular form of Christian piety reemerged in history, and thus they deny the faith of the whole course of Christian history in the interval. Although this is an arrogant solution, it is an understandable retreat from the encounter with the realism of the church's sinfulness and frailty through the ages.

Can one maintain an incarnational view of the church's mandate and postulate such a high calling, and also be an honest historian? The question, hard as it is, must be faced. To do so, we must consider another presupposition. If we are convinced that God truly works in and through history, then we must include all of history in that view. We must proceed from the assumption that history cannot exclude God from its course, although God may work in different ways and more or less imperceptibly within that history. At the same time, we must deal with the fact that the opposition to God is also virulently at work in history, and particularly in ways that result in disobedience by the people of God. What is truly there in history must be honestly confronted. The truth, including historical truth, cannot exclude God if God is truth.

When, in the name of Christ, the church has functioned in ways that contradict both the spirit and the instruction of Christ, we cannot then resolve the problem by stating that, in this particular unfortunate episode, God was absent. Nor can we make God responsible for our human sinfulness, in a sense, passing the spiritual buck. We must allow the tension to stand, just as we must accept the same tension in the long and torturous history of Israel in the Old Covenant. But we can seek to understand that tension, and we may even perhaps grasp something important about the mysterious nature of God's sovereign actions in history.

When we scan our history, we see again and again Christians distorting the calling of the church in order to serve purposes other than God's. We see the church aligning itself with political movements, diluting its message to insure its continued acceptance within a given social setting, becoming a mouthpiece for narrow nationalisms and even racisms. There are innumerable episodes in the history of the church where we honestly wonder if Christ could have reacted to what was going on in any other way than to braid a whip and clean out the temple again. Rather than being a constant force for the realization of peace, serving the Prince of Peace, the Christian church has continually aligned itself with the goals and methods of war. In some of its organizational expressions, it is still doing so.

For example, if we try to evaluate with some degree of objectivity the emergence of Marxism in the Western, "Christian" world, then we must admit, I believe, that at least part of the historical network of causes that led to Marxism was the failure of the Christian church to carry out significant parts of the gospel mandate. Much of what Marxism is about is really a possible Christian social ethic (not the only possible one), stripped of its rootedness in the law, grace, love, and justice of God. The Christian church today must see this as a very sobering indictment of our own resistance to the claims of the gospel.

Historical movements are fraught with complexity, and sorting out causes and effects is, at best, a very chancy undertaking. But I will hazard one interpretation of the disappointment of church history, which has a bearing upon our theme in this book. It can be argued, I believe, that our failure to carry out our mandate has often been caused by the very reduction of that mandate, as we have already described. That is, as the Christian church has divided the benefits of faith in the gospel from the mission of the church as the witness to that gospel, it has embarked upon a course of action that must result in failure. Concentration upon the benefits of salvation, separated from the calling and purpose for our existence as the church, leads inexorably to an analysis of "how we are saved," "how we know we are saved," and, then, "how we protect our savedness from the evils of the world around us."

We have often become a church that focuses upon its own spirituality, its own goodness, its own separatedness, and, in our modern world, its "success." The effects of God's blessing, intended to be motivators and enablers of obedient ministry, have become ends in themselves, subject to incessant reflection. We have been preoccupied with our own spiritual welfare, and thus have lost sight of the essential link between our blessedness and our call to be a blessing.

This can be illustrated in many ways. I am reminded of the portals of the great gothic cathedrals of the Middle Ages, where we usually find a sculpted vision of the final judgment, of the heavenly court in which Christ sits as Judge, surrounded by angels and saints, with depictions of the lost disappearing downward from the heavenly scene. The medieval worshiper entered that building preoccupied with the question, "Will I survive that judgment, and spend eternity in heaven or in hell?" The medieval church focused its structures of spiritual discipline on that question. The sacraments had evolved into a subtle and intricate system to deal with one's lostness and guarantee one's eternal blessedness. Luther was driven to the insights of the Reformation, as we have stated, out of the spiritual distress that resulted from his repeated discovery that he could not be certain that he had pleased God adequately enough to regard himself as saved. He later spoke of sinful man as "curved into himself," but the Christian preoccupied with his or her salvation to the exclusion of all broader dimensions of our calling is just as "curved into himself"! How different is the spirit of the apostle when he writes, "For I could wish that I myself were accursed and cut off from Christ for the sake of my brethren . . . " (Rom. 9:3).

When, in the course of modern secularization and the discovery of the vast unevangelized reaches of the world, the modern mission movement emerged, it was often motivated by this narrow definition of the gospel. This is very paradoxical, because the modern mission movement was, in fact, a rediscovery of the church's calling established at Pentecost. And yet we often did not proclaim the whole gospel as we went out to the "unevangelized world." The motivation was to "save heathens from eternal damnation," whereas the calling of the church is to be Christ's witnesses, proclaiming the wonderful deeds of God to enlist more workers for the harvest, and thus to expand the evidence of the gospel in the world through the presence of the incarnational community, the church.

We must view as evidence of God's sovereign grace the fact that the churches born out of Western missions have often developed a fuller view of the gospel than their parent churches brought them. Clearly, the Holy Spirit continues to be the initiator and enabler of the church, and although the witness may bring the Good News into a new historical situation, and there experience the response of faith and the formation of the church, the witness cannot control the course of the gospel once planted. Lesslie Newbigin has made this point in his basic book on the church's mission, *The Open Secret.* For the Western church, this means that we may well need to learn more about the gospel from the Third World churches as they expand our sense of the gospel and work as God's instruments in our continuing evangelization.

The obedient church should not be so preoccupied with the question "Are you saved?" (emphasizing the past tense), because this question betrays too narrow a view of the gospel; once again, it is the fateful reduction of Christianity to its benefits. Salvation is, ultimately, a certainty about the future tense of our faith (see 5.2, pp. 78-88): the final events are yet to take place, and they are under God's sovereign rule. Our work is that of the witness, not the final judge. And the witnesses are to continue to witness, with neither fear nor anxiety about the outcome, but with great attention to the integrity of our work as it expresses the meaning of the gospel in our actions as well as our words.

This one-sided emphasis upon our salvation presents to the world a self-centered Christianity that cannot help but convey a sense of its own spiritual superiority. In that way, the accusation of hypocrisy is not far from the truth. If we do, in fact, see ourselves as spiritually special because we are saved, and do not live with the salvation dynamic of the past, present, and future tenses of salvation (see 5.2, pp. 78-88), then we will disappoint ourselves and give our critics live ammunition. We will be tempted to pull away from the world in order to protect ourselves from the world's sinfulness. We will literally reverse the thrust of the Pentecostal equipping of the church and return to some form of centripetal spirituality, looking for or attempting to fabricate the perfect community, the perfect theology, the perfect place and time for the Christian experience of our own savedness.

To link our salvation with our mission, to see the benefits of salvation as God's equipment for the task to which he is sending us, is to be and to remain realistic about who we are in the world. We are not surprised at the disappointments in Christian history—we are ashamed of them. They are one of the reasons the Christian church lives under the sign of the cross and begins its acts of worship with a confession of sin and receives again the assurance of God's pardon. As has often been noted, it is the honest Christian who best knows the meaning and dimensions of sin, and it is the honest church that faces its own sinfulness and proceeds on its pilgrimage equipped by the forgiving grace of God. That grace is the growth-enabling power that gradually weans us away from our sins of disobedience and little faith. But we are also confident that God's purposes will not ultimately be hindered because of our sins, although the progress of the kingdom's proclamation may be obstructed or diverted.

The marvelous fact about the whole gospel, about the benefits and the mission taken together, is that it liberates us from the wrong kind of preoccupation with ourselves. We are certain that we are saved and will be saved, and that therefore we have a task to perform. Therefore, our question is not "Am I saved?" but "Am I useful?" It is not "Are we perfect?" but "Are we obedient?" It is not "Have we arrived?" but "Are we moving in God's direction?" There is great release in not having to serve as the Judge; only Christ can do that. Although it is obvious that our strategy for mission will differ depending on what we know about the faith of those to whom we go, it still is ultimately preferable that we see ourselves as witnesses who are obedient to Christ and who carry out the mandate of incarnating him and his Good News, regardless of whether or not those with whom we work are

Christians. Just as God's sun shines on rich and poor alike, and God's rain falls on sinner and just, the task of Christian witness is omnidirectional and totally nondiscriminatory. It even means that Christians are supposed to act like Christians toward each other!

The gospel mandate equips the Christian realist to view all of history and every situation with a twofold focus. There is no particular setting in our human experience from which God's sovereign grace can be excluded, but there is also no setting in which the opposition to God is not at work. Where God is most at work, where the Spirit is most dynamically present and active in people's lives, there the opposition is all the more virulent. Every revival of faith is accompanied by its distortions and abuses. Every form of radical Christian obedience can be twisted into an ideological program that betrays the gospel and its Lord. This may not be obvious in a program's outwardly admirable actions, but the betrayal takes place through the loveless and judgmental spirit that often surfaces in such radical movements.

What we know about the New Testament congregations is helpful and comforting. In Acts, we read of the distortion of the Pentecostal gift in Simon Magus's attempt to buy the Spirit. The Epistles are really a catalog of misunderstandings and distortions of the gospel to which the apostles are responding. Those churches did not necessarily have a better grasp of the gospel and our task than we do. They experienced divisiveness, pride, abuse of the spiritual gifts, heresy, and incredible distortions of the essentials of the gospel, including the meaning and work of grace and the significance of the resurrection. The Bible is disarmingly candid about this, just as the Old Testament honestly portrays the "heroes" of the faith with all their very considerable flaws. We are shown a church that is both human and divine, both called by God and defined by the sinfulness of its members. It is a disappointing church. The seven letters of Revelation document this disappointment, as the Lord of the church admonishes the churches where they need to hear it.

And yet, this church, in all its weakness and sinfulness, was the only church—and the same is true today. It is convenient to retreat to some kind of illusive "invisible church" in order to avoid the problems of historical ambiguity in the visible church. But the only church there is, as far as we are concerned, is the visible church. We certainly cannot emphasize the incarnational nature of the church and its work, and then deny that incarnation by making the "true church" into some ephemeral, spiritual entity that is neither historical nor experiential. The church is a blemished and disappointing movement, but God is not finished with it yet. It will be presented as the perfected bride, but not until the future bridal banquet that is part of the consummation of history. Until then, we continue functioning as a community in witness, pointing to Christ and not to our perfection, yet revealing who Christ is and what Christ does by sharing both our sinfulness and our forgiveness as a part of our witness.

Without any hint of apologetics, the Christian church must confess that its history is disappointing. The survival of the church is scarcely explicable if we look at the human element in it. In a mysterious analogy to the continuing existence of the Jewish nation, the Christian church continues in history in all its self-contradictoriness and ambiguity because God made it and will bring it to the end of its pilgrimage, certainly battered but still his called and chosen, his weak and sinful people. Perhaps the most compelling outward evidence of this mysterious fact is the survival of the Christian church, often with surprising virulence, under those ideologies in the world that have been openly and aggressively committed to removing Christianity from history as the remnant of an earlier and now superceded period—we think of the church in Poland, in East Germany, and in the Peoples Republic of China.

While confessing our sinfulness and living within the spirit of D. T. Niles's definition of the church ("one beggar saying to another beggar, 'I know where bread is'"), the church does live with a confidence about its calling and its destiny that does not emerge out of its reality. God gives this certainty to the church together with its calling. The Christian hope is a living hope (1 Pet. 1:3), because it is based on God's actions and promises. The Christian certainty is totally steadfast, because it is focused on the person and work of Jesus Christ, who is the Lord of the church, the One working through it and bringing it through its ambiguous and often hazardous historical journey to its certain destination. We expect the church, in its adventuresome pilgrimage, to change, to discover more of what the gospel has meant, to take steps in the direction of the "mature manhood, . . . the measure of the stature of the fulness of Christ" (Eph. 4:13), which is the definition of our goal.

Movement and growth are essential aspects of the church's historical existence. The church is not a frozen institution (more about that in the next section of this chapter) nor a museum devoted to preserving the golden past. The historical reality of the church is that of a people underway, a pilgrim nation; thus, movement verbs characterize biblical talk about the church. *Faith* itself is a term defining a relationship, a dynamic event going on between God and us. Thus it is always damaging to our concept of faith when we try to force it into propositional boxes that will not permit us to express that dynamic relationship.

The imagery for the church in the New Testament is more akin to the tabernacle in the Old Covenant than to the temple. Peter, in his first epistle, actually speaks of the Christian church as an alien people, as strangers in the land, as sojourners and members of God's diaspora (1:11; 2:11). A major emphasis of the New Testament is on the suffering and hostility that the Christian church is to expect to encounter in its historical pilgrimage. The Book of Revelation, taken as a whole, is a manual of preparation for that very intense resistance and persecution that will constantly come upon the church, and is normally a part of the church's daily experience at some point on the globe at any time in history. But the writers of Philippians, 1 Peter, and Jude also address this reality, as did our Lord himself when he instructed his disciples about the harsh realities of radical obedience to him. We do not deal realistically with the historical situation of the church if we ignore that fact. It is more realistic to see the church in that kind of hostile situation than to expect the church's situation always to be what we have been privileged to experience in the Western world in the last few centuries.

It would be wise for Western Christians to move out of their historical isolation and look more carefully at the present-day realities of the Christian church around the world. They would see that the church is growing in ways quite surprising to them, that it is grappling with pressures and opposition of which they do not know. We may count ourselves grateful that we have the legally protected rights and privileges that are the result of our long history as a "Christianized civilization." No one is going to discount superficially this history nor fail to express gratitude for what we are still privileged to be and to do in our Western democracies. But we must address the question of what our protected state is doing to the church, particularly in the West. Is it not possible that our moral strength and evangelical commitment are jeopardized by the very security we enjoy in our historical situation? Could it not be that we are being "persecuted by softness" (I once spoke of "being stoned to death with marshmallows" to describe our situation), and that we are rendered just as ineffective in our witness by such privileges and protections, which also limit and restrict us, as we would be if we we were confined to concentration camps?

We have obviously overstated the question, for the reality of the situation is somewhere in the middle. We dare not discount the rare opportunities we have for open proclamation and broad ministry in our Western society. The sad thing is the way we fail to use these God-given opportunities wisely for ministry. But we should be alert to the spiritual jeopardy present as a result of our overly comfortable relationship to our own societies and structures. In a sense, this could be one of the most disappointing parts of our historical process, that we have, in fact, so domesticated and adapted the gospel that we can be utterly at home in our culture, and find rather puzzling and inappropriate the New Testament preparation of the church for hostility and resistance to its message.

There is one other aspect of our historical reality that I need to mention as we consider the significance of change and movement as essential to the church's pilgrimage through time. In addition to suffering and hostility, we are to expect to discover more of what the gospel is and calls us to become (we alluded to this earlier). As we "grow up in every way into him who is the head, into Christ" (Eph. 4:15), we will find that the gospel is like a vast treasure, and we are constantly uncovering more of its wonders. We should speak of this as "growth" rather than "change," though, as many Christians become nervous when we speak of change in the church. They feel that somehow this implies that we are moving away from orthodoxy or the truth once given. But this is a static view of Christian truth and reality that we need to examine and correct. The point here is that the gospel, understood as the totality of God's saving purposes and work culminating in Christ, is far greater and more comprehensive in its meaning than the church has ever discovered.

The church's historical pilgrimage begins with just such a process of discovery, which we have already referred to in our review of the vision of the church in Acts. Although Christ promised that the church would be a witness to the entire world, the first hurdle was simply moving outside the city limits of Jerusalem. It was the Sanhedrin's persecution that forced the Christian community into the surrounding country of Judea and into Samaria. Thus began, almost inadvertently, the outward growth of the church. The discovery of what "all the world" really meant became a painful process as the apostolic community first confronted the fact of genuine faith in non-Jews, in Samaritans, and even in Gentiles. This long and difficult passage for the church was marked by heated controversy and ultimately by conciliar compromise (Acts 15). But, in effect, what was happening in the

Jewish/Gentile controversy of the early church was a significant chapter of growth in Christianity's understanding of the "breadth and length and height and depth" of the love of Christ (Eph. 3:18-19), expressed in the Good News.

Scripture gives us evidence of other struggles of discovery as the church pursued the path of obedience in the first decades of its existence. Paul had to grapple with a limited vision of Christian freedom that still insisted on the observance of dietary laws or the refusal to use meat offered to idols. He struggled with the perceptions of "strong" and "weak" Christians in Rome (14-15:13). We are now discovering, in our biblical research, that the apostolic communities were also struggling with the radical nature of the gospel in confrontation with social realities such as the established inequities in the roles of men and women, or of children, or even of slaves and owners. The Christian church needed fifteen centuries to begin to act upon what the gospel has always said about slavery, although many Christian thinkers had pointed out the ethical and evangelical impossibility of slavery much earlier. In the twentieth century of our pilgrimage, we are beginning to deal with the impact of the gospel upon the role and position of women in the church, and the struggle is a very real one, marked by the same heat and controversy that surrounded the Jewish-Gentile battle in the first century.

On another front, Christians are rediscovering the dimensions of the gospel with regard to our responsibility within the world. We are seeing again that the gospel of a new creation rearticulates for the church the profound significance of the creation command at the beginning of the Bible. And so it gradually becomes clear to Christians that we must be at the forefront of obedience with regard to exercising responsible authority over creation, as good gardeners, caring for the beautiful garden God made, ensuring its continuation and its productivity, and working to correct our human abuse of the world of nature. A "theology of ecology" has always been part of the creation dimension of the gospel (St. Francis knew that), but Western Christians in their industrialized and technological societies have avoided that dimension and now are finding out, rather painfully, that this too is part of our obedience.

When we deal candidly with the disappointment of our history, and learn from the New Testament how realistically we have been prepared for this history, then we can be honest about our failings and yet totally certain of God's faithfulness in bringing to a conclusion the good work he has begun. In a very real sense, we have more future with God than we have past. The fundamental orientation of the church in history is toward the future. The salvation events of Christ are not closed chapters but events pointing toward future consummation. Although we dare not speculate about the sequence of details of that future, we live our lives in confident expectation that this hard and often disappointing historical passage will end just as God intends it to. Rather than worry about it, or try to figure it out, we are called to obedience, to the work of being, doing, and saying the witness.

4.2 THE SOBERING CHALLENGE OF THE INSTITUTIONAL CHURCH

Perhaps the disappointment of Christian history surfaces most painfully when we consider that the church is a vast institution, characterized by all of the familiar drawbacks of institutions: complexity, bureaucracy, power brokering and politics, resistance to change, commitment to the status quo . . . and the list could be extended. Certainly there are few aspects of Christian reality that call forth more negative reactions, especially from young people, than the institutional realities of the church. How many groups and movements break away from the church in an effort to rid themselves of the negativeness of "the institution" and "the establishment"! How much of the world's criticism of Christian hypocrisy is actually the result of encounters with Christian institutionalism as it compromises the gospel in its accommodation to the world! If we are going to be realistic about the church as Christ's incarnational witness in the world, we must deal with the sobering challenge of the institution.

To put the problem in its most pointed form, one often senses that the fundamental criterion governing life and especially decision making in the church is not theological but rather organizational: the institution will insure its survival, which usually means meeting this year's budget and increasing it by at least the rate of inflation in the coming year. What will be said and done in obedience to the gospel will be filtered through the network of organizational concerns that includes factors such as "what will help or hinder giving," "what will least offend the membership," and "what will draw more people out." Admittedly, this is both a stereotype and an overstatement. But it is uncomfortably close to the reality of much of the institutional church. Therefore, we must deal with this question or our entire undertaking in this book, to define precisely the church's mission as one of incarnational witness, will lack credibility.

We begin with some truisms about the institutional aspect of the church. As truisms they are obvious, and yet they need to be said, because they are so often ignored in the often emotional discussions that cluster around the problem of the institution. We must affirm that the institution is a necessity. There is no way to exist within historical reality and avoid taking on the form of an institution. (In my view, Howard Snyder, in his valuable books on the church, *The Problem with Wineskins,* and *The Community of the King,* oversimplifies this problem when he calls all organizational expressions of the church "parachurch.") Those who seek to continue the life of the church and reject its necessary institutional form are involved in a totally deceptive effort, and they are becoming their own institution as they rebel.

The moment any group of people repeats what it has already done together once, that is, meets a second time or repeats any action, it has become an institution. Social existence requires institutional form. The church, as the family of faith, is an institution that functions as such in the world, just as the physical family is an institution that takes on particular ways of functioning in the world. Therefore, it will be totally unfruitful to approach the sober challenge of the institution as though there were a choice. The church *must* be institutional. The question is not "To be or not to be institutional?" but "How will it be institutional?"

The New Testament makes it clear that the church was an institution from the beginning, that it was our Lord's intention that it be so. His preparation of the disciples for their ministry was, in part, instruction about the life of a special kind of institution. It was to be very different from other institutions, having radically contrasting concepts of authority, leadership, service, and decision making, as well as a unique mission in the world. But there was to be leadership, structure, form, purpose, and action. And from the very beginning, the church was such an institution. It had, since Pentecost, ways of defining its membership, structures for decision making, processes for dealing with conflicts among its members, and assignment of varying levels of responsibility.

We know, from our study of the environment within which the church had to exist in the first century, that the conditions of Roman society imposed certain institutional realities on the early church. No group of individuals could gather without the acknowledgment and permission of the state (the underground church of the catacombs, from a later period, is negative evidence of that necessity). The early church conformed to the laws of the land, constituted itself as a collegium, and functioned in society as a recognized body. When it was persecuted, it was as an organization that did *not* have official permission to exist. And when, finally, Constantine confirmed its legal existence, it developed organizational forms borrowed from the social and political structures in which it had emerged.

The early church had to organize not only for obvious sociological reasons; it was directed by God's Spirit to become a particular kind of organization in order to carry out its mission. The New Testament does not define what kind of institutional structure the church will take, but makes it abundantly clear that the church must have concrete and tangible institutional form in order to be the Body of Christ in the world. Titles such as bishop, elder, presbyter, and deacon indicate the development of structures of leadership and service. In reference to Christian assembly, the New Testament gives instructions on what to do and what not to do when gathered. It addresses the moral standards of the community as an important aspect of the church's witness. Certain Scriptures tackle major disagreements in the church, and refer to at least one "council" convened during the New Testament period to deal with such disagreements (the so-called Council of Jerusalem; see Acts 15). Paul leaves instructions to the elders of the Ephesian church, when he meets them at the port of Miletus, and elsewhere we note that he chose elders and established roles of responsibility in the churches he founded. In 1 Peter 5, the apostle gives explicit instructions to the "elders" in the churches to which he is writing. And, of course, the Pastoral Epistles are classic statements about the organizational qualities that should characterize the early churches.

The institutional existence of the church, then, is a sociological necessity. But more importantly, the incarnational nature of the church demands, as we emphasized before, that the church be a social reality. The Word continues to be enfleshed in the realities of world history, which must include the givens of social and political structure. Retreat from the real historical world has never been an answer. The monastic foundations became as institutional as the worldly orders from which they withdrew, and amorphous Christian groups that seek to be "organic" but not "organizational" are as institutionalized as any other form of the church. (It would be instructive to review at this point the long history of "Enthusiasm," but I must refer the reader to Ronald Knox's excellent book on the subject.)

We have already stated the issue: How will the church be an institution? The negativeness about the church's institutional realities is understandable when we address the problem of "institutionalism."

It is possible, and it has frequently happened, for the necessary institutional form to become an "ism," a dominant ideology, which redefines the purpose of the church. Early in this section we alluded to many of the more obvious ways in which this has happened. It is quite pointless to deny or ignore these historical distortions of the church; it would be better to learn from them.

Institutionalism presents itself as a problem whenever the institutional aspect of the church is allowed to become the church's dominant characteristic. The institution of the church is intended to serve the witnessing community as it obediently carries out its mission. Institutional structure should be enabling structure; it should provide the ways and means for the Body of Christ to progress within history, under the leadership of the Spirit. It should not be the central model of the church, but it is an essential part of the church. (Dulles quite rightly deals with the "institutional model" as necessary but only in a secondary and supportive role to the other, more central models of the church; see *Models of the Church*.) Our task is to develop a biblical theology of the institution, and then to apply it rigorously to the church's reality, with the intention to change what must be changed based upon such a review.

As we have pointed out, there is no eternally mandated biblical institutional form. The variety of institutional approaches we find in the New Testament (often discussed as Jewish and Hellenistic trends in church organization in the first century) reveals that, while institution is necessary, it can take on various forms. What form each will take appears to be left to the "redeemed intelligence" of the Christian community. If we understand clearly our task, that is, if we grasp the nature of our calling as incarnational witness, then we can proceed to organize our life and resources in ways that will most obediently and effectively enable us to do what we are to do. The institution of the church is to be the servant of the church's calling.

Given the fact of sin, and the further fact that human sin tends to compound itself in institutional forms that conceal their roots in human rebellion, it is an important theological task to develop with our doctrines of the church those disciplines that will allow us to review our institutional forms. We should ask ourselves if the ways in which we have chosen to function in the world continue to be useful and functional to our task. A church that is future-oriented in its self-concept can, with the Spirit's enabling help, learn to examine itself critically and to set aside practices and customs, traditions and forms that may once have been functional for the carrying out of its task, but have lost that usefulness. History often forces such decisions upon the church. We can think here of the Protestant Union imposed upon the Lutheran and Reformed churches in the Prussian realms in the early nineteenth century. Or we could refer to the twentieth-century church unions that have emerged out of the insight in the Third World churches that their imported divisions were neither relevant to their task nor necessary in their non-Western settings.

It is, however, a necessary kind of Christian obedience to address the critical question of institution and institutionalism before historical crises force the issue upon us. In our secure Western societies, we are undoubtedly too complacent about the institutionalism that obviously has evolved over almost twenty centuries of Christian history. The fact that it took the old Northern and Southern Presbyterian churches in the United States one century to overcome the division of the Civil War is a sad commentary on our complacency—although we are very thankful that this particular reunion did finally come about! Our history is replete with instructive lessons about the dangers of institutionalism. So it would be wise for the church to design its own "sunset laws," to test its organizational forms regularly, to ask itself: Do we best carry out our purpose and serve Christ in the form in which we now exist? Could we be better stewards of our resources in this particular historical situation by making changes in the form—since the form is neither sacrosanct nor inspired? The stewardship that our mission requires of us will lead us to be critics of our institution and to change where change will lead to heightened obedience.

The incarnationally understood community will be very aware of the way in which our institutional forms and procedures are a part of our witness to the world. This is perhaps the more urgent reason to be attentive to the integrity of our institution and to beware of institutionalism. The world to which we are sent encounters the church as an institution—and necessarily so. The issue is then whether that encounter is a meeting with the gospel or a barrier to meeting the gospel. If the Christian church as an institution refuses to translate the gospel of love and grace into its inner functioning; if it compromises with the world and lets power, politics, and single-interest groups be its guiding principles; then it should not wonder at the recurring accusation of hypocrisy. Nothing is more damaging to the cause of Christ than the in-fighting, divisiveness, empire building, and unprincipled pragmatism that are so much a part of our churchly reality. Sadly, the Western churches can observe how they have exported precisely these problems to the younger churches in the course of the mission movement, so that we are talking about universal problems of the church when we speak of the dangers of institutionalism.

The challenge to the Christian churches today (it is necessary to use the plural here, especially when discussing the realism of institutions) is to learn from the disappointments of our history, and to submit again to the tutelage of Scripture with regard to the ways in which the gospel must govern our institutional forms. We must learn how to enflesh the gospel as an institutional church. We need to study again our Lord's instructions to the disciples when he addressed the questions of authority, servanthood, and the contrast between the world's standards of power and the Christian practice of self-sacrificing service. It will not help for any part of the church to be particularly judgmental or superior at this point. Nowhere is the fact of sin in the church so obvious as in the church's institutional struggles. But our "redeemed intelligence" and our summons to "be his witnesses" are, taken together, more than adequate resources for the process of reviewing and reforming our churches into institutional bodies that know their calling and single-mindedly go about the task of doing it.

The classic management dictum is "Form follows function." We can apply this principle, with some adaptation, to the institutional task of the church. The goal of the church is clear. Incarnational witness, as a concept, links together our call and the way we go about pursuing it. Our function is inherently an expression of our call: we enflesh the gospel in who we are, what we do, and what we say. Our institutional forms are, then, one very important way in which we "do the gospel." The task of ecclesiastical renewal and reformation is thus an eminently theological task: we must ask again what our purpose is, what the givens of any particular historical setting are, and, then, what will be the organizational and institutional ways in which we will obey Christ where we are.

We remind ourselves that the church is not an end in itself but rather an instrument created by God for the accomplishing of his great salvation purposes. When that concept is firmly in place, we can then see the institutional questions much more objectively and with greater theological clarity. Since the church is not an end in itself, we cannot allow its forms to be ends in themselves, to be self-perpetuating structures that assume the dimensions of theological necessity. Our salvation is never dependent upon what we do, including what we organize in the church. And our salvation is not our primary concern as we look at the church's institution; rather, our concern is to be useful servants of God as he completes his salvation history. This larger perspective is liberating: we can be quite open about our failings past and present, and we can be courageous in our self-criticism and church restructuring as we seek to obey the call we have received.

Part Three

DEFINING THE CHURCH'S MISSION INCARNATIONALLY

"Therefore, if any one is in Christ, he is a new creation; the old has passed away, behold, the new has come. All this is from God, who through Christ reconciled us to himself and gave us the ministry of reconciliation; that is, in Christ God was reconciling the world to himself, not counting their trespasses against them, and entrusting to us the message of reconciliation. So we are ambassadors for Christ, God making his appeal through us. We beseech you on behalf of Christ, be reconciled to God."

—2 Corinthians 5:17–20

Five

WHAT IS THE GOSPEL?

5.1 SAYING TOO MUCH AND SAYING TOO LITTLE

We were sitting with a group of friends, discussing the wealth and opulence of the papal art collections and wondering about the appropriateness of such wealth within the church—an old and often discussed question. During the conversation, a variety of statements were made about the gospel, all of them "definitions" of the gospel stated with conviction and earnestness. They had an intriguing range: The gospel is caring for people, is abiding by the Ten Commandments and the Golden Rule, is following Christ, is believing that Christ is coming again, is believing that Christ died for our sins, is concern for all that is truly good in the human, and so on. Everyone seemed to assume that the content of the gospel was absolutely obvious, and yet there really was no consensus in that group about what it really is. Most Christians would agree that the church's task has to do with proclaiming (whatever that is) the gospel—but it would be difficult to find general agreement within Christendom on the essentials of the gospel.

Several weeks before this discussion, I had been in conversation with a highly respected professor, a New Testament scholar who has devoted decades to the study of the gospel records. He said to me, "I have devoted all of my scholarly career to the question 'What is the gospel?'"; implying clearly that he believed that he still had a great deal more to discover as he continued his disciplined research on this theme. But he would also agree that there is really no scholarly consensus on the essentials of the gospel.

The skyline of any American town reveals a variety of church towers, and the distinctives of their architecture are symbolic of the many ways in which the gospel is formulated, understood, and proclaimed in our various ecclesiastical traditions. I am not criticizing the fact that the gospel is expressed in so many ways—it may well be an essential aspect of the gospel that it must find so many forms through which it is communicated. But I am concerned about the attitudes with which we approach the gospel and our particular versions of it. That discussion group in our living room was characterized by a great deal of self-assurance—several of those who spoke seemed to be totally sure about the truth of their gospel definitions. There is a notable contrast between that kind of self-assurance and the modesty expressed by my scholarly friend.

As we turn to the task of defining the church's mission incarnationally, we should pause to consider the spirit with which we define the gospel. If we understand our definition to be complete, exhaustive, and definitive, then we will probably also look upon our theology of the church as complete, exhaustive, and definitive. If, however, our understanding of the gospel is dynamic, then our theology of the church will also be dynamic, which means that it will be subject to review and possibly to revision.

That same New Testament professor said, in the course of a theological consultation, that "the gospel is always before us." This statement captures an important characteristic of biblical faith that we have already addressed but will bring back into the discussion at this point. To say that "the gospel is always before us" is to accept as a central presupposition of all theological work the fact that the gospel is bigger than any definition we have ever made of it. There is more to the gospel than any confession or creed has summarized, any dogmatic system has worked out in detail, or any particular ecclesiastical tradition has expounded in its worship, theology, and praxis. There is "more" to the gospel because the New Testament definition of *world* means more than we have yet discovered, and because the Lordship of Christ is more revolutionary and comprehensive than we have yet discovered. The gospel is "more" because it is not finished—God is still completing the salvation history he initiated. And the gospel is necessarily "more" than our understandings of it because our own sinful rebellion works as a kind of filter that forces the gospel into our historical and cultural settings, domesticates it, and seeks to rob it of much of its radical force. Ultimately, of course, these attempts to reduce the gospel will not succeed, but they can hinder or divert its progress, a mysterious possibility that God's sovereign rule does not make impossible but somehow includes.

Thus, it would be wise for us to approach with modesty the task of gospel definition, and that of the definition of the church's mission. All that we know about our own conditioning, individually and in our various cultural and ethnic traditions, should make us careful about uttering sweeping statements defining the gospel. Our history of debate and division in the church should caution us against ever assuming that we have reached the final stage of theological exploration. The course of salvation history is fraught with surprise, and just when we assume that we have reached a secured "position," new challenges confront us with which our positions are not equipped to deal.

The attitude of modesty with regard to the definition of the gospel and the church's mission will not mean that we are uncertain of what we say and believe. To be certain of the gospel does not require that we rely with confidence upon our formulations of it. Certainty, as Luther taught us, is outside of ourselves. It is based upon the person and work of Christ. The truth of the gospel is the Truth who is Christ. The utter reliability of the gospel is the reliability of the Incarnate Son and the events of his life. The authority of Scripture is the authority of the Savior and Lord whose witness we have in these written records. When we asume that our confidence is to be placed in the accuracy of our dogmatic formulations, the reliability of our particular confessional definitions of the gospel, or a particular version of the inspiredness of Scripture, we have transformed the gospel into a subtle kind of Gnosticism (salvation by knowledge).

All of this is not to say that we are not to think and to formulate the content of our faith. We certainly are intended to do that. The "sacrifice of the intellect" is not a possible expression of a gospel that promises to transform us by the renewing of our minds (Rom. 12:2). However, we must do our thinking and formulating knowing that "the gospel is always before us"; that as we state what it is, we will find it correcting our assumptions and leading us into insights that, although often painful, move us out of our ruts and into new dimensions of understanding and discipleship.

It is possible, however, to say too much when we define the gospel. In other words, we can make assertions that we have not yet worked through and appropriated, that we accept but do not even seek to understand. It can be "too much" to insist upon formulations of the gospel that have literally changed their meaning with time and confuse rather than clarify our faith (for many, the use of the word "persons" in Trinitarian discussions is an example of the kind of problem caused by the changing meaning of words). God's call to faith is not to a quantity of faith propositions but to radical submission to him and to his will.

But it is also possible to say too little, to be so modest that we say nothing at all anymore. The gospel is a message to be stated, and although it is bigger than our formulations, it is neither vague nor inexpressible. While some frequently invoke "tolerance" as a reason not to be too assertive about the Christian gospel, this dilutes the very reason for the calling and existence of the church. Modest theology will not permit us to say what we in honesty should not say . . . yet. But it will certainly equip us to say what we must say because the Word has become flesh and has dwelt among us, and we have been made its witnesses.

In this introductory chapter to our third section, I will discuss some aspects of the gospel that have a very great bearing on how we define the church's mission incarnationally. Some of this is a summary of earlier discussions in this book. I hope to demonstrate that a modest approach to the definition of the gospel does not lead to a diluted understanding of the church's mission, but does result in a theology of the church that participates in the dynamic movement of the gospel "before us," more of which we are discovering as we follow Christ.

5.2 SOME SUMMARY STATEMENTS

The gospel is God at work in our history

This has been our major assumption from the outset, and we need only restate it here in order to insure that everything that follows is in proper perspective. We are working on the biblical presupposition that human history had a beginning and will have an end, and that God is sovereign over both as well as over the entire course of events in between. Further, we are assuming here that this history under God's rule is purposeful and that, in Christ, God has revealed enough of his purposes to draw us into useful servanthood in that history (Eph. 1:3-23, esp. v. 9).

We should also look at the negative meaning of this statement, for to say that the gospel is God at work in our history is to rule out any reduction of the gospel to a set of eternal verities. This might take the form of a philosophical structure of truth we deduced from our own investigations of reality, affirmed and then used for our own thinking

and investigation. Or it might be a dogmatic system that was the result
of our reception of revealed truth cast in the form of propositions we
establish and define as the guarantee of the reliability and truth of our
faith. Both Christian philosophy and dogmatics proceed from the gospel, but the gospel always encompasses more than can any systematic
or reductive approach. It is the personal God who makes himself
known (through the entire course of salvation history and ultimately
and climactically in the incarnation of Jesus Christ) that we can speak
about, because we know him. We can initiate the formulation of
propositions about the nature of God, truth, and life—but since God is
at work in our history, our propositions will necessarily be subject to
the continuing process of discovery of the "more" which is the gospel.

Much of what we can express about the truth of the gospel will
be in other than propositional forms: the lyricism of the music of faith,
the visual evocation of God's nature in our art and architecture, the
expression of God's nature in actions that defy grammatical explanation. These, too, will be inadequate formulations of the "more" of this
historical gospel—they need the explanations provided by our propositions, by our dogmatic systems. But these other ways of defining or
describing aspects of the gospel are an essential part of the witness we
are equipped to be and to give. The scriptural record contains both
Psalms and Romans, the hymns of the Book of Revelation and the sober
history of Acts. To say that the gospel is "more" than we already know
of it, that it is "before us," is to confess our faith that the Holy Spirit
has resources for the communication of the gospel that we have not
yet begun to exploit. It is, at the same time, our certainty that the full
meaning of what God has already done in Christ is larger than what
we have already discovered it to mean.

The basic presupposition of the historicity of the gospel gives
Christians a different kind of viewpoint on our own history. Peter
formulated it succinctly: "Therefore gird up your minds, be sober, set
your hope fully upon the grace that is coming to you at the revelation
of Jesus Christ" (1 Pet. 1:13). Coming at the end of his great exposition of the past, present, and future tense of the gospel (which we will
discuss below), this summary admonition addresses the Christian's
opportunity to take a unique position within our historical context.
We are called upon to pull ourselves together, get ready for the rigors
of the mental struggle before us, and then to be sober. The sense of
this obeyable imperative is that Christians have all the equipment
needed to address the task of discipleship in a hostile world; they can
be sober, balanced, and objective about the history through which

their pilgrimage leads. Their hope, however, is not embedded in this history but is beyond it. That is a very important aspect of the Christian view of history: its ultimate resolution is beyond its boundaries, just as the present solution to its crisis comes from outside its boundaries of space and time (incarnation!). Christians are not to be fearful, as the angels proclaimed on Christmas night. Under the lordship of Christ, to whom all power has been given in heaven and on earth, the church can go about its task soberly, with its eyes open, and marshalling all the resources of "minds stripped down and ready to run," knowing full well that the enduring history is that which is happening in the service of God and the accomplishment of his purposes.

The gospel is about God's work of reconciliation

There are many biblical scholars today who state that the message of reconciliation is the overarching theme of salvation history, the common thread through the Old Covenant and into the New Covenant, leading on to the future hope of the church. Certainly any definition of the gospel will be inadequate if it does not place the concept and reality of reconciliation at its very center. The work that God is doing in history is the work of reconciliation: "In Christ God was reconciling the world to himself" (2 Cor. 5:19).

This reconciliation theme focuses our attention on the creation intention of God, laid out for us in the creation accounts of Genesis 1 and 2. There we see a created world living within the beautiful purposes for which God made it, a creation characterized by a beauty and a sufficiency that was good in every detail. This definition of creation purpose is linked, in Genesis, with the description of the other side of our reality—this creation, so beautiful in purpose and still revealing so much of that beauty even now, in rebellion against its Creator and his intentions for it (Gen. 3). Hostility, discord, and violence characterize a world at war with itself because it is at war with its Maker. The sweep of events in the prehistory of Genesis 1-11 reveals how that rebellion expands outward, drawing in ever-larger circles of creation, so that ultimately the entire world is under its sway.

But this creation is marked by a tension between its creation design and its sinful rebellion. The rebellion has not been able to obliterate the signs and evidence of the Creator. Noah can still hear God's instructions to build an ark, and Abraham can still recognize the call of God to leave his fatherland and move out into the adventure that will become salvation history. Our reality is best described as *simul creatus et peccator*—simultaneously created and sinner. Our rebellion cannot totally erase the image of God, nor can our moral and religious efforts restore it.

But the tension requires a resolution; it longs for reconciliation. The design of God's good creation still reveals his hand in its making, even though that evidence will not equip us to find our way back to him. When we understand the Christian doctrines of original sin and total depravity to mean that there is no trace left of God's authorship of creation, we distort the realism and complexity of the biblical portrayal of our situation. These doctrines rightly emphasize our inability to save ourselves. But they also express the tension and contradictoriness of a rebellious creation that knows that there is another way, that carries within itself a dim recollection of paradise, and thus can imagine what "should" and what "ought" to be—but is not and cannot, humanly speaking, be anything other than that rebellious creation.

Reconciliation is the New Testament surprise. The One rebelled against, the One denied and rejected by his own, comes to his own to restore the relationship between Creator and creation. This results in a new and totally unforeseen possibility: the old creation can be replaced by a new creation. The human incapacity for self-salvation (in spite of all its sophisticated and often admirable attempts through human religion, philosophy, and morality) is replaced with the divine offer of reconciliation. Reconciliation is the work of God that results in our salvation. In terms of reconciliation, we begin to understand that salvation is a way of describing the other option made available by God: rather than having to experience to the very dregs all the necessary consequences of our rebellion, God's loving act of reconciliation removes that cup, rescues us from that ending, and replaces it with a beginning. "Set your hope fully upon the grace that is coming to you at the revelation of Jesus Christ" (1 Pet. 1:13).

God conquered the rebellion that is the source of our tension and our human dilemma in his reconciling work. But we need to grasp that just as our rebellion affected all of creation (those ever-widening circles of Gen. 4-11), God's work of reconciliation makes its impact upon every part of creation. Reconciliation and new creation are ways of talking about the total scope of God's work—which we call the gospel. Thus, when we use "reconciliation language" to define the gospel, we must be prepared to have the gospel mean much more than Christians often have wanted or expected it to.

Sin brought human alienation—Cain killed Abel. Reconciliation restores human community. Reconciliation with God redefines my neighbor, forces aside the discriminatory categories by which sinful humanity sorts out the types of classes of people who will be cared for and receive justice—for God so loved the *world!* When we define the gospel as God's act of reconciliation, we must mean a reestablishment of the creation commands and the creation order as our new mandate for obedience. That is, in effect, what the Beatitudes do—this description of life, so often held to be impossibly idealistic, is the new possibility of life when rebellious humanity is reconciled with God, and thus with its world, with nature, and with the human family.

Reconciliation makes possible an entirely new view of the human situation: where human and historical realism would make us all pessimists about the possibilities of overcoming our divisions and setting aside our hostility, the gospel as reconciliation creates hope and gives us our marching orders. Those who are reconciled must now understand themselves as agents of reconciliation—"We are ambassadors for Christ." These familiar words, spoken so often in the last several decades, must be reiterated and translated into the action of Christian witness. If we understand the gospel in terms of reconciliation, then our theology of the church will necessarily include a major focus upon the reconciling ministry of the church—in all the dimensions of that evangelical event.

Reconciliation with God introduces into our concept of the gospel the whole breadth of God's intention for his good creation: its orderliness, its justice, its adequacy of resources for all God's creatures. A gospel of reconciliation must be a gospel that becomes political and social, because the body politic and social is a part of the creation made by God and included within his definition of its intended goodness. Put very bluntly, this means that it is an evangelical concern to deal with hunger, because God's creation is sufficient, if we administer and tend it properly. It is an evangelical concern to struggle against injustice and oppression, because God's creation is marked by a good order that excludes exploitation of some by others and expects all creatures to experience God's goodness in every dimension of their lives. The reconciling work of the cross makes peace an evangelical concern, for the division into friend and enemy has been set aside by Christ, and the church has been sent into that historical no-man's land between the fronts of human hostility, to be a witness to the impossible possibility: reconciling love, forgiveness, community, and common purpose under God.

Obviously, defining the gospel as reconciliation means to embark upon a long process of both discovery of what that really means and correction of all our narrowing definitions of the gospel, which do not take all the dimensions of reconciliation seriously. Under this term we address Christ's model of ministry to the outcasts of his day. We are challenged by the Prince of Peace who draws Gentile and Jew together over the walls of human separation. We are forced to see the Samaritans of our day as our neighbors—and we may have to ask ourselves if they are not, in fact, all those whom we have marked as enemies and whose possible destruction we are willing to justify as we continue to play with the power of sinful rebellion and deny that the gospel of reconciliation both convicts us of that sin and enables us to be healed of it.

A gospel defined as reconciliation is a hard gospel for a divided church to preach. The lessons of the modern ecumenical movement are hard lessons that threaten the complacent churches of the West, but they are confrontations with the meaning of reconciliation. How can we proclaim the Prince of Peace and yet divide his people with our differences, and then justify our divisions as though they were virtuous acts of faith? The church of reconciled people does, in fact, bear within it the divine power to be reconcilers, but we must be willing to be evangelized where we are still unreconciled—and that is so often our refusal to be reconciled with our own family of faith. The family of God is more diverse than any of us is comfortable with, but comfort is not an acceptable criterion for our theology of the church. That is the challenge to us of the gospel of reconciliation. Like Peter with the vision of the unclean animals, we need to continue discovering how vast this world is for which Christ died, how comprehensive the concept of "all nations" is to which we are being sent, how all-embracing the definition of the neighbor is in the New Testament—the person and peoples whom I must deal with are, quite simply, my and our neighbors, and no one can be exempted from that definition.

If we are to be witnesses to a gospel of reconciliation, we must be willing to learn what reconciliation means. It is a reality woven through all the images of the gospel in the New Testament. It is the fact that God accomplished upon the cross. It is the power that raised Christ from the dead and is available to us. The church has for too long restricted its meaning to the personal dimension of one's relationship with God—which is clearly at the heart of the fact and the doctrine. But until we realize that reconciliation with God enables and requires us to be ambassadors of that reconciliation, we will have a less than biblical theology of the church's mission.

The gospel is the past, present, and future tense of salvation

Much of what we have already said bears upon what remains to be said. It is necessary, however, to stress all of these accents separately, for they are like the facets of a diamond, all expressions of the one central reality that we are seeking to define—the gospel. If we are going to read the New Testament carefully, then we will have to become attentive to grammar, and especially to the grammar of salvation. As we have already argued, for centuries Christianity has been preoccupied with our "being saved." Out of that one-sided focus upon the benefit of the gospel to the neglect of its mission, we find ourselves reading the scriptural record one-sidedly. We tend, especially in evangelical circles, to read everything in the past tense: "I have been saved," "We are saved," and "Are you saved?" The biblical definition of the gospel will require a more careful reading and understanding of the record.

In the New Testament, salvation is discussed in the past, present, and future tenses, and an adequate understanding of the gospel requires that we grasp all these dimensions and hold them together. The Word has happened, and we must accept this presupposition before there can be a "Word witnessed to" and, after that, a "Word proclaimed" (Otto Weber). The past tense of salvation is foundational: it is all that God has already done in Christ for us. The incarnation is the fulfillment of all that the Old Covenant had been looking forward to. That incarnate life includes the teaching and ministry, the redemptive death and victorious resurrection of Christ, followed by his ascension and the gift of the Holy Spirit at Pentecost. This past tense of salvation is unrepeatable and irreplaceable. It is the history out of which our history unfolds. Our "living hope," as Peter teaches us (1 Pet. 1:3ff.), is based upon the firm foundation of God's action in raising Christ from the dead and making our faith possible. Thus, we must begin our proclamation with what God has done, just as Peter did in his sermon at Pentecost.

But the past tense of our salvation is very different from that of any other history. When we have read and digested the historical facts of the Napoleonic campaigns, we go on to other things. Our daily lives and our total reality are not truly affected by the past facts of Napoleon's life. But the events of the gospel are not closed chapters: that history is still happening; its pastness does not mean that it is over. Those events, that "Word happened," have been witnessed, and that witness has been written down and passed on in and through the church for all these intervening centuries. This combined Word as event, witness, and proclamation now makes it possible for that history to become our individual and corporate history, and for us to be drawn into that history as it continues toward its promised conclusion.

The past tense of salvation leads inexorably into the present tense of salvation. What God has done directly confronts us now in such a way that our lives are changed and our direction converted. The present tense of salvation refers to the present meaning of the gospel, to the way in which the gospel is an event that is happening now. This is the reality of the church as witness: the Spirit is equipping us to be a witness in such a way that the past tense of salvation becomes the present reality of those who respond to the gospel. To hear the gospel of the cross and to come to the realization that this suffering and death were for *me* is to experience a past event as a present reality. We cannot do that with any other historical event. The Spirit does that through our witness, and it is the ongoing work of the Good News that grips people today and calls forth a response like that of the hearers on the first Pentecost Day in Jerusalem: "What must we do to be saved?"

The present tense of our salvation also refers to the fact that each Christian is in the process of "being saved." This is where it is misleading to speak only of one's "having been saved," to dwell solely on the past tense, and neglect the present and future tenses. There is a sober realism in the New Testament about the struggle and suffering that are part of the salvation process. To be saved, in the past tense, means that we are certain of the sufficiency of all that God has done to reconcile us to himself. To know that we are being saved, in the present tense, means that we are prepared to experience our Christian lives as an ongoing process of discovery of what it means to be saved, what it costs, what must necessarily be changed, and how much of each of us remains to be saved.

The present tense of salvation is the tense of realism. Peter describes this reality in his first epistle, where he writes of the present suffering of Christians. He compares it to the process of refining gold, in which the assayer's fire renders the gold pure, although it is a painful process. Paul knew that struggle in his own life and gave eloquent testimony to the inward and outward suffering through which he went as he was "being saved." The present tense of salvation, then, is the understanding of faith that confronts the tension of our being both the old and the new person at the same time. It is the way we grapple with the fact that our sinful natures, although ultimately vanquished, still contend for us and create genuine crises through which we must go. The candid confession that we "are being saved," while we know that we "have been saved," makes us more useful witnesses, because it permits us to let God speak through the ambiguities and mysteries of our current experience. This is the tense of the still darkened glass (1 Cor. 13:12) in which we see dimly what we need to see but not all that we would like to see. Yet we live patiently in this present tense of our faith, knowing that the call is for obedience and for endurance—as the Book of Revelation constantly reminds us.

Without a proper sense of the present tense of salvation, we will define the gospel in triumphalist and often arrogant terms that divide the Body of Christ. We will have little sympathy for the real struggle through which so many in our family are going, both individually and corporately. We will take the past tense of the gospel and make it into a closed definition, thus, we allege, making it possible for *us* to decide who truly believes and who does not. But Paul admonishes us to be patient with the weak and to be understanding of those who still need more milk and can digest little meat. Paul models for us a marvelous ability to uphold with vigor and conviction the truth of the gospel he proclaims and simultaneously to deal lovingly and firmly with all the problems, distortions, and dilutions of that gospel, which immediately emerged in the churches he himself had founded. He knew that God's promises were certain; his grasp of the present tense of faith was such that he delighted in the evidence of what God was doing while he also addressed himself to all those areas of misunderstanding and disobedience where obviously much still had to be done. But he did not accuse any of heresy, not even those in Corinth who denied the heart of the gospel, the resurrection (1 Cor. 15). Rather, his confidence was in the future: "He who began a good work in you will bring it to completion at the day of Jesus Christ" (Phil. 1:6).

Paul understood that the often harsh realism of the present tense of salvation, as it stands confidently on the certainties of the past tense, is bearable because of the future tense of our salvation—possibly the most neglected dimension of the gospel in many of our formulations today. Peter says that "as the outcome of your faith you obtain the salvation of your souls," (1 Pet. 1:9), referring to that inheritance which is the object of our "living hope" (1:3), which is "imperishable, undefiled, and unfading, kept in heaven for you" (1:4). The whole sweep of the gospel is toward the certainty of God's completion of what he has begun. The past tense of our faith focuses our vision on what God is working toward, what God will do at the "day of Jesus Christ." How sad that so many Christians for so long have made the promise of that day into a formidable and frightening day of judgment. Certainly it will be that judgment, but the New Testament message is that the Judge is the Savior, and the judgment that is coming is part of the greater and marvelous completion and consummation of what God has been doing all through salvation history. For that reason, the visions of that coming day in the Book of Revelation are marked by joy, celebration, praise, worship—a great festival of completion!

This future tense of the faith is really what makes it possible for Christians to deal with the struggle and tension of the present tense: the end is sure! We can be certain that we have received what we need for the present struggle ("You are not lacking in any spiritual gift . . . "), knowing that God will bring to its promised conclusion this salvation history of which we have become a part (" . . . as you wait for the revealing of our Lord Jesus Christ"; 1 Cor. 1:7). Thus, the future tense is not a utopian speculation that diverts us from the hard realities of today, but rather a serene certainty that enables us to address these realities with strength and purposefulness. The exciting thing about New Testament studies in our century, as they have discovered more and more of the meaning of New Testament eschatology (teaching on the "last things"), is the way in which these discoveries apply to our lives now. We distort the biblical concept of the future and waste Christian energy when we speculate about the times and details of the future. The intent of New Testament eschatology is to equip us for more faithful obedience *now* and to assure us of the faithfulness of God.

The future tense of our faith, therefore, does not make us complacent about the present ("it's all going to turn out all right, anyway"), but rather makes us more effective in our present work as witnesses to the gospel. Nor does it divert our attention from the present but focuses us upon what we are to do and frees us from all fear of the future, for God is sovereign over that future. Finally, the future tense of our faith makes it possible for us to deal with the imperfection and ambiguity of our present experience, because we know that this tension is an essential part of "being saved" but will result in the final perfection or completion that God has promised and that only God can accomplish.

A theology of the church that deals with the past, present, and future tenses of our faith will emphasize the centrality of this process character of salvation in the church's preaching and teaching ministry. Such a theology will also reflect that dynamic in the way it is formulated. As a part of the process of salvation, that is, as the people called out to be God's instrument as his witnesses for the accomplishment of his saving purposes, the church will understand and interpret itself within this past, present, and future. This has several implications for a theology of the church, which we will briefly state in conclusion.

5.3 DOING MODEST THEOLOGY OF THE CHURCH

The church's self-understanding, expressed in its doctrine (ecclesiology) and in its practice (ecclesiastics), must begin with the past tense of the gospel. This is the foundation upon which the church stands. As we have already developed extensively in Chapter One, the church knows itself to be at a particular place for a particular purpose in salvation history. In classic language, the church is defined as apostolic; it is authentically Christian when it continues the apostolic ministry, passing on the teaching and preaching of the apostolic college of the first century, and remaining faithful to that heritage.

The past tense of the faith, which rightly goes back to the initiation of the Old Covenant, constantly reminds the church today that it is the result of God's continuing action in history, and that it is informed and strengthened by what it can know of God's work through and with his people in earlier generations. Church history is a study that equips us for responsible witness in our world today. In addition, the study of our past has a liberating effect: it constantly reminds us that the work of the church is God's work, often carried out in spite of and even through the frailty of the human witnesses. The church's past tense, even though often disappointing, is still a testimony to God's grace and faithfulness, and a rich tradition from which we may continue to learn. We ignore the past tense of the church to the detriment of our intelligent ministry today.

But the church is not a museum. And the ministry of the church is not the curatorship of an impressive but now antique tradition that interests us for its aesthetic merit but little affects us today. Whenever we see the tradition of the church, the past tense, functioning as a restrictive burden and preventing the church from moving through its present tense toward its future tense, we must call for change. This may be painful, but the church must constantly remind itself that it is most comparable to Israel in the wilderness. It knows God's immediate presence and guidance; he has provided for all its needs. But it is no longer in the security of Egypt and has not yet arrived in the Promised Land. At times it will long for an alleged golden past (in the Egypt of slavery), and at times it will seek to preempt the future before God's timing, but it will be most useful to God as it recognizes and accepts its situation between the past and the future.

The rock foundation upon which the church stands is that part of its past which is unchanging: it has happened once and for all, and from those gospel events the church moves out on its pilgrimage of witness. Indeed, its witness is to those events. But that witness is given in the present tense, to the world in which the church finds itself now. The event of Pentecost equipped the church to move into this perpetual *now* of Christian witness and obedience, taking the gospel into new languages, cultures, and epochs. The past leads to this *now*, and in this *now* the church must see its primary call. "You shall be my witnesses wherever you are, and wherever you are, that is the time and place to be my witnesses."

We must be careful, however, not to violate the present tense of the faith by seeking to force it into the past tense. This could happen if the Christian church were to try to return to what it was at one time, whether that be the first century or the sixteenth. Or it could happen when the church insists upon expressing itself in forms and practices that are no longer relevant and useful ways to communicate the gospel, whether it be Latin in an age that no longer speaks that language, or the methods of nineteenth-century revivalism in an age sensitive to mass manipulation and impersonal communication.

But the church also may be weakened if it attempts to minister in the present tense while totally preoccupied with the future tense. The task of the church is the time and place in which God has put it, and speculation about chapters of salvation history that have not yet happened (but will happen!) is an effective waste of time and energy. The future tense of our faith throws its light upon the present tense, providing a sense of focus and direction toward which the church is moving in time. But the present tense calls for a witness to the present Lord, who can be known and served now just as his Word is being proclaimed and witnessed to in the lives and words of his servants. The sacraments are to be experienced as God's preparation for the now of our faith and work; they are the real self-giving of God so that we might be nourished and enabled to carry out the task which he has entrusted to us.

Our theology of the church will then be dynamic, moving from the past to the present, and looking confidently toward the future. It will be a modest theology, knowing that our concept of the church will grow and mature as our grasp of the gospel grows and matures. It will be careful to avoid arrogantly superior and exclusive definitions and prescriptions. Our theology of the church, summarized under the imperative "Be my witnesses," must be open to the enormous diversity of Christian modes of expression and thought. It should be written in such a way that alternative ways of saying what it says are both possible and encouraged. It should seek to be alert to its own cultural bondage and find ways to present the church that do, in fact, transcend the limits of any individual culture and make it possible to do theology in a universal fellowship of faith.

In short, the way we do our theology of the church should reflect the way we define the gospel. The humility characteristic of the latter task must be shared by the former. This is, in effect, a call for an "incarnational" way of doing theology, a theological method that reveals the dynamic tentativeness of any formulation, coupled with faithfulness to the traditions already given, and openness to what God's Spirit will surprise us with in the future tense of our faith.

Six

BEING THE WITNESS:
THE EQUIPPING COMMUNITY
AS WITNESS

We have defined the church's task as "to be the witness," and we have further stated that this means that the church and the Christian are to *be* the witness, *do* the witness, and *say* the witness. This means that we are beginning this triad with an emphasis upon the first meaning of witness, the *martys,* who is both the person and the community called to faith and service. We will then move to the *martyria* aspect of this New Testament word group: what the witness, as a person and as a community, *does* and *says* is the witness or testimony. The witness in the personal sense *is* the *martys* and thus *does* and *says* the witness as activity in the world, that is, the *martyrion.* The *doing* and *saying* of the witness, however, must be understood in terms of the person who *is* the witness. To divorce them is to arrive at a disembodied witness, a message without a messenger, and thus to fail to grasp the incarnational nature of witness. We begin our definition of the task of witness then by turning to the person and the community who *are* the witness.

6.1 THE RISKS OF DEFINING WITNESS AS PERSONS

When we use phrases like "being the witness," we alarm many Christians who have struggled with regrettable extremes in the history of Christianity. The danger is very real that this kind of language will force us into a one-sided concentration upon the benefits of being a Christian, on the privilege of one's calling divorced from the responsibility of being a called people. Concentration upon who Christians are and what makes them different very easily leads into this trap. Closely linked to this issue is the Reformation concern that our salvation not be understood as based upon our own works—certainly a vital issue but still one that tends to emphasize our own salvation and how we attain it and understand it.

Clearly the pathway here is theologically treacherous, and we can easily overemphasize personal salvation at the expense of our calling to serve, or else ignore the personal dimensions of faith and stress only our task. One effect of that unfortunate division between the benefits and the mission of the gospel has been to make the church into a "salvation agency" (the Germans say *"Heilanstalt"* with a delightful double meaning!), concentrating upon the provision (or withholding) of the benefits and assurance of salvation, while reducing the mission of the church to the guardianship and administration of an already given and possessed salvation. Thus, although our route may be difficult, it is necessary. The New Testament, with its words about being the witness, its descriptions of the changed persons and the changed community called to this mission, and its many admonitions about the character of Christian community and individuals as witnesses demands that we begin here. Our task will continue to be to relate the calling and the equipping for that calling, the benefits of knowing Christ, to the purpose for our having been given that privilege, so that our theology of the church embraces both aspects. To do so, we need to explore the roots of this misunderstanding of the church's mission.

In the long course of medieval theology and spirituality, an understanding of the gospel evolved that emphasized human cooperation in the work of salvation. Although ultimately salvation was dependent upon God's grace, certain elements of creation within the human person could respond and act for that person's salvation, making grace conditional in a sense, and making the human person God's partner in the attainment of salvation. Beyond that, there was an even greater emphasis upon the spiritual responsibility and capability of the human person to maintain the state of salvation. The sacramental system, the spiritual exercises, the pilgrimages and Crusades, and the exemplary piety of the saints—all were woven together into an impressive system of human religious accomplishment that contributed to the ultimate salvation of an individual.

The role of the church was manifold: to serve as the administrator of the benefits of salvation, to guide the pious in the spiritual pilgrimage toward complete sanctification, to reprove and discipline those who violated the disciplines and doctrines of the faith, and, also, to carry on the evangelistic mission of the church. Undeniably, that focus never disappeared: the expansion of the boundaries of the "Christian world" continued throughout the Middle Ages (K. S. Latourette's six-volume history of this expansion gives impressive testimony to this unceasing mission movement in the church). But that work was viewed as the task of the very special and the few—a priestly and monastic task around which evolved an understanding of a special spiritual "estate" that ascribed to those who took on such tasks and accepted such "holy orders" a particular kind of holiness that the laity could not share. They were, perhaps, the only ones who could properly understand themselves as "witnesses" in the sense we have defined it. The gospel they proclaimed was, generally speaking, the gospel of the benefits of faith. The clergy of the institutional church carried out the mission; the laity, those who received the grace transmitted through the church, enjoyed the benefits but also had to work to maintain them.

The church needed the reaction of the Reformation. The total dependence of the human person upon God's grace and action both to be saved and to remain saved had to be reformulated and restored to the center of the church's teaching and practice. This meant that the biblical doctrine of sin had to be reworked and broadened to its full scope. The human incapacity to save oneself needed reiterating. The doctrine of justification by grace, through faith alone, became the resounding cry of the Reformation movements.

Coupled with that reform of the Christian doctrine of salvation was, however, a tendency to downgrade the actual results of God's saving actions in one's life. Out of a fear of assigning too much importance to human decisions and actions and a desire to avoid the structures of spirituality that had been rejected when the monastic orders were abolished, the human was left almost totally passive and inactive as far as the gospel of salvation, or, more particularly, as far as the Christian response of witness to that gospel was concerned. Although the Reformers' primary concern was, in fact, to correct the doctrine of salvation, they did not clearly emphasize the mission for which we are being saved, that is, our calling to be God's witness; thus, there was still a tendency to "halve the gospel." They viewed justification as forensic: we were in fact justified before God, in the heavenly courtroom, but the actual effect of that fact would not necessarily be obvious or experienceable. It was generally feared that too much preoccupation with the effects of God's saving work could easily lead to a renascence of works righteousness.

We've already pointed out that this one-sided emphasis quickly brought its own reactions. There is, quite simply, a very great deal in the New Testament about the concrete and historical effects of God's work in our lives. Obedience and Christian action are dominant themes in the New Testament, and it is hard to deal with justification and salvation as abstractions that we believe, while at the same time avoiding to look for their effect in our lives out of a fear of becoming spiritually proud and reliant upon our own works. Thus, various forms of Christian piety, often legalistic, soon emerged again, emphasizing what one must look like and must do to be considered a Christian. This movement, often resulting in what has come to be called the "believers' churches," looked for concrete evidence of one's salvation before affirming one's right to call oneself a Christian and share in church membership. The fronts were defined: on one side was the broad Reformation position with its emphasis upon grace, its insistence upon faith, and its tolerance of a great breadth of reactions and levels of seriousness among those who called themselves Christians; on the other, the determined and disciplined structures of the radical Christians who looked for clear commitment and change, conversion and radical discipleship, who were impatient with what they looked upon as diluted and ineffective Christianity in the great traditions. (Luther revealed his own awareness of this tension when he discussed "those who with all seriousness would like to be Christian" in his preface to the German Mass—but he concluded that he did not have people of that kind!)

Much of this dichotomy found intriguing expression in the Wesleyan (later broadening into the Holiness and Pentecostal) tradition, where the biblical emphases upon our real sanctification and our observable experience of God's Spirit changing us were linked into a vibrant movement that often revived piety and invested the more abstract forms of traditional Christianity with great personal excitement. The tendency to dwell upon human spirituality and to elevate experience to the level of a work that was (in fact) necessary either for salvation or for the retention of salvation was obviously present and has continued to be a problem for this particular branch of the church. But Wesleyan scholars rightly remind us that the New Testament makes strong statements about the reality of holiness, change, newness, and even perfection.

However the understanding of salvation developed, all of these movements became involved in a reawakened concern for the church's mission, although it was normally formulated as the task of "saving people." The Great Commission reemerged as a central definition of the church. Unfortunately, what the church understood "discipling the nations" to mean, and how it went about "teaching them all things that I have taught you," would appear to have been more on the side of a gospel proclaimed and received for its benefits. It has consistently been difficult to proclaim salvation as God's great goal for his creation, and our calling as a summons and enabling to serve that purpose as his witnesses in the world.

We can see this happening in many places today. In the West, the "born again" movement claims impressive statistics, but it does not seem to have the transforming effect upon American society that should result from such a large number of "born again" people. This difficulty is also documented today in the problems the Third World churches frequently have when they seek to develop an educational or catechetical ministry. The religious experience is widespread, and we constantly hear about the marvelous spread of the gospel and ongoing revivals in the younger churches. But upon closer examination, we discover that the hard work of learning and growing in the faith and thus translating the gospel into its disciplined expression in a new culture appears often to lag very far behind.

Much of the expanding church in the Third World grapples with the tension between salvation understood in terms of life beyond this world and salvation as the call to be a force for wholeness and reconciliation within this world. The dichotomy between benefits and mission makes it hard for the evangelistic mission of the church to confront the world with the total scope of the gospel, the ministry of reconciliation, and the dynamic of salvation as it stretches from the past tense to the future tense of faith. Young churches often struggle with the political and social challenges of the gospel, as do their parent churches in the West. We should not be surprised when this tension produces division and rancor within the church, and sets up theological fronts that appear unable to hear each other. Although working out of the same gospel, we create enormous problems for ourselves if we allow ourselves to impose our own boundaries on the gospel.

Personal salvation that does not express itself in mission and service is at best a very truncated gospel. It permits the suspicion (which may not become an allowable judgment) that we may be dealing more with "religion" than with "Christianity" (we will return to this distinction later).

To "be the witness" must mean, however, upholding this essential connection. We must receive and understand the benefits of salvation as the blessing God has provided for us so that we can be the witness to which he has entrusted the ongoing ministry of reconciliation. The gospel is not merely *"my* salvation" but God's great work of salvation for his entire creation, and my part in it is as one of the firstfruits of that salvation. In other words, the problem with the dichotomy of benefits and mission in the church, in all of the various forms in which it has surfaced, is the lack of a future tense of faith. The gospel as certain salvation is too securely our possession, and is, in fact, more sight than faith. We must understand "being the witness" in terms of the long future perspective of God's saving work. We are to be the servant people whom God has called and enabled, confident that God will complete the good work he has begun, because he is faithful (1 Cor. 1:9).

Rather than allow ourselves to be caught in the riptide of either one of the reactionary movements in our past, we should attempt to see in the constantly fluctuating history of the Christian church essential components of the gospel that have been underemphasized in preceding epochs. The Reformation had to correct the inadequate definitions of grace, faith, and sin that had become operative in Christian theology in the Middle Ages. The Catholics could, quite rightly, react to this by saying that Protestant Christianity is all doctrine but little experience and practice. Protestant radicals said the same thing. But the debate tended to be within the confines of the concern for salvation, and seldom moved out to the mission and witness dimensions of New Testament calling—until the emergence of the younger churches in our modern day. Now the concern for ecumenically responsible theology has begun to coalesce in a new search for a theology of the gospel and of the church's mission that is biblical *and* relevant to our history.

6.2 BEING AND BECOMING THE WITNESS

Most of the New Testament is addressed to the plural *you.* The Gospels and the Epistles were written, as we know, for the instruction of the whole church, in response to the challenges to the gospel that the early church was experiencing as the first century advanced. It is, therefore, most appropriate to discuss the character of witness in the plural and corporate sense. We have already spoken of the impossibility of separating the individual from the corporate aspects of New Testament teaching. The Christian church is a called people made up of called individuals, and the individuals receive and experience their calling in the context of the entire body. What we say about "being a witness" must apply both to the individual (the tongues of fire were distributed on the individual heads on Pentecost) and to the body. But the accent is more biblical if we use plural language. To do so is probably a necessary corrective to the one-sided individualism that marks so much contemporary thought about Christianity.

The very nature of Christian existence is that the Christian community is different. To be the witness is to be something distinctive. Before we can talk about what the witness as person does and says, we must understand that the witness's nature is a transformed nature. Leonhard Goppelt, my revered professor of New Testament at the University of Hamburg, once said that one could develop a theology of the New Testament by carrying out a careful study of the words *new* and *now*. God has acted decisively in history, as we have so strongly emphasized, and the result has been something new that continues to be new in the experience of our now. The apostles can compare the earlier life of the first Christians to their present reality, and see a clear change, and have reason to expect further change. Ongoing change is an essential aspect of the definition of the witnessing community. It has become and is becoming something different. The imagery used to express this new being is diverse.

In Jesus' conversation with Nicodemus, he describes the newness of the life of the believer as a new birth. He uses this radical image to convey the character of new being: to experience the life that God gives, one must be born "from above" (the translation preferable to "born again"). This image emphasizes two things about Christian existence: it is the result of God's initiation, and it is radical transformation, comparable to physical birth. Peter uses a similar image in his first epistle (1:3) when he speaks of God, the Father of our Lord Jesus Christ, "begetting" us to a living hope: the picture is literally of the Father providing the seed for new life.

These emphases stand necessarily at the beginning of any discussion of Christian existence. As heirs of the Reformation, we must stress that our new life as Christians is the result of what God has done for us and in us totally apart from any merit or qualification on our part. We have received this newness in the concrete reality of our lives, within the ongoing gift of enabling newness that the Spirit has been giving ever since Pentecost. To respond to God's love revealed in Christ is to receive the assurance of forgiveness, because Christ has covered the penalty for our sin in his death on the cross. It is to receive the unmerited gift of a new life, a new being: to become a new creation.

Through the practice of the sacrament of baptism, the church from its beginning has confessed its faith that this is in fact what God is doing in the life of the Christian. Baptism, however its timing and method are understood, is the celebration of God's work in a person's life. In baptism the church confesses that it recognizes the hand of God in the life of an individual, either through that person's birth into the Christian family or through that individual's confession of faith. The individual cannot baptize himself or herself. Only the Christian community can perform that act of witness and worship. The words proclaimed at baptism are words of authority, stating our conviction that God changes life, reverses rebellion, converts direction, and implants in those whom he calls the power to believe and to confess their faith. The Christian confession of faith, "I believe," must necessarily be a humble statement, because it is not the result of anything that person has done, but is rather the response to what God has done.

For that reason, the Christian church may well look upon the birth of faith in any individual as the greatest miracle. There is no method or program that can produce faith. The changed person, who knows that he or she is a child of God and has received the "downpayment of the Holy Spirit," is the continuing evidence of God at work in our history. There is no greater privilege than to be present when God works that work and to discover that the faith of the whole community is confirmed by that miracle. This is why baptism is undoubtedly the most meaningful when celebrated in the midst of the entire assembled community.

As a child of the Reformed tradition, I might add that one of the many reasons I am a proponent of infant baptism (while respecting the theological concerns of those who disagree on this issue) is that this celebration and practice do in fact emphasize the nature of Christian existence as God's gift, not the result of one's decision or action. The infant, whose own confession of faith will have to follow as a confirmation of this congregational confession (more about this below, pp. 213-15), is a symbol of the state of all Christians over against the grace of God: we are receivers of grace, responders whose response has been empowered by God, persons who are called but who must now discover what that calling necessarily means.

Unfortunately, many churches that practice infant baptism neglect the preaching of the meaning of the sacrament. I am grateful to Professor Hans-Joachim Kraus for pointing this out to me when I was going through the typical theological student's struggle with the ins and outs of baptism. The proclamation of the gospel to the church needs to include a frequent exposition of what it means to be "the baptized." The Christian community needs to hear about the source of its identity, and about the power made available through God's promise when baptismal vows were made and baptismal proclamation was uttered. We are the baptized; we have been called and claimed by God through Christ's redeeming death and victorious resurrection; we have been brought from the realm of certain death into the family of even more certain life and hope. Ours are all the resources of the power that raised Christ from the dead (Eph. 1:19). The evangelization of the Christian community is the appeal to become in all fullness what we already are. There are other problems with the discipline of infant baptism as it is practiced that I will not address here, but its emphasis upon God's action and God's grace as the sole source and cause of faith is particularly clear—and that should be stressed in our celebration of the sacrament.

Being Christian and becoming Christian are, thus, two ways of talking about Christian existence. The reticence of some orthodox traditions in Lutheran and Reformed theology to talk about the reality of Christian experience, Christian obedience, and even Christian works can be understood as a desire to emphasize the "being" as God's act—which is certainly true but often not actually experienced—thus downplaying the "becoming." But the New Testament clearly expects the Christian community to become what it is.

One way to see this is to examine the indicatives and imperatives in the New Testament. Much of the instruction of the Christian community takes the form of imperatives: commands to be followed. We must accept it as a fundamental principle of New Testament interpretation that biblical imperatives are obeyable. The apostles did not intend to subject the Christian church to futility by establishing expectations for their behavior that could never be carried out. Biblical imperatives, if they are in fact inspired direction for the church, are obeyable imperatives.

However, they are not obeyable because of our ability to obey them. They are obeyable because of the indicatives that precede them. The New Testament imperatives follow on New Testament indicatives, that is, on New Testament statements of fact, on what is true because God has acted and is faithful. The indicatives of the Christian faith are all of the elements of the past tense that we have already discussed (see 5.2, pp. 78-88). God has acted; he sent his Son, empowered the proclamation of his kingdom, enabled and accepted the Son's sacrifice on the cross, raised him from the grave and enthroned him as Lord, and sent his Spirit to make the church into the company of witnesses. The church cannot debate those actions: they are the indicatives. Faith in Christ is a possible response to established facts. God has said his Yes to us, and thus made possible our Yes in response.

These indicatives precede and enable the imperatives and their obedience. Paul shows us this in his letter to the Philippians, where he discusses the nature of Christian community as unified and characterized by mutual service and concern. He then says, "Have this mind among yourselves, which you have in Christ Jesus . . . " (Phil. 2:5). Christ Jesus is the given, already there, already true; and because he is there and has done what he did, it is possible now to claim his presence and his power. It is possible to move from that indicative to the imperatives of Christian witness.

We can be his witnesses because "all authority in heaven and on earth has been given to [Christ]" (Matt. 28:18). We can be ambassadors of reconciliation because God has reconciled us and the world to himself in Christ. We can love one another because our souls have been purified "by [our] obedience to the truth for a sincere love of the brethren" (1 Pet. 1:22). The biblical imperatives are not impossible—they are feasible. But this is not because they make such eminently good sense, or correspond to the highest human aspirations, or elevate man to the level of his greatest potential. They are possible because God makes them so when he makes us into his children and his witnesses, and commences his work of salvation in us.

Thus, Jesus can describe the existence of the Christian community as light and salt (Matt. 5:13ff.), because he will make it into a source of illumination and a community that will preserve and give savor to life as his witnesses. The effects of light and salt will result from being that kind of community, made up of individuals who are Christ's disciples.

The relationship of indicative to imperative in the New Testament is the relationship between what God has initiated and what must now necessarily follow in our growth into the fullness of our calling. The indicatives can lead to imperatives because we already are what we are to become. As we have emphasized before (3.1, pp. 35-40; 4.1, pp. 55-65), the givens of our faith must be discovered in our pilgrimage as that process we call Christian growth. But we do not grow beyond what God has already made possible in the indicatives of the gospel. Rather, we experience the unfolding of all the potential already present in the work of God in Christ. The ministry of the Spirit is to teach us all things, bringing to remembrance all that Jesus has said to us (John 14:25).

The New Testament writers expect the Christian community to become something more and other than it has been. They invoke the power of the gospel because they know that this gospel is both a once-and-for-all event and the ongoing enablement of its full discovery within the community of faith. Thus, Peter, in his epistle, describes the nature of faith as obedience, stressing that faith is the hearing of the gospel and then acting upon what one has heard. Faith is the enfleshing of the gospel's meaning in the historical and personal experience of the church, constantly finding that the same power which raised Christ from the dead is now at work in the church's members. Thus, faith and power are linked in New Testament teaching, because the indicative behind faith is God's power at work.

The experience of the Christian community will, therefore, include the possibility of looking back to see where it has been, and recognizing that it has "become" more of what it was called to be. It is not an act of Christian arrogance to recognize growth and change in one's Christian pilgrimage. Scripture quite realistically addresses immaturity in the church (1 Cor. 3:1ff.; Rom. 14), but it includes the expectation that growth will follow (1 Pet. 2:2; Eph. 4:13ff.).

Another way Scripture describes this process of growth and becoming is with the word *transformation*. Paul appeals to the Romans to present their bodies, their entire existence, to God as the only truly reasonable response to what God has done in Christ (Rom. 12:1). Then he goes on to say, "Do not be conformed to this world, but be transformed by the renewal of your mind, that you may prove what is the will of God, what is good and acceptable and perfect" (v. 2). This succinct imperative brings together the themes of being and becoming, benefit and mission, in a very instructive way. The goal of the imperative is the recognition of the will of God. Seen against the backdrop of salvation history and the definition of the gospel in Romans, this must refer to the salvation will of God, which reached its historical apex in the incarnation (Rom. 1:1ff., and chaps. 1-11 as the full exposition of the gospel), and now is to be worked out in the obedience and ministry of the Christian community (Rom. 12-16). But Paul's statement about the will of God is a promise: when everything else has happened, the will of God will be recognizable in all its perfection and goodness. What comes before the promise is what concerns us.

The recognition of the will of God, which will include our obedience to that will, results from two processes, both of them basic to our becoming what we have been called to be. The first of these processes has to do with the reality out of which we come. Paul recognizes that we are conformed to this world. Because of all that we can learn from the contemporary behavioral sciences, we know more about this conformity than first-century people could have known. The fact of our conformity is psychologically and sociologically demonstrable. The gospel does not address us as unwritten slates, but rather as individuals who are sinners, who are conditioned in our various cultures to reflect the values of those cultures. Just as the Greeks in Corinth brought their religious and social systems with them when they responded to Christ, we bring our histories and our cultural programs with us to the gospel. Conformity is another way of talking about original sin. It is submission to the powers and structures of this world, which we have allowed to replace God as our operative deities. That conformity must end. That is the necessary presupposition for transformation.

It is a clear either/or in the New Testament: either the world or God, understanding the world here as the network of pseudo-deities we allow to assume power in our lives. This means that we as a Christian community must face the sober fact that we are continuing to live our lives in patterns of conformity to "this world" from which we are called to depart. We are instead to become what God has made us and proclaimed us to be in our baptism. This entails confronting and recognizing our conformities. Paul frequently holds up the mirror of the gospel to his churches and forces them to face their conformities, especially when he appeals to them to lead lives worthy of the gospel with which they have been called (Eph. 4:1ff.; Phil. 1:27ff.; and elsewhere). Continuing in conformity to the world must mean stunted Christian growth, immaturity in faith, a Christian existence that does not begin to develop into what God intends it to be.

This is an obeyable imperative, for Christians have experienced and now have within themselves the resources of God to recognize their conformities and set them aside. In more classical terms, this is a summons to the ongoing process of repentance, which is part of the Christian experience. And it is an enabled process: God has given us eyes to see our conformities because he has released us from their ultimate consequences, those wages that we must no longer fear, because "Christ has overcome the world." But it is also an imperative that calls upon us to labor with the task before us. There is much pain involved in recognizing our conformities. Repentance is not to be taken lightly—it is internal surgery, the necessary removal of what is no longer a part of the Christian's being.

For Christians in our Western world, this must mean asking and working through such difficult questions as: How have we conformed the gospel and the church to our world, so that we fit more neatly and find it less threatening to our well-being to call ourselves Christians? How have we allowed our society to determine for us what Christian witness will be? How have we prevented the gospel from exercising its "searchlight function" on our current reality, so that it does not reveal the darkness that is really there? How have we diluted the gospel, so that it does not force us to face embarrassing questions? What are the assumptions we have brought with us from our world and mixed with the gospel to produce a palatable message?

The Christian community, if it will be transformed, must be intentional about searching out its conformities. This will be the result of disciplined study of all of God's word. The swordlike function of the word directs itself primarily against our conformities. A confrontation with all that Scripture teaches us will challenge our "lukewarmness." The problem is that we are too selective about what we want to read and learn from God's word. We avoid all the uncomfortable portions and thus evade confrontation with our conformities. But in so doing, we will never experience the promised transformation, and we will find it impossible to recognize and do the will of God.

When we recognize and remove our conformities, however, we find an amazing new possibility opening up before us: we can be transformed. In fact, Paul's words here make it plain that this *will* happen to us, if we are willing to struggle with our conformities. The way this transformation will happen, as God's work in us, is through the renewal of our mind. This is a particularly important way of describing how we are to "become what we are." We have to recognize that the most fundamental conformities are mental: they are the deeply ingrained attitudes that subtly but powerfully control our decisions. Sin expresses itself most profoundly where it is least recognized as sin—where the issue is not immorality but deeply rooted resistance to the truth that is God and his will. It is comparatively easy to set aside all the bad things we should not do, especially if our society legislates against most of them so that we get punished for doing them anyway. But it is not at all easy to change the attitudes that produce our decisions.

Secular behavioral scientists have studied the power of attitudes and agree that these powerful components of human personality are by no means easy to change. The attitudes of racism are a sobering example. In spite of laws, public crusades, marches, school curricula, and church preaching and teaching, racism persists, defying God's grace and love and continuing to permit injustice in our societies and, even more deplorably, to justify and condone racist attitudes within the church itself. The outward pressures of laws and programs have a minimal effect upon such deeply rooted attitudes. The apostle rightly sees that it is necessary to have one's mind renewed. That means that it is necessary to learn to think as a Christian. One must accept an entirely new set of presuppositions and assumptions and build one's understandings of life from that new beginning.

For the Christian, the question of the worth of the human person is an example of the kind of "new attitude" that must result from the renewal of the mind. Whereas apart from Christ human worth is measured in terms of productivity, or birth, or education, or race, in Christ there is only one criterion: every person on earth is an individual for whom Christ died; thus, every person possesses a worth measured by the shed blood of Christ. This "alien dignity" of the human person, to use the medieval phrase, must become the Christian community's starting point when it approaches the task of witness. The worth of all people is established by the gospel.

Our fundamental attitudes about the created world are another example of what must change when the mind is renewed. The nature of creation is defined by the theology of creation. What God has made is good, and the human responsibility is to administer that goodness for the benefit of all. This must become the operative presupposition of the Christian community as it becomes what it has been called to be.

But our conformities with regard to these and many other basic questions are numerous, and to change them is hard. Hard, but by no means impossible. Our minds *can* be renewed! We can become what we have been called to be! It is not a comfortable or easy process, but it is the divinely enabled process that is essential if we are to be the witness that God has called us to be. Our minds are renewed as we learn to think Christianly. That means that our study of God's word and the meaning of what he has done must lead to changes in our ways of thinking and deciding (which is the subject of the next chapter, "Doing the Witness").

To become what we are, then, to have our minds renewed so that we can be transformed and recognize God's will, means that we must refine our definition of the Christian community. The community, in order to be the witness, must be the "equipping community."

6.3 THE "EQUIPPING COMMUNITY" AS THE PRESUPPOSITION FOR BEING THE WITNESS

To *be* the witness, the Christian community must *become* the witness. The indicatives of the faith must result in obedience to the imperatives, and the Christian community's responsibility is to bring that about. The "therefore" of the New Testament Epistles, when the writer moves from the exposition of the gospel to what that gospel must mean in historical experience, defines the existence of the Christian community. We address this aspect of the church at this point because we view this as basic for what will follow. We have emphasized that we are to become what we already are before God as his adopted and reconciled children, and thus we are to become the witnesses God has called us to be. "Becoming what we are," however, is an empty phrase if the process does not become definitive for what the church is. The individual Christian cannot become what he or she is and is called to be apart from the ministry of the church. And we are defining that ministry, so essential to the *being* of the witness, as the work of equipping.

I referred earlier to the helpful approach to ecclesiology developed by Avery Dulles in his book *Models of the Church*. I would like to use that approach, but develop it further. Father Dulles discusses the church in terms of the institutional model, the mystical communion model, the sacramental model, the herald model, and the servant model. I am proposing here a sixth model, the equipping community model, to define how the church is to enable its members to be and to become the witness to the gospel.

Dulles adopts a helpful approach to the definition of his models by discussing them in terms of

(a) their characteristics;
(b) their unifying bonds;
(c) the beneficiaries and
(d) the benefits of the model;
(e) the model's definition of the church's mission;
(f) the biblical basis of the model, and both
(g) the assets and
(h) the weaknesses of the model.

This analytical approach makes it possible for the student of the church to grapple with the vast variety of understandings of the church and make useful judgments in terms of one's biblical presuppositions. We will use this approach to examine my equipping community model.

(a) Its *characteristics* are an integrating combination of the major features of the five models proposed by Dulles. In this equipping community model, the central thrust of the church is seen in its calling to be the witness to the gospel. The combination of *kerygma, koinonia,* and *diakonia,* under *martyria,* is accepted here as the fundamental definition of the church. For Dulles, this is the herald model. However, we must link it intimately with the community model, because the message is committed to a called out people and is enfleshed by them. That is the "incarnational understanding" that we have been developing. The insights of the servant model are brought into the equipping community model immediately: the meaning of *witness* must include action that reveals the gospel (see the next chapter). The emphasis upon the servant model is a necessary corrective of the tendency of our church theologies to emphasize the proclamation of the message without realizing that the message is to be expressed in actions and events as well as words.

The sacramental model, which is obviously more difficult for many Protestant Christians to grasp, is a helpful approach because it stresses that God's work through the church is really happening in experience-able history, that the Word does become flesh through the church's presence and action, and that the sacraments themselves are to be understood as historical experience of the reality of God. Finally, the institutional model is necessary as the visible and orderly form of the church's obedience in the world, but we must remember that the institutional form of the church is to serve this witnessing community as it carries out its mission, not dominate it.

(b) The equipping community model, then, is rooted in the mission of the gospel. It is *unified* by the work of God, who calls it into being and gives his Spirit to enable it to function. It has received its task from God and has been sent out to Jerusalem, Judea, Samaria, and the end of the earth, to carry out that mission. The message and the community together with the work of service comprise the witness that is to be given. The unity of the equipping model is thus given to it, and like so much of the gospel, it is now to be discovered and realized as part of its obedience.

(c) and (d) When we consider the *beneficiaries* and *benefits* of this model, we must be aware of the immediate danger of dividing the gospel and the church's mission into benefit and mission. Therefore, at this point, I suggest that we consider these analytical categories in terms of the inward and the outward dimensions of the church. A brief digression is therefore needed.

Our detailed analysis of the church and its mission obviously will have to address the particulars of churchly reality. It will be helpful, when we seek to be specific about the church, to recognize that the church exists in the world in two overlapping and interdependent spheres of action. I call these the inward and the outward dimensions of the church.

The inward dimension of the church has to do with all that the church is and does within its defined structures, its membership and tradition. Much of what takes place in the church is intended properly for its own members. Most of its worship life, fellowship, study and instruction, and spiritual discipline is intended rightly for those who call themselves Christians and have taken the step of identifying with the Body of Christ.

Thus, it is important to recognize that much of what takes place in the community of Christ inwardly is unintelligible to the outside world. Worship services, if they are what they should be, will seldom function well as evangelistic offerings to an unbelieving world. They are, rather, special times and experiences where the community of faith receives the equipping needed in order to carry on as the witness in the world. (This theme will be discussed in the chapter on ministry, "Ministry for Incarnational Witness," pp. 204-25.)

It would be fair to state that the Reformers addressed much of their work and concern to this inward dimension of the church, which at that time was the whole picture. The outward dimension of the church has reemerged as a concern in the modern age as a result of secularization in the West and the discovery and opening of the une-vangelized cultures outside Western traditions. The outward dimension of the church is its mission, its calling to the world to serve God there as the witness to the gospel of salvation. To use our earlier language, the outward dimension of the gospel is the *martyria* rendered by the church in obedience to its election and enabling.

Concern for the inner dimension of the church is quite clearly both necessary and good. However, a problem arises immediately if we consider this dimension only. The inward dimension of the church easily concentrates on the benefits of faith, leaving aside the mission, or redefining the mission to mean that the purpose of the church's existence and ministry is to concentrate upon the faith experience of those who are in the church. Some have spoken of the church as constantly reevangelizing the evangelized—although it is undoubtedly necessary that evangelization continue both in the inward dimension as well as in the outward dimension! But concentration upon the inward dimension with no concept of the outward mission of the church is certainly too small a definition of the church if witness to the gospel is the central purpose of God's election of his people.

Thus, we need to learn to consider the outward dimension of the church's call as the dominant motif in our ecclesiology and then link it functionally with the inward dimension. It is my contention that the outward dimension of the church's call defines the purpose and the function of the inward life of the church. We shall be approaching this from various directions—but the fundamental concept I am advocating is that the inward life of the church is to be developed around the central purpose of equipping all its members for the mission of the church to the world, which is its outward dimension. That is why we are describing the church here as the equipping community.

Returning to our description of the equipping community model, then, using Dulles's analytical outline, the *beneficiaries* of the church in this model are both inward and outward. Inwardly, Christians are clearly the beneficiaries as they are equipped for the ministry of witness. Externally, the "world" is the beneficiary because the equipping and equipped community is God's instrument to present the gospel to the world. The witness of the community is God's gift to the world, the way in which his love continues to be enfleshed so that faith may be awakened.

Similarly, we are to distinguish between the internal and external dimensions of the *benefits*. We have frequently alluded to the benefit for the members: the experience *now* of what salvation means and brings—the blessing of knowing God and living in relationship with him while being restored to the fullness of life for which he created us; the excitement and completeness that are the necessary results of encountering and experiencing the love of God as a historical force that changes people and even societies. Membership in the witnessing community is thus a very great benefit of the church in this model. But that internal benefit is functional to the external benefit, which focuses the existence and work of the church on the task of mission. The world is to experience Christ through his church, to see and to hear the witness that the church is and does. If the effect of the church is not to be a witness in the world, then the church is restricting the gospel and selfishly reducing its self-definition to the enjoyment of the benefits of faith and calling, excluding the mission to which it is called.

(e) Thus, the *mission* of the church is to be Christ's witness in the world, being, doing, and saying that witness as the continuation of his ministry, incarnating the gospel for the sake of a world for which Christ died. And the internal mission of the church is to be equipped and to equip itself, under the ministry of the Holy Spirit, for this work as witness.

(f) The equipping community model, I suggest, is firmly rooted in the *scriptural* doctrine of the church. It builds on the theology of the church in the Book of Acts; it reflects the theology of ministry in Ephesians, especially chapter 4 (to which we will return in Chap. 12, pp. 226-35); it links the New Testament imperatives directed to the life and integrity of the church with the mission of the church within salvation history. It incorporates the rabbinic model of our Lord's preparation of the disciples for the ministry of the early church, and also builds bridges to the synagogical tradition, which most likely influenced the structural development of the early church. It takes the Great Commission seriously and yet deals with the incarnational fact of the called people who, as a result of God's action, are present in the world from day to day and whose mission bears directly upon that historical existence in all its forms and ramifications.

(g) The *assets* of this model are obvious. As a strongly biblical model, this approach obviously is presented as a corrective to other models, which too narrowly focus on one or the other aspect of the church. Over against the traditions of ecclesiology out of which we come, it argues for the preeminence of witness as the fundamental definition of the church. It seeks to direct the church's understanding away from itself and its own survival and toward Christ and his work in history. We view the church "functionally" in the equipping community model, in an attempt to draw God's incarnational way of working into our doctrine of the church. To "be the witness," the church must understand that its election is a privilege leading to responsibility, and that all that it is (and does) must serve that purpose for its election. God allows his Good News to continue to become flesh in the corporate and individual reality of the church in order to make his love and grace known to the entire creation, which Christ died to save. Thus, the "being" of the church is itself functional to the purposes of God.

(h) The *problems* of the equipping community have to do with its realization in a Christendom characterized by a pluralism of ecclesiologies often at odds with each other, and by churches whose concentration tends to be upon their inward continuation with an inadequate understanding of their call to be a witness in the world. Even where evangelism is strongly emphasized, we have to ask about the division between benefit and mission so common in the presentation of the gospel solely as a "means of salvation" separate from a "call to service." We will explore the ways in which our current ecclesiologies need correcting (see Chap. 9), but first it is necessary to complete our discussion of the church's mission as being, doing, and saying the witness to the gospel.

Our purpose has been to emphasize the transforming power of the gospel to make people into witnesses, into a community of witness. This "being" of the witness must be stressed in order to maintain the biblical wholeness of the church's definition. Those who do the witness do so as those who are, by God's gracious work in their lives, witnesses—and as those who are becoming witnesses. Those who say the witness do so out of the changed identity of lives that are new creations.

Finally, then, this emphasis upon "being the witness" renders it impossible to define Christian existence as "anonymous." One currently popular approach to the discussion of the Christian presence and task in the world is to use the image of salt, seeing the Christian presence as invisible and often unconscious, although having its impact. This is probably an understandable reaction to the often arrogant and self-certain way in which Christians have related the gospel to the world. Understandable as it may be, however, it is still a denial of the work of the Spirit in making faith, because it implies that this faith must not become known to its bearer, is not conscious and decisional, and thus not really expressed in submission and obedience to Jesus Christ as an act of faith.

The Christian response is highly varied, ranging from childlike to mature faith, and is always characterized by the perplexing tension of our sinful humanity and our redeemed humanity linked in the existence of the individual Christian and the church. We never move beyond the *et* in Martin Luther's classic definition of the Christian (*simul justus et peccator*—"simultaneously justified and sinner"). But we do "know whom we have believed," and we confess that our existence is defined by the gospel of God's Yes to us. To divorce the "being" of the Christian from his or her awareness of that being and his or her decision to make that confession is to redefine Christian reality in a way that is radically different from the New Testament record.

We *are* Christians who are then to *do* and to *say* what God has given us to do and say. We are also *becoming* the Christian witnesses God intends us to be, for which purpose his Holy Spirit is at work in us. We know that it is wrong to define Christians only in terms of who they are, so we must immediately turn to what they do and say. But we have begun where we must: at the pivotal point of God's real action in entering into the lives of individuals and calling forth their faith so that they can say of themselves, "We are Christ's witnesses."

Seven

DOING THE WITNESS: CHRISTIAN ACTION AS WITNESS

7.1 INCARNATION INSTEAD OF ABSTRACTION

When God commenced his intervention in history to accomplish the reconciliation of his creation to himself, he entered into a relationship with Abraham. His action in Abraham's life resulted in decisive action on Abraham's part: he left his homeland and ultimately established himself and his tribe in the land that was to become the land of promise. God's purposes were "enfleshed" in the call to Abraham and in his obedient response and action. For Abraham, faith was demonstrated in what he did, in the fact that he obeyed, and that God's will became for him the purpose and definition of his own life. Faith was not an abstract proposition for Abraham, but was in fact doing the will of God. For this, Abraham became the model of faith for the New Testament church.

Similarly, Israel's faith was not the result of a philosophical process of reflection, argumentation, and abstract formulation. No Athenian academy produced the tenets of Old Testament faith. Rather, the faith of Israel, with all of its formulations of truth about God's nature and purposes, and about the human situation, is a confession of conviction in response to God's actions within experienceable history. We need to understand "confession of conviction" Hebraically; that is, as actions that reveal conviction. Israel "does" its faith—and also "does" its disobedience! Rebellion against God is not the changing of one's mind about the truthfulness or falsehood of various theological propositions, but willful disobedience, doing what God does not want us to do rather than what he wants us to do.

At the apex of salvation history, God did not articulate a message that could be mentally perceived and then accepted or rejected. He came in the form of his Son and presented his will in the life and actions of Jesus. In the end, he accomplished the reconciliation that was his purpose in the obedient death of Jesus, ratifying that sacrifice in the resurrection and enthronement of the Messiah as Lord.

When God then set about the task of making known his actions, he did not content himself with a treatise on what he had done. He called forth a people to be the enfleshed testimony to his actions. Their lives and actions were to be made into the channels through which the Good News of God's favor toward us could be communicated. The message was implanted in messengers. This is what we have called the "incarnational" way in which God has chosen to carry out his intentions.

By its very nature, biblical faith cannot be reduced to abstractions and is difficult to render into systems. Our division of the theme of witness into "being" and "doing" is itself an abstraction that produces its own problems. From a Hebraic and biblical perspective, it is quite impossible to distinguish between who a person is and what a person does. Human actions reveal the truth about human identity, and all of the statements we make to the contrary cannot alter the fact that what we are is not reflected in our theoretical statements but in the actual living of our lives.

Thus, as we move from our discussion of "being" the witness to "doing" the witness, we need to stress that we make this distinction only for the purposes of reflection and analysis. To be true to the biblical witness, we must insist that the identity and the action of the witness are inseparable. The work of God changes in one whole process both who we are and what we do.

Immediately, of course, the rejoinder must come: But do we not in fact make that separation in the reality of the church? Do we not talk about "being Christian" and neglect "doing Christian witness"? Is there not a depressing amount of evidence that this "impossible distinction" is frequently made by Christians and even whole theological and ecclesiastical traditions? The candid answer is Yes, that distinction is made. And over against that weakness of the Christian church the incarnational concept of mission must stand as a corrective.

The separation of that which is inseparable takes place in at least two ways:

1. Christian action is divorced from Christian existence when the emphasis is on *being* Christian, primarily as a way to insure that one's

own salvation (after death) has been guaranteed. The Christian identity is then that of the person who is "saved" (past tense only). This
understanding can limit the necessary expression of that benefit in a
variety of ways: it may reduce faith to a set of spiritual exercises that,
although good, are not a full expression of what the gospel means; it
may redefine faith so that its effect is transposed to "eternity," and
historical reality is left largely untouched. Further, some may see any
concern for the present expression of the meaning of the gospel as a
reintroduction of works righteousness, or may reject it as an undesir-
able mixing of the "religious" with "real life." The emphasis on *being*
may even reduce Christianity to the affirmation of doctrinal statements,
so that faith is basically subscription to a religious system of thought.

This way of separating the inseparable concentrates upon what I
have called the inward dimension of the faith, the personal experience
and enjoyment of the benefits of the gospel. Where there is an outward
dimension, it tends to be an evangelistic emphasis upon being saved in
order to avoid judgment and damnation. The real purpose of the
church, in this kind of separation between being and doing the witness,
is to expand its membership; thus, the church, rather than the world,
becomes the central focus of the gospel.

2. Christian action can be separated from Christian identity when
the emphasis is on *doing,* and identity is discounted. We see this
happening whenever the effect of the gospel is taken to be a program
of morality or education, or a platform for political and social reform
that should be advocated and perhaps even imposed upon a needy
world. Those who hold this view often dismiss as old-fashioned, myth-
ical, or passé the concern for linking action with personal Christian
conviction.

The effects of the gospel, even when separated from the life-
transforming power of Christ known and served as personal Lord and
Savior, are undoubtedly a desirable program for the reform of society.
Who would not rather live in a world governed by the principles of
behavior articulated in the New Testament, whether or not Christ is
served as Lord? In effect, that is approximately what has evolved in the
Western world after twenty centuries of Christian tradition, and for
these effects of the gospel upon our world we can be grateful. (At the
same time, we must recognize that massive distortions of the gospel
have also been at work in the development of Western civilization, so
that often today the gospel is rejected in many parts of the world more
because of the Western reshaping of it than as the result of an encounter with the biblical message of grace and salvation.)

The problem with this separation, however, is that the doing of the gospel is ultimately impossible if it is not the expression of a life-transforming relationship with the Lord of the gospel. Because of human sin, every social and political program based upon the humanitarianism of the gospel will distort those tenets of our faith. Good ideas become tainted practice because we cannot do what we do as though we were not sinners. Even though certainly the second table of the Ten Commandments describes a human order in which we genuinely would prefer to live, we see today that even these so-called basic values can be set aside under the new ethical principle, "I can do what I want as long as it doesn't bother anyone else." Apart from the relationship with the Savior God who establishes himself in the first four commandments, the latter six ultimately are relativized, or enlisted in the service of a value system totally foreign to biblical faith.

This second form of separation is, then, a concentration upon the external dimension of the gospel with a corresponding underemphasis or discounting of the necessary inward dimension. The gospel becomes an idea, and Christian witness is made into the intellectual defense of that idea, or the political or social program to translate that idea into action.

Thus, we must understand and experience as inseparable the "being" of the witness and the "doing" of the witness, the essential link between the *martys* and the *martyria*. The inward dimension of the gospel must focus upon and equip the outward dimension of witness to the gospel. To do the witness to the gospel, which is our mission, we need to accept the enabling power of God to whom we come in faith through Christ's ministry on our behalf. In that reestablished fellowship, the doing of the witness becomes both our unforeseen opportunity and our necessary obedience.

Before I am accused of anti-intellectualism with regard to Christian witness, let me emphasize that much can be learned about the gospel through abstract analysis of all that our faith says and means. Theology is far richer because of the way in which human minds have done that kind of abstract reflection. But the abstract method, which we have learned largely from ancient Greece, has its notable limits, especially with regard to the biblical message. In general, the Hellenistic approach leads us to separate the inseparable, to divide being from doing, inward from outward, and, thus, to separate the benefit from the mission of faith. Historians of Christian thought have dealt extensively with this problem of our Hellenistic heritage, and certainly the last word has not been spoken on how to understand and appreciate the evolution of theology in the first several centuries of our era.

It appears to me, however, that biblical faith has a genuine problem when it confronts Hellenism's tendency to make a distinction between the spiritual (or mental) on the one hand, and the physical and material on the other. Generally, this distinction is accompanied by a value judgment: the spiritual is essentially better, and the physical less worthy. In some forms of Hellenism (and later in Gnostic religions), the physical and material were regarded as the enemy of the human person. The goal of spiritual advance was to free oneself from the dictatorship of the physical and become more truly spiritual. Obviously, in such a system an incarnational approach to truth and to ministry would be unacceptable. The "doing" of the gospel could easily become the concerted attempt to move "being Christian" out of the structures of human limitation and history: to identify the eternally true principles of faith, or to discipline oneself toward a spiritual existence that was as little subject to the realities and limits of physical being as possible. Many forms of asceticism expressed this separation.

In our incarnational understanding of the mission of the church, we assert that God intends to have his grace made known through human instruments in the events of human history. Rather than withdraw from history as monks, we enter into history as servants of God in whom he is graciously willing to make his presence and love known to the world. (There are obviously other excellent reasons to consider celibacy and the monastic life as one valid expression of Christian obedience; monasticism does not have to mean withdrawal from the world and rejection of the physical as part of God's good creation.)

Our doing of the witness to the gospel is the necessary expression of our being called to be witnesses and our having been given the faith to become witnesses. We cannot hoard this treasure but must make it known through the opportunities for communication that God's Spirit brings about. Doing the witness means that we understand that God's Spirit brings about those opportunities in the course of all of life, and not just at special times, in special places, and through special rites and words.

To *be* the witness is to *do* the witness. To become a witness is to learn how to do this witness to the gospel. The *martys* is commissioned to give the world his or her *martyrion*, to continue doing what Christ did as he both spoke and acted as God's Son to reveal the heart of the Father. In grappling with what it means to "do the witness," we will find ways to overcome the dichotomy between the benefit and the mission of faith.

7.2 "SAVED TO SERVE"

The Lord commissioned Moses to go to Pharaoh and say, "Thus says the Lord, the God of the Hebrews, 'Let my people go, that they may serve me'" (Exod. 9:1). The exodus from Egypt, which ultimately resulted from the confrontation in the Egyptian court, became Israel's great experience of salvation. To this day, Jews continue to celebrate Passover as the active remembrance and proclamation that God is a redeeming God and has acted to redeem his people. The people of the Old Covenant defined salvation in terms of the historical experience of the exodus and looked forward to God's future work as the consummation of what he had done when he freed Israel from slavery.

But God's word to Pharaoh does not dwell solely on the salvation of Israel ("let my people go"); it does not speak only of liberation and freedom. Rather, God's purpose is stated emphatically: "that they may serve me." Just as God blessed Abraham and his seed so that they might become a blessing to all nations, God freed Israel so that they might serve him. This is a fundamental theme of the entire scriptural record of salvation history—the inseparable link between the benefit of salvation and the mission for which we have been called and saved and which, I am suggesting, we must see as the foundation of our theology of the church. If we can grasp the essential relationship between the two parts of Moses' statement to Pharaoh, then we can grapple with the mission of the church in its proper biblical context.

The questions that necessarily follow are these: How do we serve God? What does it mean to serve God? If God liberates his people so that they can serve him, what does he then expect that they will do? What does the "doing" of the witness really look like?

These questions are justified because there are many ways of understanding the meaning of "the service of God." This variety of understandings is already found in the Old Testament, in what one might call various theologies of Israel's mission. And certainly there is a similar variety within Christendom when we seek to define what "the service of God" is. We shall attempt to address this question by reviewing some central themes of scriptural teaching.

To serve God is to be obedient to his will as he has disclosed it. From the first pages of Scripture and throughout the Bible, we encounter the revelation of God's will for his creation. In the creation com-

mands given to Adam and Eve (Gen. 1:28ff.; 2:15), we see that it was
God's intention that his creation be responsibly managed, and that to
serve God would mean to be good gardeners and reliable stewards of
this good world committed into human hands. Thus, in the creation
accounts the service of God is expressed in the exercise of God-given
human capacities to multiply, to fill, to subdue, and to have dominion.
This service was world-directed and was intended to be the way
through which God's own purposes for his creation would be fulfilled.
The human person, created in the image of God, is to know God and,
out of that relationship of knowledge and communion, is to do God's
work within the structure established by God—which means, as well,
that God sets a limit over which his creature is not to go. That limit is
the tree of the knowledge of good and evil, and the issue is obedience
to God as the appropriate form of his service.

God's will for his creation is later restated in the Decalogue, a
legal codex. By this time, this reformulation of God's good design must
necessarily be phrased in negative commands as well as in positive
ones, because human rebellion has led creation very far away from the
original relationship of service to and fellowship with God. But the
basic intent is the same. God intends to have his creation well managed, and wants his creatures to experience its goodness as they serve
him by carrying out his will. And so the service of God is defined in
terms of human actions and attitudes that are a part of the very routine
of daily life. The quality and shape of interhuman relationships are the
arena of obedience to God. Here we serve God as we live with one
another in the good way that God intended us to live. The service of
God is the doing of his will, and his will embraces the wholeness of
life, both for individuals and for the entire nation. It is appropriate to
remember that "Torah" means "instruction for life"—we too narrowly
understand "law" when we define it as legalistic regulations only.

When we examine the nature of obedience and the actual content
of God's commands in creation and in the law, we are struck by the
fact that the definition of God's service is not very "religious." By that,
we mean that we find here little emphasis upon activities that relate
exclusively to religion, such as the rituals and liturgies of worship,
sacrifice, and the spiritual exercises that help us to concentrate upon
God. These aspects of the life of faith emerge soon in the Old Testament tradition, as we see in the Levitical Codes. But the larger context,
found throughout the Old Testament, is that the service of God takes
place in the conduct of all our lives, and very especially in the conduct
of our daily affairs and the living out of our relationships. The world in

all its diversity appears to be the place in which God will be served. Thus, the laws given to regulate the life of Israel touch upon every area of life, not only upon the ritual.

But Israel's history demonstrates the general human capacity to distort what is essentially good into its own perversion. The worship of God in its organized and structured forms, as ritual and formalized celebration, can become a way to avoid doing God's will. The disciplines of religious practice, all inherently good and necessary, can and did evolve into systems that provided their participants with a sense of security but at the same time failed to focus them on their true calling, which was to do God's will in every area of their lives. Sacrifices became so distorted in their meaning that the prophet said, "Your burnt offerings are not acceptable, nor your sacrifices pleasing to me" (Jer. 6:20b). Whenever the practice of religion became a source of security, divorced from obedience and unrelated to the way in which God's purposes were being intentionally carried out by his people, the prophetic voice was raised to call the people back to the reason for their existence and for their worship: "Has the Lord as great delight in burnt offerings and sacrifices, as in obeying the voice of the Lord? Behold, to obey is better than sacrifice, and to hearken than the fat of rams" (1 Sam. 15:22).

We see that the one-sided concentration upon the benefit of knowing God can degenerate into an emphasis upon religious practice as an end in itself, and then as a (false) source of religious security and even a distortion of the revealed purposes of God. God focuses his will upon the reconciliation of all his creation to himself, and to lose that perspective will invariably lead to perversions of the faith. To use language made popular by Barth and Bonhoeffer, the danger is always there that we will allow faith as a God-enabled reponse to his love for the purpose of serving him to degenerate into "religion," as a system under our control, intended to manage God and the experience of him in our lives for our purposes, thus violating the second commandment and creating a god after our own image.

Central to the worship life of God's people, then, is the constant need to revise radically our own "religious interpretation" of God's purposes, so that as his people we can serve him again. The pathway to that radical revision is the repentant prayer of a people who know that their sinfulness leads them to appropriate the God-given opportunity to know and serve him and to make it into an instrument for their own sinful purposes. Both the worship literature of Israel and the prophetic message confronted Israel constantly with this need. "The sacrifice acceptable to God is a broken spirit; a broken and contrite heart, O God, thou wilt not despise" (Ps. 51:17).

But contrition must result in renewed commitment to doing God's will. And his will is that his creation be restored to the goodness of its original design, that all of his creatures know him as the source of their life and its bounty, and, thus, that justice be done and all humanity know a life marked by righteousness and peace:

> I hate, I despise your feasts,
>   and I take no delight in your solemn assemblies.
> Even though you offer me your burnt offerings and
>   cereal offerings,
>   I will not accept them,
> and the peace offerings of your fatted beasts
>   I will not look upon.
> Take away from me the noise of your songs;
>   to the melody of your harps I will not listen.
> But let justice roll down like waters,
>   and righteousness like an everflowing stream.
>
> (Amos 5:21–24)

Human rebellion has perverted God's creation. His gracious purpose is to restore it to himself, to save it. Those called to serve his purposes will discover that an essential part of their obedience to his call is to work to reverse the effects of human sin within creation. Where there is injustice, obedience will require that his people work to restore justice. Where there is suffering, they will seek to relieve that suffering. They must address poverty as contrary to God's gracious design of his world. They must recognize inequity and oppression as forms of disobedience that reveal hostility toward God's rule, which is the very core of sin. Therefore, if God's people are to serve him, then they must accept his purposes as the agenda for their action. The prophets made that very plain.

Jesus came, proclaiming the kingdom. His words and actions were the revelation of God's desire for his creation. They were both good news for the world and a word of judgment over every distortion of the will of God, especially every reduction of God's disclosure of his purposes to a religious system that concentrated upon itself and ceased to be a witness and a channel to the world of God's blessing. Jesus demonstrated that obedience to God's will is the only possible form of worship. To serve God is to do his work in the world. And so Jesus stands in the great tradition of Isaiah, Jeremiah, Amos, and Hosea when he begins his proclamation of the kingdom of God: "The Spirit of the

Lord is upon me, because he has anointed me to preach good news to the poor. He has sent me to proclaim release to the captives and recovering of sight to the blind, to set at liberty those who are oppressed, to proclaim the acceptable year of the Lord" (Luke 4:18-19).

The difference in Jesus' proclamation was that he was to bring about that kingdom, whereas the prophets of the Old Covenant could only look forward to its coming. Jesus proclaimed the will of God for his creation in a radical way that restored to the center the creation intention of God and the salvific intention of the law. In the Sermon on the Mount, he made it very plain that God's purposes have to do with all of creation, and with the rectification of every perversion of that creation. We are not to understand the law as an obeyable code of behavior that guarantees its faithful adherent a sense of religious security. Rather, Jesus reveals its true purpose as God's design for life lived in total responsiveness to him and to his purposes. Thus, he addresses the heart and the actions of the believer, which are to be in concord. When they are not, then the law is a summons to repentance and cleansing, so that the faithful can be made again into useful servants of God. Radical obedience is the only possible way to serve God appropriately. Those who are privileged to receive this revelation of God's purposes are to accept it as God's equipping for his service.

"Let my people go that they may serve me!" The issue for Moses was not merely release from Egyptian bondage, but liberation for service. Jesus, too, is about the business of liberation from the bondage of sin and death, but his liberation is not an end in itself. He accomplishes this release so that those who respond in faith may serve God in the continuation and completion of his saving work . . . with eternal implications for all of creation. In that process, he warns the disciples (and through them the church) of the continuing danger that obedience to him will be reduced to "religion" understood as a system of religious observance under human control that produces effects desired by rebellious humanity. This possible distortion will always be present in the church. Jesus' polemic against the religious leaders of his day was, in effect, a preparation of the Christian church for the problem of "religious manipulation" and the danger of reducing the gospel to the shape of ritual and religious celebration for its own sake.

Our history documents that the Lord's warnings were not in vain. We need to turn to the gospel accounts in order to discover again that obedience to Christ means accepting his cross, following him, and setting out into the world to do the witness to which we are called. His death and resurrection have both revealed God's saving love and accomplished the reconciliation upon which humanity is dependent. The "acceptable year of the Lord" is here, now. As Paul reminds us, "now is the acceptable time; behold, now is the day of salvation" (2 Cor. 6:2b). But the danger is also great that we might "accept the grace of God in vain" (2 Cor. 6:1). To divide the call to salvation from the task of witness would produce that very religious vanity about which the apostle warns us.

For the New Testament church, then, obedience to Christ must mean the service of God within his world. Knowing that we are saved through faith, out of God's grace alone, and that our own works could never have contributed to that marvelous fact, we must then know that "we are his workmanship, created in Christ Jesus for good works, which God prepared beforehand, that we should walk in them" (Eph. 2:10). This is the reason that God has made us a source of light in the world, so that we might let our light "so shine before men, that they may see [our] good works and give glory to [our] Father who is in heaven" (Matt. 5:16). Clearly, our good works are not to draw the attention of the world to us, but are to be a form of witness that will turn humanity toward the God who loves his creation and desires to reconcile it to himself.

We cannot divide *being* the witness from *doing* the witness. Christian obedience is active work in the world, doing the work Christ began, and following his instructions as we do his ministry. The task before the Christian church today, after twenty centuries, is to learn to read the four Gospels as the Holy Spirit's equipping of the church for its ministry in the world. We must move on from seeing the accounts of Jesus' teaching and miracles, his parables and sayings, as demonstrations of his deity and authority—although they are certainly that—and read them again as detailed and adequate teaching on how to go about incarnational ministry. The resources of New Testament research today make the gospel teaching available to us with remarkable clarity. We can, in fact, discover much more of what was the original intent of the accounts than earlier generations knew. But these discoveries are an uncomfortable challenge, because we now see that the gospel accounts are a radical summons to obedience, a revolutionary call to serve God in the world by continuing to do the work of Christ as our witness to him.

In a sense, our tendency to emphasize the word, the *kerygma*, at the cost of doing the word, the *martyria* of actions, is a way of retreating from the cost of discipleship and the demands of the gospel. The early church discovered that witness must mean the gift of one's entire life, and so the word for the witness became our term *martyr*. We need to remove the halo from that term and realize that it applies to every Christian and to the whole church. We cannot be Christ's witnesses and then not do the task of witness, and we cannot reduce the definition of that action to narrow programs of charity and comparatively safe forms of cooperation with a world that does not want a more radical witness to this radical gospel.

Doing the witness must mean that we return to the prophets of the Old Covenant and learn from their polemic against the religiosity of their day. Doing the witness must also mean that we explore the New Testament concept of "neighbor" until we begin to see how uncomfortably challenging it is to our mindset. Doing the witness must mean accepting Christ's call and following his example in going out to the outcast and rejected ones of our society, demonstrating that God's love is as much intended for them as for the respectable classes of society. Doing the witness to this gospel will make of the church a movement more threatening to the orders of the world than is any ideological program. And yet doing the witness will also mean that the way we do it is as much a part of our message as the actual gospel content. Never do the ends justify the means in Christian witness; rather, the means are an essential part of the witness.

Studying the life and ministry of Christ as the school of Christian obedience is a sobering and often disturbing experience. The temptation is great to explain much of what we find in the Gospels as culturally determined, or perhaps only eschatologically realizable. To be sure, those factors are important in the interpretation of the Gospels. But let us examine our hidden agenda carefully. Since we know that radical obedience will certainly mean that there are crosses to be borne, it is not surprising that we might find ourselves seeking to find interpretations that will lift the onus of that obedience off our shoulders. We will protest that the realities of history do not permit us to turn the other cheek, and that the facts of politics and power must make us revise the injunction to "love our enemies" so that it does not apply any more to the real enemies in a real world.

Such a reduction of doing the witness to the limitations of what is safe and acceptable in our particular historical setting will necessitate that we spiritualize and privatize the gospel. The lessons of Hellenism are not lost: we still know very well how to withdraw the gospel from the world of real people, real problems, and real sin, and make it purely a matter of the invisible, ahistorical, irrelevant, "spiritual." Yet Christ was not a Hellenistic philosopher, but one who did the will of God to the great annoyance and ultimately homicidal anger of the power structures of his day. We must examine our theology and praxis today to see how much of that spiritualization we are still doing. We must recognize that the gospel can be made so private, so intimate, so isolated from the world into which we are sent that we really cannot be either salt or light. And we are back at that fateful separation in which we emphasize "being" but rule out "doing."

The process of rediscovering what "doing the witness" means is by no means easy—it is terribly threatening and often painful. It engenders controversy within the Christian family, and is already expressing itself in mutual judgment and accusations of heresy. As we shall emphasize later, the challenge here is to do the witness in our labors with each other, as we seek to find out what this radical obedience will require of us in the world to which we are all sent. The end of clarifying what doing the witness means for us today cannot justify the means of mutual recrimination and rejection, which have already begun to be a sad part of the contemporary debate about the church's task. There is a profound testimony to be given to the world today in the way in which the church works through the painful process of discovering what the action of witness is in obedience to Christ. The inward dimension of the church is, at this point, of great significance for the outward witness of the church.

7.3 THE INWARD DIMENSIONS OF DOING THE WITNESS

We have discussed the inward dimension of witness in several ways: we spoke of the church as "the Body of Christ" (2.3, pp. 27-32); we defined the community in terms of "witness" (3.4, pp. 48-54); we defined the "equipping community" as our model for the church, which is to be and to become the witness (6.3, pp. 105-11). Building upon all that we have said, we proceed now to consider how this community "does witness" in its inward dimensions. It is at this point, especially, that the inward life of the church does, in fact, become a major form of witness to the world.

Our concern, again, is with the character of the community that arises as a result of God's calling and equipping of the church. He has called a people to enflesh the gospel, to be the Body of Christ. This fact necessarily makes the theme of relationships very central in our theology of the church. Although I am fully aware of the problems of so-called relational theology—its superficiality, its emphasis upon "feeling good," its lack of doctrinal clarity and focus—still, I cannot discuss faith and community apart from the reality of relationship. Faith we may define as an ongoing relationship with God, who is known personally as he makes himself knowable. The result of that action on God's part is the formation of a community that is truly historical, truly experiential, and thus truly incarnational. Its relationships are an essential component of its obedience. In fact, it is through these interpersonal relationships within the community of faith that much of its witness is done.

Our Lord said to his disciples in preparing them for the ministry that was to follow, "By this all men will know that you are my disciples, if you have love for one another" (John 13:35). Paul expounds that fundamental principle of Christian obedience in community all through his writings, but especially in his great exposition of spiritual gifts. There (in 1 Cor. 13) he develops the nature of love as the supreme expression of faith and obedience, and his examples make it plain that he is referring to the actual doing of love among the members of the church. Lovelessness within the community of faith is virtually a contradiction of the gospel. Similarly, he deals with divisiveness and division as totally unacceptable behaviors in the church. They are nothing less than a denial of Christ and his work in the lives of those who call themselves Christian. As we have already pointed out, an unreconciled community cannot really be a witness to the gospel of reconciliation (5.2, pp. 78-88).

To do the witness to which we are called, then, the Christian community must learn to practice love as it is defined in the New Testament. If the world is to see our love and recognize that it is present because of God who makes us his disciples (John 13:35), then we are going to have to love in concrete, visible, experienceable ways. That is, of course, the proper definition of *agape*, love which acts, which self-sacrificially accepts responsibility for the needs of the other person, and acts on his or her behalf.

We have long assumed that, as far as love within the church is concerned, Christian love can be exercised only toward those Christians with whom we are in total agreement (in fact, many Christians find it easier to love the "pagan" than those Christians of a different theological persuasion!). As we have pointed out, though, we do not see this model of love in Jesus or in the apostles. Their love was a powerful force that bonded them with those with whom they had to disagree. Such love motivated them to persuade not through harsh judgment but through argument and service, both displaying that their love was greater than their disagreement. The church today, in its sinful dividedness, must regard it as the first and most urgent demand of the gospel that it learn to lead its inward life lovingly, translating into its structures, decisions, and processes the action of love modeled by Jesus and the apostles. We have permitted our diversity to become a reason for division rather than an opportunity to do the witness by demonstrating inwardly and outwardly that Christ is the Lord who is greater than our differences, and that his peace draws together what humanly speaking would remain apart.

This concept of the inward witness of the church does not mean that we brush over our differences. Quite the contrary! Just as our forgivenness is a primary form of our witness, that is, just as we display the meaning of sovereign grace in the ways in which we struggle with our own sin and experience God's continuing victory of grace, we can also display to the world that the sin in the church, which produces division, can be overruled by the Holy Spirit. But to do so, we need to learn to disagree with each other in a Christian way. We have to learn to extend the right hand of fellowship to those who differ from us, and really to mean it as a sign of our common identity as Christians. We have to discipline ourselves to reserve judgment to God alone.

We are not doing the witness honestly if we ignore the tensions and the historical reality of division. There are no easy answers to these major forms of disobedience within churchly reality. But complacence about the dividedness of the church only compounds the sin. Our motivation for the unity of the church is not merely organizational: it is evangelistic. Our witness is impeded as long as we devote our God-given time and energy to maintaining divisions, defending them, and resisting the repeated New Testament imperatives summarized by Paul: "[Be] eager to maintain the unity of the Spirit in the bond of peace" (Eph. 4:3).

The inward life of the church will do the witness as it reveals the power of God in Christ to overrule our differences and make us into one body. Further, the inward dimension of the church will do the witness as we rigorously examine all that we do as the community of faith in light of the central reason for our existence: are we being equipped for our common task through all that we do together in our worship, fellowship, and churchly activity? Is all our inward life focused on the doing of the gospel outwardly, in and toward the world? The realization of the equipping community model (6.3, pp. 105-11) will insure, I believe, that the inward life of the church will, in fact, "do the witness." We must insure, at the same time, that the gospel we are proclaiming in our inward life is the *whole* gospel (5.2, pp. 78-88), which means that our inward life will be a disciplined and intentional process of discovering what that whole gospel means. Such a discovery process will force us to face hard questions about the limits we have set on the gospel, especially those which are sexist and racist.

Christ's victory on the cross and at Easter was a victory over God's enemy and over the effects of human rebellion against God. Whatever human sin introduced into the world as a part of the curse (Gen. 3) cannot be regarded any longer as unavoidable fate; Christ is the glorious victor who has removed forever the threat that the curse of sin could be eternal. Thus, a necessary part of the inward dimension of doing the witness will be for the church to allow the new and restored order of God's good creation to emerge in its midst. Jesus began to demonstrate what that would mean when he crossed over the social and religious taboos of his day and included within his fellowship children, women, publicans, fishermen, lepers, Samaritans, and prostitutes. The world has built its value systems, and in particular its hierarchies and authority structures, on the results of sin. The gospel reverses that curse and removes that necessity from the church, as the firstfruits of the new creation.

Paul summarizes this radically new way of living in community when he explains what it means to be "in Christ Jesus": "There is neither Jew nor Greek, there is neither slave nor free, there is neither male nor female; for you are all one in Christ Jesus" (Gal. 3:28). He was simply stating what Jesus had already done in his earthly ministry, as the model for the church's doing of the witness in the world. And the early church began to move in this direction under the tutelage of the apostles, even as they struggled with the meaning of this radical newness. Paul's instructions to Philemon regarding the runaway slave Onesimus introduce a slow process of realization that slavery cannot accord with the gospel. Similarly, his descriptions of marriage, building upon the already existing social structures of his day, transform that relationship into a mutual ministry in which human categories of domination and authority are simply replaced by the servant model of Christ himself, to whom we do witness as we lead our marital lives in mutual submission.

The Christian church does the witness as it seeks to unfold all the concrete and tangible outworkings of this radically new order of life in Christ. This has always been the source of great struggle within the church, for as a human and social institution it is prone to live within the categories and customs of its historical situation. But it is called to move beyond what sinful human history can achieve. It is summoned to a new kind of existence that is quite literally a prefiguration of the new heavenly society in which, finally, sin will no longer have any sway at all. The barriers between Jew and Gentile, the value distinctions between slave and free (or employee and employer), the various forms of sexist discrimination—all are a part of the results of sin and thus not normative for the witnessing community. Like all the other "givens" of the gospel that the church in Acts had to struggle so hard to discover, these continue to be a source of controversy in the church. But the integrity of the church's internal doing of the witness is at stake here.

Do we, the church, truly believe that God has done a new thing on the cross, and called forth a new people to be the witness to that event? Do we expect that God's amazing work will lead to practical conclusions and differences in our life? Or, do we not prefer to restrict the possible impact of the gospel, even upon the forms of social structure in the church, so as not to disturb our own conformities and the expectations of the sinful world that surrounds us? The issues of racism and sexism in the church challenge our willingness to be witnesses to Christ who do the witness in the world. Like the problem of division and diversity, these concerns indicate the seriousness of our obedience and the depth of our trust. To do the witness within the church will mean to move where we have not been before, and to discover that there is still more newness, often threatening and strange, before us—out there, where the gospel has already gone, but where we have yet to follow.

Our biblical study of the whole gospel will constantly require of us that we examine our own subtle agenda to see the ways we are importing into the faith unevangelical and even disobedient motifs and attitudes. In this endeavor, we will painfully discover how God's word is always a two-edged sword. If it is not cutting away at our sin as it cuts into the rebellion of the world into which we are sent, then we are blunting that word for the sake of our own comfort.

7.4 THE OUTWARD DIMENSIONS OF DOING THE WITNESS

We have already addressed the outward dimension of the action of witness in our discussion of the diaconic model of the church (3.4, pp. 48-54), and, more extensively, in our exposition of the meaning of reconciliation as the central definition of the gospel (5.2, pp. 78-88). We shall discuss another aspect of doing the witness when we turn to the theme of "living hope" (9.2, pp. 159-67).

It is in the outward movement of the church into the world that we reveal whether or not we are overcoming the heretical division of the church's task into mission and benefit. The evidence will be in the doing of the gospel in the world. It has been said that the Christian must experience at least two conversions, one to Christ, and then one to the world. This is really another way of saying that the response of faith to Christ, of which conversion can be the marvelous and miraculous initiation, must become a response expressed in obedience to his call to be his witness in the world. And that witness must be to the full gospel, the gospel of the kingdom, the gospel of reconciliation and restoration to God's creation design. That must mean, necessarily, that the doing of the gospel will be a continuation of Jesus' own ministry to every area of human need, as a sign of the "coming near of the kingdom."

It will also mean that the church will have to look constantly for more of what the gospel means as it seeks to do witness in the world. As instructive as our history is, we may never assume that we have exhausted all the possibilities for Christian witness in the world in the past actions of the church.

The church's corporate ministry cannot be selective. We cannot, if we are obedient to Christ, choose those parts of the gospel that will not offend, and make that the content of our outward witness. Nor can we decide in advance what the gospel will not be allowed to mean and thus limit the scope of witnessing action in the world. To proclaim Christ and him crucified is to proclaim the redemptive work of God, which is valid for the entire creation he made. To accept the Great Commission must mean to go to *all* the world, and teach *all* that Christ taught. Every attempt to reduce "the least of these my brethren" to a select group of those whom we, for any number of reasons, would like to favor while rejecting the social and political dimensions of the gospel for the rest of the world, must be firmly rejected as poor exegesis and wrongful restriction and dilution of the gospel.

Such exploration of the "whole gospel," the gospel that is always before us (5.1, pp. 75-78), raises questions within the church, which are often highly controversial. Various groups within the church define Christian witness and obedience in mutually contradictory ways. Passions run high, and subtle commitments to lords other than the Lord of the church betray themselves in the programs and polemics of disagreeing factions. There is no area of evangelical obedience where disagreement is more painful than the question of Christian obedience and witness in the world. The hostility between theological camps at this point is a particularly tragic example of willful neglect of the biblical imperatives to be and to become one. We often allow our national and political backgrounds, and our particular ideologies, to overtake and revise the gospel. Thus, we see that "doing the witness" becomes the subjection of the revolutionary gospel to other revolutionary programs, which are permitted to redefine what the kingdom is all about and what we are supposed to do for it. Our critique of this process of co-opting the gospel for other purposes must be done with an evangelical spirit, and it is extremely difficult to maintain that spirit. Perhaps one of the reasons for this kind of difficulty within the church is our failure to grasp the preliminary and penultimate nature of *all* our gospel interpretations and adaptations.

If we are committed to doing "modest theology" (5.3, pp. 88-90) then this will be the place where that modesty is especially needed. In particular, we will need to remind ourselves constantly that the future tense of the gospel makes all of our applications of our witness provisional and subject to change. Our political programs will not usher in heaven, and our economic systems will not recreate Eden. But our obedience to Christ must mean that we will be radically committed to doing justice, condemning oppression, and working toward the good stewardship of this world's blessings so that all may enjoy what God has provided. Those blessings begin with the most basic needs of human existence, for which God has adequately provided: food, shelter, clothing, health, life with dignity. To be made in the image of God must include these dimensions, if we are to understand the Old Testament Hebraically and not separate the spiritual from the physical. Therefore, the outward dimension of the church's witness may well focus on precisely these areas of human need, not as diversions from the evangelical purpose of the church, but as its very expression.

As the church, in its inward life, constantly studies the gospel records to determine more of what the gospel means (it is "always before us!"), this will translate into the external doing of the witness. Creative imagination, inspired by the Holy Spirit, will increasingly discover ways of doing the witness that reveal the gospel in its ever-expanding dimensions of love and grace. This adventure of discovery will be free of all utopian expectations. It functions out of the motivation to be obedient, not to be successful, and thus it can endure through its failures, through its rejection, through all of the hostility such a witness will certainly experience in the world.

If our emphasis upon the "doing of the witness" is correct, then there is a direct connection between our theology of the church's mission and the complex study of Christian ethics. Without claiming the competence to enter into that field, I would still raise the concern that the church needs to do a great deal of work on its understanding of the ethics of the gospel. The tendency of our history to treat ethics in terms of rational and verifiable propositions or principles (which is a very productive approach) needs to be brought into dialogue with our understanding of the church in terms of salvation history. In what sense do we also need to learn to do ethics modestly, and how do we understand ethics as an evangelical function of the church? My question and my appeal are directed toward the Bible's challenge that we should lead lives worthy of the calling to which we have been called (Eph. 4:1). That seems to imply that our understandings of ethics must be developed in response to our calling. That, in turn, means that both the being and the doing of the witness will require definition and review from the perspective of the ethics we develop. Christian behavior is Christian witness, and thus the principles established for the determination of Christian behavior should be directly related to and result from our knowledge of God's saving purposes.

Next to a Christian community that shows forth Christ in the way it practices love and deals with its differences, a Christian ethic that formulates how we shall do the witness will be the most persuasive response that the church could make to the accusation of "hypocrisy." It is rightly observed that the Christian church, especially in the Western world, must "earn the right to be heard." This will happen when our actions as the church already express the gospel before we say anything about the content of our faith. Love experienced is a powerful witness that can open up hearts and ears to the message of love, which is available and accessible.

This is a particularly important aspect of witness in those places in the world where it is difficult—if not impossible—for the Christian community to say very much about the gospel. Under those repressive circumstances, the doing of the gospel is the primary form of witness. But it is certainly authentic witness! And the doing of witness in this comprehensive sense ultimately makes the saying of the gospel possible, even there where the harsh realities of politics appear to make any kind of evangelistic witness impossible. We can point to the modest but decisive witness of Christians in the Socialist world as a prime example of this kind of process.

The discipline of Christian ethics must be taken very seriously as we consider the mission of the church. An incarnational understanding of that mission is inherently ethical in both its structure and its application. To be concerned with both the "what" and the "how" of gospel communication, to define witness in terms of being, doing, and saying, to relate the inward dimension of the church to its outward dimension as equipping for ministry to the world—all of this is to say that the ethic of the church's life and work is essential to its obedience. We must be deeply concerned about the ethics of communication (see Emory Griffin, *The Mind Changers*), and we must call upon the contribution of the discipline of Christian ethics to assist us in understanding how the being, doing, and saying of the gospel are a coherent and harmonious witness.

Eight

SAYING THE WITNESS: UNDERSTANDING EVANGELIZATION

8.1 "EVANGELIZATION" RATHER THAN "EVANGELISM"

When, in evangelical circles, one uses the word "witnessing," he or she usually means a certain kind of talk. This talk could be understood as a preset order of steps in the presentation of the gospel, or the argumentation of the truth of the Christian faith using various logical and rhetorical approaches, or it could be simply "sharing one's faith." We have seen that the concept of "witness" must be viewed far more comprehensively, for the being of the person or community who is the witness and the doing, or the activity, of that personal witness are essential parts of the total ministry of witness. Much that is witness, and that bears the authority of the Holy Spirit working through it, will not necessarily become verbal. The day-to-day example of that witness lived out by obedient Christians in all the spheres of life is perhaps the most powerful and most persuasive form of witness. Ethics understood as witness will point to the lordship of Christ in many situations in which speech is not possible, as we have already noted. So, as we turn to "saying the witness," we shall stress that this saying of the Good News must emerge out of being and doing the witness. In other words, being and doing the witness provide the context and also the validation for what we say.

Having established that necessary context, we must now emphasize how crucial to our understanding of the church's mission is the saying of the witness. To stop with being and doing, which is the tendency of many Christian movements today who have problems with "evangelism," is to reduce drastically the biblical mandate and the very nature of the Good News. We are seeking to define the saying of the witness in such a way that it will not be isolated from the total scope of witness. But we must insist that our definitions are incomplete, and our concept of the church is less than biblical, if we do not focus the task of witness ultimately on the verbal communication of this Good News. The witnesses (*martyroi*), as the witnessing community, must address the witness (*martyria*) to the world.

When we discuss the saying of the gospel, we are moving into the area commonly called "evangelism." However, this term does not always mean the same thing. When we listen to the way Christians and Christian organizations talk today, we note that the word *evangelism* covers a broad variety of activities in the church. Some use it in the very narrow sense of "soul-winning," usually connecting it with the experience of conversion. Others use it in the sense of Christian activism in political and social concerns (frequently to the exclusion of the verbal presentation of the Christian faith), arguing that such activity is the prophetic proclamation of the gospel in specific situations. In many churches, "evangelism" refers to the recruiting and winning of new members, so that the definition of the church's mission becomes simply "getting people into the church." Traditional denominational circles are using the term more frequently now, but again, in each denomination it seems to mean something different.

I have found it helpful to make certain distinctions in our terms, in an attempt to define the church's mission clearly and cleanly. Thus, at various times in my ministry I have proposed that we use the term *evangelism* for the saying of the gospel. My thought has been that we could, in this way, define *evangelism* as one aspect of the overarching task of witness. At this stage in my own thinking, however, I prefer to use the term *evangelization* for the saying of the gospel. In doing so, I am borrowing from the usage of our Roman Catholic colleagues, who have arrived at some important insights about this aspect of our mission, as they have moved so dynamically in their concept of the church's mission since Vatican II.

There are some tactical reasons as well for saying "evangelization" rather than "evangelism." The term *evangelism* has become highly misunderstandable, precisely because of all the meanings attached to it. It creates barriers for some and awakens such concrete associations for others that discussion of it almost always requires a long process of terminological clarification. Further, the use of any "ism" is increasingly problematic. There appears to be a tendency in society today to make a particular emphasis or concern, as valid as it may be, into an

ideology that controls the whole fabric of Christian thought and practice. Many "isms" are obviously hostile to the gospel or strongly distort
it: sexism, racism, consumerism, militarism, even nationalism, and
often rationalism. It is questionable whether we do well tactically by
ranking the evangel among such "isms"!

When we look at the concept of evangelism from the organizational perspective, we see a rather curious trend toward dealing with
this theme as "one of the many things the churches do." Thus, we have
departments of evangelism, programs for evangelism, and even ministers for evangelism in large churches. When we set up such specific
designations and compartments, we certainly open ourselves up to the
criticism that we have reduced the meaning of evangelism within our
theology of the church. I recently heard an Episcopalian bishop ask the
obvious question: Can we conceive of any valid activity of the church
that should not be considered in some way a form of evangelism? If we
define the church's mission as witness to the gospel, and we know that
the gospel is the evangel, then everything the church is and does and
says should be "evangelistic."

But, as Stephen Neill once observed, if everything is mission then
nothing is mission. The danger of generalizing our terms in order to
insure that everything is always being said can result in vagueness and
platitudes that never define anything, and never challenge anyone.
Obviously, everything is evangelism, if we define evangelism as the
witness to the gospel. However, we can analyze and reflect upon the
saying of the gospel, which is a clearly recognizable action of the
church corporately and of Christians singly. There is proclamation to
those who have not heard or believed and who should have the
opportunity to hear. There is the address of the gospel to the church
so that it will grow in its faith and obedience. This aspect of the
church's mission is integrally linked with being and doing the witness,
but, as we said, the verbal statement of the message must take place.
And if our concern for incarnational ministry is valid, then we must
examine very carefully how we say the witness!

Thus, for this specific activity of the church I propose to use the
term *evangelization.* It is, I believe, a more biblical way of speaking.
There is no biblical word for "evangelism," but the family of terms that
we translate as "gospel" or "evangel" has its verbal expression in the
New Testament: "to evangelize" means "to proclaim the Good News
with power," just as the "evangel" itself is the Good News of Jesus
Christ, reported with life-transforming power so that those events
become the truth and the experience of reconciliation with God for

all those who respond in faith. Scholars generally agree that "to evangelize" is synonymous with "to proclaim" (the root verb for *kerygma*), and that both terms are the verbal form of *euangelion,* the Good News. (For background on the terminology, see the standard New Testament reference works, such as Kittel or Colin Brown.) There are very few places in the New Testament where we find the term *evangelist* used (Acts 21:8; Eph. 4:11; 2 Tim. 4:5), but here again the reference is to the verbal proclamation of the gospel, both for those who have not yet believed as well as for those within the church.

Finally, I prefer "evangelization" because the term implies activity and process. It speaks of an ongoing aspect of the church's life and work, "evangelizing." We need to understand that it is both possible and necessary to say this gospel, and that there are both inward and outward dimensions of that verbal proclamation. Our task is to "enflesh the gospel" in our spoken witness, just as we have understood the necessity of doing that in the way we *are* and *do* the witness.

8.2 THE POSSIBILITY OF EVANGELIZATION

Just as the Word became flesh, the gospel can be formed in words and uttered and explained in statements that can be heard, received, and responded to. The once-and-for-all events of the gospel, together with their saving significance, can be reported in such a way that they become the personal experience of the believing hearer. In our discussion of the vision of the church in Acts (Chap. 3), we emphasized that the gift of the Holy Spirit was to enable and empower the early church to become the witnessing community that Jesus had promised they would become (Acts 1:8). The immediate result of that event was the proclamation of the gospel in Peter's sermon. A further result, still at work in history, was the gift of the spiritual power and authority to state the gospel in all the languages of the world, spoken by those gathered in Jerusalem at that time.

We must begin our theology of evangelization with the centrality of God's grace as the presupposition to our response and activity. It is possible to evangelize because the Holy Spirit equips us to do so. That is the very purpose of Pentecost, and the church is truly Pentecostal as it continues to exercise the power to proclaim the gospel. Thus, evangelization is an expression of enabled faith, a response made possible in us by God's precedent action. The very nature of faith is that it wants to communicate itself to others, so that they will become a part of this witnessing community (see 1 John 1:1-4).

Evangelization is possible because God has acted to make it so, and that action has not ceased in the course of salvation history to this day. In the Second Helvetic Confession, the Swiss Reformers went so far as to say that the "proclaimed word is the Word of God." That is a bold statement of faith about the gracious way in which God makes this Good News knowable through his servants—and not a description of the spiritual qualification of the preachers!

Not only is it possible to respond to the gospel and to become its evangelizing witnesses, but it is possible to do so effectively. Here, we must proceed very carefully. The temptation is very great to import standards of effectivity and success (and even efficiency) into Scripture and to develop both criteria and methods of evangelization that are marked more by our secular value systems than by Scripture. What is "effective evangelization" in biblical terms? What is truly "possible" as the result of the Spirit's enabling of the church to say the witness?

First of all, the Spirit's enabling of evangelization means that the Good News can be stated understandably. It is a message for *all* the world, not for an intellectual or religious elite. It is a message for all languages and cultures. It is to cross over all boundaries and call forth faith among all nations. We observe in the apostolic church an astonishing freedom with regard to the ways in which the gospel is to be proclaimed. At the same time, we see a struggle in those early Christians as they painfully discover how much freedom they have received, and how responsibly they have to use that freedom in order to say the witness understandably and universally.

Paul's strategies of mission are clearly intended to make the gospel understandable wherever he proclaims it. He has the freedom to use the philosophical and religious curiosity of the Athenian scholars on Mars Hill (Acts 17:22ff.) as well as his own Jewish tradition and his personal experience in his defense before Agrippa (Acts 26). He could claim his freedom in the matter of eating meat offered to idols but also refrain if need be to advance the gospel (1 Cor. 8). He counseled the "strong in faith" to devote their strength to the support of the weak (Rom. 14). In his overwhelming sense of the mandate of his mission, Paul can become "all things to all men" (1 Cor. 9:22b); that is, he can adapt himself to the culture in which he is to minister, not to compromise the gospel, but to make it known. "I do it all for the sake of the gospel, that I may share in its blessings" (1 Cor. 9:23).

The incarnational understanding of ministry means that evangelization is to be understandable. The gospel is not an arcane secret, nor is it special knowledge granted only to the few. Rather, it is God's grace for all people, and it is to be made known to all people. It can be translated and reformulated; it can be phrased in thought systems of an infinite variety; it can find its expression in the art and literature of every human tribe. It must, in fact, continue to cross over human barriers until it reaches "the end of the earth."

But its effectiveness will not necessarily be measured by its so-called success. For at the same time that we are prepared by our Lord and the apostles to be empowered witnesses, we are warned that our effective communication of the gospel can lead to contradictory and even hostile consequences. The "effectiveness" of the gospel includes the effective communication of the biblical message about our sinful situation apart from God and in rebellion against him. That is, the proclamation of the gospel includes the theme of repentance. And the listening world may understand that message so well that it rejects it! In the parables of the kingdom, especially in Matthew 13, our Lord carefully prepared his church for the variety of responses that evangelization will receive. The seed will fall into all kinds of soil, with all kinds of results—and, ultimately, there will be a marvelous harvest. The response to the gospel is in the realm of spiritual mystery. We can no more produce faith as the manipulated result of our proclamation than the farmer can make the seed sprout once it is planted.

Thus, we may properly understand effectiveness as obedient witness, which God uses to present the gospel in its power and truth. The response may be one of faith; if so, God has made that response possible—or it may be one of rejection; if so, God has mysteriously permitted the message to be heard in its power and yet not received. Our theological systems cannot and should not seek to explain that mystery, but rather should remain open to the future tense of God's action, as Christ taught us to do in his parables (see Matt. 13:24-30, 47-50). We need to learn the apostolic attitude of patience with the process of evangelization and confidence about the certain results of God's work (1 Cor. 3:4-9).

When we define "effective witness" in terms of measurable results, especially in the sense of numerical growth, we create major problems for the practice of incarnational ministry. Others have discussed these problems adequately elsewhere (see Lesslie Newbigin, *The Open Secret,* pp. 135ff.), so I will simply summarize the issues here. Focusing on measurable results will easily lead us to dilute the gospel in order to insure the success we are seeking. Much of the subtle motivation, I believe, for the benefit-mission dichotomy in evangelical proclamation is to be found here. To present the gospel of grace as a summons to servanthood will necessarily reduce its attractiveness. We would rather have the sword of the word be one-sided than two-sided; that is, we want to proclaim the gospel that meets the human need for wholeness and salvation, but we hesitate to proclaim the claims of Christ as Lord over all of heaven and earth, the prophetic gospel that summons us to an obedience and service that will move us into our world as those who no longer truly belong to it. But, as we have argued, this limitation and dilution of the gospel are unallowable.

Therefore, we must examine our motives: are we defining our success in terms of obedience to the gospel mandate, or in terms of statistical results that provide us with visual and immediate gratification, and even guarantee organizational growth? Certainly one can be ineffective for the wrong reasons—for instance, when we fail to make the gospel as understandable as it needs to be and can be. But to conceal the full meaning of the gospel of the lordship of Christ in order to "win souls" is a questionable, if not unethical, reduction of our mission.

We will find a further variation of that unallowable reduction when we measure the effectiveness of our proclamation in terms of other goals, outside the gospel, that we may seek to meet through our evangelization. One obvious tendency here is to link the requirements of good citizenship in a particular social and economic order with the proclamation of the gospel. Another one is to make the gospel into a need-fulfilling psychological and emotional therapy. These alien goals imposed upon the gospel constitute what I have called the "cultural bondage" of the gospel, to which I will return below (10.4, pp. 197-203). Our history is replete with depressing examples of evangelization in the service of the state, the system, or of the human need for an emotional and psychic panacea. Marx's criticism that "religion is the opiate of the people" must be understood against the backdrop of the Prussian kingdom's regulation of churchly proclamation to produce obedient and submissive subjects to the king! And who has not heard proclamation of the gospel as the way to achieve a fulfilled and successful life? The possibility of evangelization is, at the same time, the opportunity for the distortion, reduction, or even heretical perversion of the gospel. Where God's Spirit is at work, God's enemy is all the more virulently at work as well.

Finally, "effective evangelization" is to be defined as the saying of the gospel in full harmony with the being and the doing of the witness. What we say must be congruent with who we are and what we do. That means that our evangelization must deal with the unevangelized aspects of our own life and witness as Christian persons and Christian community. The problem of the "holier than thou" attitude of Christians can be traced to this major incongruence: we talk about the gospel in one way and we reveal our true convictions about it in actions and attitudes that contradict our language. This is why it is important to emphasize that the possibility of evangelization is always directed toward the inward dimension of the church as well as the outward dimension (see 8.4 below).

"Effective evangelization" is, then, understandable proclamation of the gospel, based upon the Spirit's enabling power, which equips the witnessing community to make its witness clearly. Another way of saying this is to state that the Holy Spirit works in and through the church, empowering us to use our creativity for the task of evangelization, as we have observed in the variety of ways in which the apostles proclaimed the one gospel. However, we will be cautious about postulating one particular kind of response as an indicator of our "effectiveness," such as numerical expansion, the growth of church budgets and membership rolls, or a particular kind of conversion experience. The Spirit-enabled possibility of evangelization will always call forth response and will always be effective, but the effect may be rejection, hostility, or possibly even persecution of the witnesses. That is not necessarily always going to be the case—we certainly should not make evangelization into a spiritually masochistic process! But we should be very careful when we see that our evangelization fits too well and too successfully into our society. That almost always indicates the "cultural bondage" of the gospel.

8.3 THE NECESSITY OF EVANGELIZATION

Because of the Spirit's enabling work in the church, we *can* evangelize. We have already stated that it is crucial that we not separate the *saying* of the witness from its *being* and *doing*. Now we turn to the necessity for evangelization: not only *can* we evangelize, we *must* evangelize. Like the prophets of the Old Covenant, we are compelled to make known to the world the Word that has come to us. We must make known this understandable, perceivable, believable Word of the Good News as the central act of our obedience. Our understanding and practice of witness is inadequate if it does not result in the *saying* of the witness.

I began this book with the statement, "The God of the Bible and of biblical faith is a God who makes himself knowable." The self-

self-communication makes human history and, especially, human speech and hearing the means by which God reveals himself to us. The Word always becomes flesh in order for us to hear it, and it must constantly be enfleshed to be heard by others. There is no other way to respond to God's gift of the knowledge of himself than through hearing and responding.

The "knowledge of God" that he makes possible is a special kind of knowledge: it is the knowledge of experienced relationship. To know God is to know him as personal, as one who addresses himself to us and who hears and responds to our answers. This special relationship of mutual knowing and experiencing, which the Bible affirms to be basic to our creation design, is called faith.

Again, we are conscious of the particular problems of dealing with the concept of relationships in order to understand the nature of faith and the way by which it is made possible (see 7.3, pp. 124-28). But we cannot define faith in any way other than as an event taking place in the form of a relationship between God and the believer. It is God-initiated, but it includes the real response of the believer. The theology of the creation accounts reaches its climax with the assertion that the essence of human existence is being in the image of God, which means, centrally, being made for a relationship with God. Martin Buber expounded this in classical form when he worked out the meaning of the I-Thou relationship that defines true humanity as well as the basic biblical design for our relationship with God. Such a relationship actually takes place in two-way communication. To plumb the meaning of this fact is the ultimate task of that Christian philosophy which truly helps us understand what God has done by disclosing himself to us (see E. Jüngel, *God as the Mystery of the World,* for a thorough and challenging study of the fact that God has made himself knowable and discussable).

Just as communication between persons is the way in which relationships actually happen, so also communication between God and the believer is the form in which faith, understood as a relationship, occurs. This was basic to our understanding of the *being* and the *doing* of the witness, but it is all the more so to our understanding of the *saying* of the witness. The witnesses "know whom they have believed" (2 Tim. 1:12), and their testimony arises out of that knowledge and that assurance. All of the witnesses, both in the Old and New Covenants, knew the God to whose words and actions they testified in their reports. It was out of their relationship with God that they made their witness; they "knew" God as intimately as a man "knows" his wife sexually, and thus they could speak of him so forcefully and with such certainty (see Heb. 11).

As witnesses, we are to make known "to all the world" the possibility of such a relationship. The purpose of God's act in sending his Son was that the whole world would experience his love for it. "For God sent the Son into the world, not to condemn the world, but that the world might be saved through him" (John 3:17). In his gospel John deals with the cosmic scope of the gospel, repeatedly using the term *world,* and making it plain that the church is to be the witness to God's purposes for all of his fallen creation. He recounts Jesus' prayer, "As thou didst send me into the world, so I have sent them into thy world" (John 17:18)—making it plain that Christ's cosmic mission is now the definitive task of the church that will issue forth from the ministry of his disciples (v. 20).

Similarly, Paul states that in Christ, God reconciled the world to himself (2 Cor. 5:19). In response to God's action, Christians are to be ambassadors of reconciliation to that world. This is the necessity of evangelization in terms of Paul's theology of reconciliation. Paul firmly expects that the ministry of witness will result in a salvation of cosmic dimensions: "Therefore God has highly exalted him and bestowed on him the name which is above every other, that at the name of Jesus every knee should bow, in heaven and on earth and under the earth [Paul's very Hebraic way of saying 'world'], and every tongue confess that Jesus Christ is Lord, to the glory of God the Father" (Phil. 2:9-11; see also Col. 1:20).

Jesus stresses that same necessity in the fourfold "all" of the Great Commission (Matt. 28:18-20). The witnesses are to go out into *all* the world, over which Christ has *all* authority as the Lord; *all* nations are to be discipled and to hear *all* of Christ's teachings. Evangelization must happen so that *all* will hear. Anything less than a worldwide vision for the church's mission is less than the biblical definition both of the world and of God's love for it.

God gave his Spirit at Pentecost to enable the witness of the church, and that witness is go out to the end of the earth. The church does not really have a choice here: evangelization is its necessary obedience. Only in this way will God accomplish his purposes. That necessity becomes a constraint, a driving energy, a focus of obedience that makes Christians into witnesses wherever they are. The apostle Paul repeatedly speaks of the fact that he can do no other than to serve Christ as his witness: "For necessity is laid upon me. Woe to me if I do not preach the gospel!" (1 Cor. 9:16).

But as Paul asks, "How are men to call upon him in whom they have not believed? And how are they to believe in him of whom they have never heard? And how are they to hear without a preacher? And how can men preach unless they are sent? . . . So faith comes from what is heard, and what is heard comes by the preaching of Christ" (Rom. 10:14-15a, 17). The preaching here is quite clearly verbal; that is, saying the gospel in understandable language. We are not here reducing the central significance of the concept of witness as being and doing, but simply stating that the Word must be said and heard as well. If we read Paul's series of rhetorical questions in this text backward, we can state that the church is sent into the world to preach. That is an outline of the plot of the Book of Acts. There will be no preachers unless they are sent, and the Spirit has entered the church in order to send the witnesses (the word *mission* is based on the Latin verb for "to send"). The possibility and the necessity of evangelization are two sides of the same spiritual truth: what God has willed must happen, he also makes possible. The Spirit was given at Pentecost, and then Peter proclaimed. The world cannot believe unless it hears . . . and what the world must hear is the "preaching of Christ."

Apart from hearing the story of Christ, hearing who he is and what he has done, there is no faith. Jesus defines our mission as "discipling, baptizing, teaching" (Matt. 28:19-20), all of which are by definition verbal events. The gospels themselves are tangible evidence of the fact that the story of Jesus can be communicated in words: what was originally the oral tradition of the early churches became finally our written record, for us to read, to hear, and to pass on so that others may hear and respond.

When we emphasize the essential nature of the saying of the witness, we need to be aware of the many ways the New Testament itself describes this form of witness. There is a remarkable tendency in our Christian vocabulary to restrict the saying of the witness to "preaching." In the King James Bible, fourteen different Greek terms are translated as "preach" or "preaching," while in Martin Luther's German Bible thirty-three Greek terms are translated with a form of *"predigen"* or *"Predigt."* This obviously produces significant problems in our understanding of the saying of the gospel, which we shall examine briefly.

The New Testament terms translated as "preaching" or *"predigen"* all deal with the verbal expression of the gospel. Their actual meanings

in English range from "to herald" or "to proclaim" to broader terms
such as "to say" and "to utter." The strong implication is that all
Christians are, in various ways, to say the witness, although clearly
some are "gifted" for particular kinds of utterance, such as proclamation to nonbelievers, teaching, or prophecy. The effect of our limited
translations is to create the impression that only a few Christians—the
preachers—are to say the witness. I suspect that Martin Luther, with
his concern for the proper preaching and teaching of the Word as a
corrective to the general neglect of biblical preaching in the tradition
out of which he came, intended just this. In addition, he insisted on
the "right gospel," one centered on justification by grace alone. To
insure the proper preaching of that Word, he wanted the church to
define clearly the preacher's task and responsibility. Thus, while all
Christians shared in the vocation to serve Christ, only some were to
"say the witness" as preachers.

This view also implies that the witness could only be said in the
form of the sermon, thus restricting Christian talk to those profession-
ally equipped to say things about our faith, and only in the formal
setting of the worship service of the church. With all the concern in
this century for a "theology of the word" and for "kerygmatic theology," it is intriguing to see how frequently "proclamation" appears to
be limited to preachers' preaching in church services. Undoubtedly,
this is one of the most important forms of evangelization (and we shall
return to this theme in our next section, 8.4); but evangelization to
the world must take place throughout the world! The Spirit's enabling
is not restricted to the twenty to thirty minutes of a sermon on Sunday
morning. And those tongues of fire at Pentecost did not settle only on
the heads of the preachers in that room but on the heads of everyone.
Although not all Christians are called and gifted to be preachers, all
are called and equipped to say the gospel.

A variant of this restriction of evangelization to preachers and
sermons is evident in the understanding of "witnessing" found in many
parts of the church family today; we alluded to this at the beginning of
this chapter when we discussed our problems with the term *evangelism.* The "saying" of the gospel is often defined in terms of a method,
even a progression of statements that should be presented in a particular order. We are taught to manipulate conversations in order to
create "opportunities to witness." This understanding of the nature of
evangelization generally does not place much emphasis upon the relationship between the Christian witness and his or her hearer. The
important thing is that the witness or testimony be said, that the

opportunity to make a decision be offered, and that, if possible, a soul be saved. Although this understanding of evangelization rightly emphasizes the responsibility and possibility of every Christian to say the witness, these approaches do, in fact, divide the saying from the doing and the being; that is, they divide the message from the messenger (and often from the community) so as to make of the gospel a kind of salvation formula. It is characteristic of such reductive approaches to evangelization that the gospel is defined almost solely in terms of its benefits, without reference to the mission for which we are saved. Even the lordship of Christ can be described in such personalized and privatized terms that the consequences of that lordship within the world (the questions of ethics, political witness, social responsibility, incarnating the gospel within the world) are never addressed, or are even disregarded. In effect, such reduced and diluted forms of evangelization summon us to receive the benefits of the cross of Christ, but seldom to take up our cross and follow him.

We need to free the saying of the gospel from the one-sidedly institutional captivity of evangelization (preaching done by preachers at certain times) as well as from the narrow definitions of "witnessing" that have emerged in various forms of evangelicalism. Both of these extremes contain accurate insights into the nature of saying the witness. From the one side we will remember that evangelization must be central to the "inward life of the church," and thus that it is directly related to the preaching ministry of the church. From the other side we will remember that all Christians are called and equipped to say the gospel. But if the saying of the gospel emerges out of the being and the doing of the witness, as we have stressed, then we must say more than either of these approaches has said.

Thus, we must return to our basic concept of incarnational witness, and to our emphasis upon the relational nature of faith. The tendency of both above-mentioned extremes is to disregard the essential and central role of relationships in the saying of the gospel. In order to say the Good News, we need to precede and accompany our words by the demonstration of the gospel's meaning in our lives and actions. In order to evangelize, the power and the reality of the evangel should be evident and effectual in the relationships between those who speak and those who hear. The saying of the gospel needs to be enfleshed in the sayers, in order for it to be heard and given credence. For the words to have meaning, the witness must "earn the right to be heard."

146   DEFINING THE CHURCH'S MISSION INCARNATIONALLY

This does not mean that the saying of the gospel must wait until the witness has reached some predetermined level of spiritual perfection or maturity in order to have the right to be heard. The incarnational understanding of witness is not perfectionistic, with regard to either the Christian person or the Christian community. It does mean, however, that the message must be congruent with the life and actions of the witness. The message is about both sin and grace, and the life and actions of the witness contain both. Forgivenness, rather than perfection, is the content of the Christian testimony. Dependence upon God, rather than arrogance, is the message we both say and do. We know that we have nothing to boast of in ourselves, so that we only boast of Christ. Rather than misunderstand incarnational witness as a revival of Christian perfectionism, we seek to define it as that Christian obedience in which the opportunities of our relationships become channels for God's work.

It is a truism to state that all humans have relationships. But it is at that simple and central point that our concept of incarnational evangelization begins. The relationships in which we live are the primary arena for Christian witness. The New Testament defines our neighbor as the person with whom we are going to have to deal anyway, who is unavoidable (in German the term is *der Nächste,* "the next person"). That is the person who is to encounter something of the reality of the gospel in our relationship with her or him. The Christian opportunity for incarnational witness is the fact that Christians are present in the world, working and playing and participating in everyday events. In that already given setting, relationships are constantly developing. And in and through those relationships, the witness (*martys*) is to be, and the witness (*martyria*) is to be done and said.

The New Testament model for this understanding of incarnational evangelization is Jesus himself. In his encounters with people, he constantly revealed his love for those to whom he ministered. He dealt with individuals as individuals; he communicated with his hearers in terms they could understand, and he did not always say everything there was to say. He accepted the measure of faith that was brought to him and worked with that faith, regardless of how immature or inadequate it might have been. What Jesus said and what he did were congruent, and the heart of his message was that God was a loving Father to whom the prodigal could return home, just as he was himself a friend to whom the outcasts, the prostitutes, and the publicans could come and find help.

The network of relationships within which we live is the primary place where evangelization is to take place. This is where every Christian is a witness. But it is also the harder place to say the witness, because congruence between being, doing, and saying is hard to achieve. It is, ultimately, easier for the preacher to go straight from the study to the pulpit and proclaim the word. But it is more incarnational to go from the study to the people, to share in their life, and to share one's life with them, and then to grapple with the ambiguities and shadowy sides of normal life—and out of that crucible to go into the pulpit and evangelize.

By the same token, it is easier to approach a total stranger, develop a conversation in which a "testimony" is given, and then present the gospel. It is far more difficult to live with one's "neighbors" daily and to put words on one's convictions, explaining who one is and why one lives in a certain way, called Christian. It is, of course, more "natural" to say the witness in such a way that the gospel surfaces out of the interactions of daily life. Through his relationships, the Christian explains and shares himself.

This way of saying the gospel must be rigorously honest. Jesus was "full of grace and truth" (John 1:14) and "grace and truth came through" him (John 1:17). That is the goal of Christian witness: to be full of grace and truth, to be channels of God's grace and honest communicators of what that grace is and means in one's own life. The saying of the gospel, understood in this way, will be going on in many kinds of conversation in which the terminology is not theological but the meaning is grace. Christians say the gospel as they share their lives in honesty, listen to their neighbors with unfeigned concern, and struggle for honesty and integrity in all of their dealings with other people.

It is not "intolerant" to say the gospel in this fashion. This form of evangelization does not present itself as judgment of those who hear it. Rather, it is the transparency of Christian lives in which and through which Christ is working, revealing what God's love is and does, even in spite of our resistance to it. It is the offer of the reality of Christ with no calculation as to whether or not the offer will be accepted or rejected. Such saying of the gospel cannot be manipulative and is not motivated by its success. Obedience to Christ is its motivation, and thus it is more often than not "unconscious" witness—that is, it is the revealing of the reality of Christ without the strained attempt to create the opportunity to do so. God's Spirit puts us in the world of our relationships and has thereby already created the opportunity for witness. The necessity that constrains us does not produce forced, unnatural, awkward statements about what we believe. This necessity leads us to love, to share, to serve our neighbor, and, as a part of that service, to make known who Christ is as he enables us to serve him in these relationships.

This understanding of incarnational witness cannot be "hypocritical" because it does not point to the perfection of the witnesses but rather demonstrates their liberated dependence upon Christ. Because of Christ, the witnesses have the freedom to love and to serve unmarked by self-centered concerns. Obviously, Christians themselves must learn to claim such freedom and live it out. That should be a great part of the teaching and equipping ministry of the church—to teach us how to be, do, and say the freedom that we have in Christ, for it is the freedom to serve him in our relationships with others without fear of the consequences. We need to learn this, and we can learn it.

Finally, understood incarnationally, the saying of the gospel is always a work of the entire Body. No one witness ever says all there is to say. The evangelization process is a choral statement of the whole church—many voices saying the various themes, and the total composition expressing more than any single voice could. Clearly we must be concerned with the problems of the discords in that choral statement. But our point here is again the issue of freedom and interdependence: each witness has the freedom to say what he or she can say in the opportunities afforded by relationships, and each can rely upon the rest of the Body to complete the verbal communication of the gospel. "I planted, Apollos watered, but God gave the growth" (1 Cor. 3:6).

8.4 THE INWARD DIMENSION OF EVANGELIZATION

If our understanding of evangelization were restricted to "witnessing," as we discussed above, then we would probably not have very much to say about the inward dimension of evangelization. Understood in that fashion, witnessing is primarily oriented toward the nonbeliever and his or her conversion—clearly part of the outward dimension of evangelization. However, if the "gospel is always before us" (5.1, pp. 75-78), if there is a "future tense" to salvation (5.2, pp. 78-88), if our task is both to be and to become the witness (6.2, pp. 96-105), then the gospel must be said inside the church as well as outside the church. It is important to deal with the way the church is continually evangelized internally before we address the evangelistic task of the church in the world.

Evangelization is the term we are using for the saying of the witness to the gospel. Thus, what evangelization is will be defined by what the gospel is, just as the being and doing of the gospel are defined by the character of the gospel itself. Much of what I have to say at this point will summarize earlier portions of this book.

The relational nature of faith will mold the way that we say the gospel within the church. This relational faith is, by definition, an ongoing event, a process and a pilgrimage. In other words, the life of faith is characterized by change, discovery, advance, and retreat. Our internal evangelization will, therefore, be a continual addressing of the gospel to ourselves in order to discover more of what it means for us. Within the community of faith, we need to hear the gospel in ever-renewed readiness to have it confront and convict us as believers whose faith is as yet too small. Our modest theology should make us into attentive listeners to the gospel, expecting that God will say more to us than we have yet heard. The ancient liturgical practice of selecting a gospel text for every Sunday of the church year, and then of preaching on that text, should be a constant reminder that we need to be evangelized within the community of faith if we are to be those who can evangelize in the world. We need to hear baptism preached and taught, as a constant summons to claim all that God has promised us as he makes us his own in Christ (see 6.2, pp. 96-105). The imperatives of the New Testament should be studied and then continually applied as the indicatives of the gospel. In this way, we will continue to inwardly evangelize the church.

Evangelization within the church takes place both formally and informally. Formally, it is happening in all our assemblies where the word is proclaimed, taught, or celebrated in worship and sacrament. Every opportunity for the hearing and expounding of the gospel within the life of the community is another step in the evangelization of the church. One aspect of the goal of such formal evangelization should be the growth of the faith of all the members of the community. We are assuming, of course, that all faith must grow, that no one's faith is perfect yet, and thus that we all need continuing evangelization toward the whole gospel, "which is before us." The cycle of Christian worship and celebration regulated by the church year should be experienced as a spiral of growth: we return, year after year, to the same events and themes; but, as we return, we find that we have grown in our comprehension and our responsiveness to the gospel. When we celebrate the birth of Christ each year, we should be discovering more about the meaning of incarnation and the wonder of God's entry into our history. The annual observance of Easter should become a celebration of Christ's victory making itself greater and more comprehensive in its definition of our lives. Christian worship that is primarily memorial in nature, that looks backward and even seeks to recreate the atmosphere and emotions of earlier ages and experiences, fails to grasp the con- temporary need for evangelization within the church.

The writer to the Hebrews admonishes us to move beyond "the elementary doctrines of Christ and go on to maturity" (Heb. 6:1). There is a genuine danger that we will constantly keep the inward life of the church at the level of initial evangelization, that preaching will be primarily a call to conversion as the first step of faith, and that the church will not fulfill its calling to be the "equipping community" (6.3, pp. 105-11). Inward evangelization is not a continual altar call, but rather the probing and exploring of all that God calls us to be and to do when he makes us his witnesses. In that sense, it is a process of continuing conversion, of the ever-expanding rule of Christ in our lives individually and corporately. Although some will call it "sanctification," it is the process of becoming what we already are in Christ, to which we must address our minds and wills in response to the instruction of Scripture. It is, at the same time, a continual process of repentance, for we discover from within the experience of forgiveness how great our sin is and how virulent our rebellion continues to be. With Paul, we need to see that we, in the church, are "the chief of sinners," in order to accept anew the wonderful and cleansing power of the gospel. That, too, is continuing evangelization.

Using other ecclesiastical terms, we could say that the catecheti- cal or Christian education ministry of the church is a necessary form of ongoing internal evangelization. I have always regarded the sacra- ment of infant baptism in the Reformed tradition as the mandate for the educational ministry of the church. When the church baptizes its young as a confession of faith in response to God's action in putting these children in Christian homes, it is accepting the responsibility of rearing these children under the tutelage of the gospel. Although the initiation of faith may be gradual, it still must grow, and evangelization must take place in and through the educational ministry of the church. We provide this Christian education for our children as a way of leading them into their own personal encounter with the gospel, to which they will have to respond individually at some time in their life. The nurture of faith in Christians of all ages is best understood as an evangelizing process, through which all of the members of the church are led into an ever greater understanding of the claims of the gospel, and thus to expanding dimensions of discipleship and commitment.

The relationships that make up the community will provide many opportunities for ongoing, informal evangelization. Small groups, Bible studies, prayer groups, friendships, task forces, committees, and, most importantly, families of believers are just a few of the innumerable informal forms of community in which we are challenged to discover more of what the gospel means. Much of the New Testament teaching on the Christian community addresses precisely this informal internal structure of the church. Here we find rivalry and divisiveness, rumor-mongering and judgmentalism at work. Here is where we must experience the practical impact of the gospel of reconciliation. Within all of these Christian relationships there will always be a need for more gospel and more evangelization. We need constantly to restate the gospel as it applies to the myriad of challenges that our daily lives present to it. The "dailiness" of Christian living is often the greatest threat to our credibility as witnesses. And so we must "say the gospel" within our routines and relationships in order to be converted further.

The inward evangelization of the church is, moreover, the fundamental form of equipping for our calling to be Christ's witness in the world. We have defined the church as the "equipping community" (Chap. 6, esp. 6.3, pp. 105-11). Both formally and informally, we need to be heralds of the gospel to each other within the church, in order to be strengthened and prepared for our common ministry in the world. Just as it is essential that we *be* and *do* the witness toward each other within the community of faith, it is also essential that we *say* that witness to each other as mutual encouragement and admonition. Just as the various members of the Body have different functions, we all have a responsibility to say the gospel to each other in whatever way we can do so, according to our gifts. When we free ourselves from the narrow idea that the gospel can be said only in certain terms and ways, then we will discover that we can say the Good News to each other through our prayers with and for each other, through our conversations, our compassionate listening, our sharing of our experiences, as well as through the teaching and preaching to which some of the Body are called. To assure one another that we are, in fact, forgiven of our sins by God's grace is a way of continuing evangelization. To stimulate each other to praise and celebration, as well as to meditation and study, is a way we continue gospel ministry with each other. When Paul wrote, "Let the word of Christ dwell in you richly, as you teach and admonish one another in all wisdom" (Col. 3:16), he was not directing these instructions to the leaders of the congregation alone. He fully expected that all Christians would have this ministry to one another. We are called to evangelize each other by saying our faith, our experience, our praise, and our needs so that we can "bear one another's burdens" as well as encourage and challenge each other.

Saying the gospel within the church is, finally and most importantly, the way in which Christ continues to give us our faith. We know that our faith is God's gift to us. He continues to give it as we continue to hear and to respond to the gospel, as it is expressed in all the ways that the Spirit makes possible. The sacraments are the "visible word," as Augustine taught us, and they are a continuous source of faith—a means of grace, as the Reformed tradition puts it. The proclaimed word, in all its forms (not simply in the form of preaching), is the Word of God (Second Helvetic Confession) coming to us through human agents and yet still God's work in our midst. We cannot witness outwardly to a reality that is not vibrantly at work in our life inwardly. That again would be a separation of the inseparable. To be sure, the evangelization we experience within the church is the benefit of faith, and our language will never exhaust the wonder of that benefit. We know that we are to receive it in order to serve God in the world. But we cannot serve God in the world without receiving this gracious benefit.

As evangelization continues within the church, that word does not return void, but works within the community to make faith stronger and braver. Our compulsion should be that of the apostle Paul: "I long to see you, that I may impart to you some spiritual gift to strengthen you, that is, that we may be mutually encouraged by each other's faith, both yours and mine" (Rom. 1:11-12).

Nine

SAYING THE WITNESS
IN THE WORLD:
INCARNATIONAL EVANGELIZATION

9.1 "EARNING THE RIGHT TO BE HEARD"

The church exists because God has called it forth. Its mission is to be, to do, and to say the witness to God's saving actions and purposes. The motivation for its work in the world is obedience: obedience to its Lord as it continues to do the work that he has sent it out to do. The church can carry out this mission only because God enables it to do so. God has provided his Spirit as the enabling and equipping power for the church's obedient ministry.

Proceeding from that understanding of the church's mission, we now turn to the theme that many would consider the first and most obvious subject of discussion concerning the church: its task to say the gospel in the world. What I have defined as "evangelization" is for many the primary thrust of the church's work. But in defining evangelization as one expression of witness, I have taken what I hope is a broader and more biblical approach. We should develop our understanding of the spoken witness out of this comprehensive definition of the church's mission.

But many consider this emphasis upon evangelization as a spoken witness to the world too narrow a definition of the church. Some say that it must be seen as one of many tasks, while others insist that it is no longer an acceptable way of doing religion in a pluralistic religious world, which calls for toleration and cooperation rather than evangelization.

I cannot agree that, in some sense, the "religious situation" has evolved in such a way that the church is no longer supposed to evangelize. The witness must be said, as I emphasized in the last chapter. That is central to the church's mission. And the saying of the witness must be addressed to the world, not restricted to one cultur-ally defined religious group (the church in its many forms) as its particular internal activity. Religious toleration is an extremely impor-tant expression of advanced civilization, and it should be protected and upheld with great energy. However, religious toleration is not necessarily the opposite of Christian evangelization. To put it another way, the announcement of the Christian gospel does not necessarily have to mean that some people (believers) are telling other people (nonbelievers) that they are "wrong."

It is perhaps at this point that the damaging results of the benefit-mission dichotomy become especially obvious. Where the focus of Christian evangelization is upon the "saved" trying to get the "unsaved" saved—that is, where the focus is upon drawing those lines so that those who are "right" go out to correct or rescue those who are "wrong"—the gospel becomes a "way to get saved," rather than the Good News about God's action for his entire creation. (The reader who fears by now that I am espousing some form of "universalism" may be put at ease—God's purposes and work in history include the mysterious possibility of their rejection, which is a spiritual reality that we know but cannot explain.) God does not call the church to practice that kind of Christian evangelization which is characterized by a spirit of judgmentalism, which uses manipulative methods to "win souls," which concentrates on the measurable results of evangelization, and which reduces the gospel to a particular experience, be it conversion or "being born again" or however defined. Such methods and move-ments of Christian evangelization do not "enflesh" the gospel, do not carry on the ministry of Jesus as he modeled it for us, and do not expose the full meaning of witness in the New Testament. Therefore, we must reject all extremes in favor of a theology and practice of witness that will not separate the real benefits of salvation from the responsibility of that call.

In our Western world, both extremes—the reduction of the gos-pel to individual salvation, and the rejection of evangelization because it is intolerant—are widely represented. They are constantly reacting to each other. Those who sense that the gospel must mean more than a "salvation panacea" criticize or reject much of evangelization. Those who are concerned that the gospel be heard and responded to are quick to condemn the more scrupulous as "liberal" or "modernist," or to adjudge them as heretics and non-Christians. These issues erupt, quite predictably, around discussions of the ecumenical movement, or of the church's role in political and social issues, or of personal piety, or of biblical authority and interpretation . . . or, quite practically, when an evangelistic crusade comes to town. In this maelstrom of action and reaction, assertion and rejection, the concern for the whole-ness of the gospel and the unity of the church (which cannot be separated in the New Testament, for the latter witnesses to the for-mer!) is obviously far removed from its biblical place as a major and central theme. At the same time, both sides throw terms at each other as weapons, whether they be "fundamentalist" or "liberal," and little Christian communication really takes place.

If, however, obedience to Christ as his witnesses in the world is our major concern, then the proclamation of the kingdom of God, with all that means, and the unity of the witnessing community as its tangible expression in the world must be central to us. If Christ calls us to serve him among the poor and the outcasts of the world, then our obedience must be to do just that. If Christ's teaching and actions require of us that we become agents of change in our society, then we must become such agents if we are to obey Christ. Evangelization must be the saying of the whole gospel, or it is itself a form of disobedience. We must, as Christ's church, recognize that our most virulent disobedi-ence is not the refusal to proclaim the gospel, but our insistence upon our particular versions of the gospel, which, because of their limita-tions and dilutions, easily falsify the gospel.

Thus, when we approach the world to say the witness, we must do so as those who know that we are and we do the witness in order to say it. Young Life, the paraparochial mission with which I have worked, constantly emphasizes that "we must earn the right to be heard." That right has to be earned even with adolescents. It is all the more necessary with the adult world to which the church is sent.

The reasons for this are obvious. Christian talk has become so routine, so stereotyped, that the words have largely lost their meaning. Christianity has been a part of our Western society for so long that the assumption is widespread that this is one thing our secular society really does know and understand. (This is illustrated in the way that secular academicians teach about, dissect, and dismiss Christianity in numerous American colleges and universities, as though they knew everything there was to know about it!) And, therefore, the dismissal of Christianity is often based upon the conviction that it has been tried, tested, and now fails. Of course, the Christian church must respond that those who reject the gospel are too often rejecting a perverted or diluted form of it. That is precisely the point: to correct the myriad of misapprehensions about what the Christian faith is, the witnessing community must earn the right to be heard. The words we are commissioned to say must explain the witness that we are living out as a Christian presence in the world. Unfortunately, the words and phrases we use are so hackneyed and have become such cliches that many are arguing for a change in the language. We must allow our language to become new because it is expressing a gospel that is surprising and new.

It is a healthy exercise for Christians to talk about grace, love, and hope with other words that express these possibilities in a fresh and gripping way. However, most of the words we use are from our biblical vocabulary, and we cannot really replace them. Rather, our understanding and practice of witness must function in such a way that the words of our faith have meaning again. To understand "love" as *agape,* the world must observe that love at work both within the Christian community and in its service in the world. "Grace" is the irreplaceable name for the marvelous way in which God acts in our lives and history, and enables us to act toward each other. But if there is no grace in our being and doing, there is not much sense in talking about it. If there is no forgiveness in our lives, then we really cannot say anything intelligible to the world about the offer of forgiveness in the gospel.

We are the heirs of traditions that, next to providing us so much for which we are grateful, have also diluted the language and the meaning of our faith words. Christian evangelization in the Western world must struggle with the fact that the misunderstandings of the Christian faith, which are profound in our tradition, are a much greater obstacle to our witness than would be total ignorance of the gospel.

Coupled with that dilution of meaning is the problem of "insiders' language," Christian jargon, which has also emerged in the institutional church. The technical language of theology may well be useful as theological "shop talk," but it should never be the form of communication with which the church addresses the world. Similarly, the language of Christian pietism concentrates so much on the internal life and experience of the church that it is neither interested in nor capable of communicating understandably with the world outside its boundaries. However we obscure the gospel, to do so is to reject the Spirit's enabling of us to say it understandably in the world.

If we are going to earn the right to be heard in our world, then we must return to the full meaning of the gospel and discover whether or not we are, ourselves, sufficiently evangelized. That is the inward dimension of evangelization we discussed in the last chapter. Then we must examine our understanding of the gospel to find out how it is diluted (for it certainly is in some way) and allow our concept of the gospel to be expanded and corrected. In the process, we must review our language and discover the obscurity we impose upon the Good News as we use believers' talk for communication with nonbelievers. We have many resources available today to help us do so, ranging from the continuing and ever-growing world of theological research, which can help us to correct our limited versions of the gospel, to studies in communication, which can show us how we fail to make the gospel understandable.

Our chief concern, however, in order to earn the right to be heard, must always be congruence: the integration of the person of the witness (*martys*) with the actions and words of witness (*martyria*). The world should see and hear the same gospel in the lives and words of the witnesses. Summons to faith should be perceived as a summons to a new and reconciled relationship with God, which issues forth in a new life of service and obedience. If the gospel is rejected, it should be the result of the congruent presentation of that gospel in the world. The witnesses who say the gospel should be people who "incarnate" this Good News, not in their perfection, because they are still sinners, but in their commitment to Christ, their allegiance to his calling, and their desire to be his ambassadors in their lives and actions. The message is not to be separated from the messengers. Christian witnesses must be credible witnesses—and then their saying of the witness can take place. Then it will have earned the right to be heard.

What I have said about the necessary congruence of evangelization with the lives and actions of the witnessing community means that the mass media, when separated from the witnessing community, are a questionable means of evangelization in our world. The media, especially those which make their receivers primarily into consumers of their presentations, such as television, radio, and often film, do in fact often separate the message from the messenger. These media can convey little experience of the lives and actions of the witnesses. The message is removed from the interaction of relationships between persons, and thus the "enfleshing" of the gospel does not really take place.

There are wonderful exceptions to this, and I realize that I must be careful with generalizations at this point. Film can be used to tell the story of faith in a marvelous way, so that it is enfleshed more powerfully than is even possible in other settings. That cannot be

denied. But there is always the problem of authenticity in that enfleshment. The skill of the actor and the cinematographer can create a
sense of credibility and authenticity that is most persuasive. But the
viewer of the film can never experience through that medium all that
faith is and means to those who made the film—and it is entirely
possible for talented unbelievers to make powerful movies about
Christianity. God undoubtedly works through that medium, but it is
clear that it cannot be the sole form of evangelization. The hearer
needs to experience the meaning of the gospel in the lives of people
with whom he or she is in relationship, needs to encounter the
Christian community, and needs to respond to the realism of faith in
the ambiguity and struggle of Christian existence.

The written word, although obviously a major medium, draws the
reader into a relationship with the author, and thus overcomes many
of the dangers of a purely consumerist response, which is my concern.
But even a book or article does not replace the direct interaction
between persons, which is the primary channel of incarnational witness. This medium is effective to the degree that it does create a
relationship. Its limitations are at that point where the relationship
cannot develop further: the reader cannot probe and question the
writer and discover what he or she may have omitted or correct the
reader's own images of what the author is really like. Even Scripture,
as the written word, is dependent upon the personal work of the Holy
Spirit to make it the powerful Word of God addressing the reader and
calling forth the response of faith. We must always bear in mind that
the New Testament was not written as an evangelistic tract, but is a
collection of writings for the church, instructing and equipping the
church for its ministry in the world. Thus, the personal interpretation
and application of the written word through those gifted by God to do
so is an essential part of the Spirit's equipping of the church.

The art (for there is true art involved) of Christian evangelization
is in avoiding manipulation and dishonesty by omission, and in insuring
that the receiver of any communication through any medium is always
aware that there is more to the gospel than any particular medium or
message can convey. The challenge to use the media responsibly in
Christian evangelization is very great. My concern is that it not be
permitted to replace our fundamental call to be, do, and say the
witness where we are. The film cannot replace the people who are
sent out to "lead lives worthy of the calling with which they have been
called," and who are the true channels of God's work in the arena of
daily relationships. The powerful medium of the written word must be

seen as one part of the church's organic life, one way in which Christians minister to each other in interdependence upon each other, but also requiring the embracing experience of Christian community and relationships in order to communicate the gospel in its fullness.

My greater concern is that the enthusiastic use of the media for evangelization is tied in directly to the reduction of the gospel to its benefits. The media, especially radio and television, are useful tools for spreading a message of salvation as an answer to all of humanity's problems. This message can come across as one of many "answer-alls" to the challenges of living. The gospel begins to be heard as a solution, even an elixir, offered in the marketplace next to headache pills and new cars. The summons to service and the prophetic dimensions of the gospel do not "sell well" on television. There is no opportunity to test the words of the speaker against his or her life and actions. The congruency is lost. And the impossibility of translating that congruency into the media leads to their abuse. The gospel that comes forth from so many television and radio broadcasts is simply not the whole gospel. And one cannot experience the Christian community through this restricted medium.

This is not to say that the media cannot be extremely important tools in ministry. They can serve to nurture the Christian community in ways that we have only begun to explore. They might well be a way to initiate evangelization, to awaken interest, and to put the gospel on the agenda of many people who will not come into a church building to hear it. But the media can never serve as the total means for evangelization; rather, we must link them with the enfleshing of the gospel in the lives and actions of the Christian community. The media can help the church to learn what understandable communication is. They can force us to examine our language both for its dilutedness and for its obscurity. They can make us take seriously the world that we address, if we want to be heard. But they are only one of the church's tools for saying the witness, and their opportunities should be carefully examined and applied with great attentiveness to the requirement of congruence in witness.

9.2 EVERY WITNESS AN EVANGELIST

Saying the witness to the unbelieving world means that we take seriously those individual tongues of fire on the heads of every Christian in the upper room at Pentecost. Every Christian is to regard herself or himself as a witness, called upon to render witness in the world.

Every Christian shares in the ministry of Christ as a part of the Body of Christ. Peter was addressing every Christian when he wrote, "Always be prepared to make a defense to any one who calls you to account for the hope that is in you, yet do it with gentleness and reverence" (1 Pet. 3:15). We may use this text as a summary of New Testament teaching about the meaning of "saying the witness," and allow Peter to define for us the evangelistic task of the individual Christian and the Christian community.

Evangelization is based upon "the hope that is in you." At the beginning of his first letter, Peter establishes the theme with the statement that "God has borne us anew to a living hope through the resurrection of Jesus Christ from the dead" (1 Pet. 1:3; my modified translation to render the Greek more accurately). The saving work of God makes its permanent impact upon the believer in the form of "living hope." That living hope is the life-encompassing certainty that God will complete his work and bring all those who believe to their inheritance; they shall receive, "as the outcome of [their] faith," the salvation of their souls (1:9). Thus, the saying of Christian witness is an outworking of the transforming work that God is doing in the life of the Christian, which Peter calls hope.

This is another way of saying that the being of the witness, and the doing of that witness, must presuppose and accompany the saying of the witness. The hope within us is an observable difference in the lives of Christians, the distinguishing factor of the Christian faith. Those who are hopeful are then able to function in this world under the sign of that hope. The doing of the witness is the translation of this living and certain hope into our actions. The effect of such hope is endurance, patience, certainty about God's future, fearlessness, the serene ability to live toward the fulfillment of God's promises because of what he has already done. It is the God-enabled ability to "set your hope fully upon the grace that is coming to you at the revelation of Jesus Christ" (1:13).

This observable difference in the very nature of Christians' lives and behavior calls for an explanation. To live without fear in a fearful world is not "normal" and demands a reason. To be able to forgive and really have it make a difference in one's relationships is revolutionary behavior. To make one's decisions and judgments on the basis of criteria other than self-interest is so threatening a difference that the world must know how this can be. Here (and throughout the New Testament) we can understand "hope" as a confidence about God's faithfulness and the fulfillment of his promises, which makes it possible for Christians to lead very distinctive lives now; it is not wishful thinking but a certainty that translates into the present tense of our lives and changes them. It is for reasons of our inner hope that we will be called upon to make our defense, our apology—which quite clearly refers to the things we will say to explain ourselves.

The apostle's emphasis upon our hope clearly links his summary statement to the future tense of salvation (5.2, pp. 78-88), and thus to the dynamic nature of the Christian witness as it makes its impact upon the world. To stress our hope as that aspect of the Christian's life that will evoke the questioner's asking for a reason is very significant. It means that the Christian's spoken witness is not so much about who he is or what she has, but who they are becoming. The witness that challenges the world is the life that is changing and growing toward wholeness. Hope describes that quality of life which is based upon the firm knowledge of what God has done (the resurrection of Jesus Christ from the dead!), what God is doing (" . . . by God's power [you] are guarded through faith"; 1:5), and thus the unshakeable certainty of what God will do.

Perhaps more significant is what hope is not. Hope is not security based upon what the believer knows or has or affirms. It is outward directed—it focuses upon the utter reliability of God. It can withstand suffering (Peter's whole epistle is addressed to a suffering church!) not because of the moral fibre of the Christians but because of the enabling power of God. Hope is not self-satisfied, for it looks forward to the "more" of the gospel (5.1, pp. 75-78), and cannot assume that everything the gospel means is already understood and applied. Hope is not arrogant, because it is the result of God's action (God begets us to a living hope, according to 1 Pet. 1:3; we cannot do it ourselves) and is dependent upon God's continuing work. Hope is not self-centered, because it knows that God's work of salvation is far greater than what we already have experienced of it. Of course, hope is not divisive, because it is motivated by the consummation of God's work of salvation, and that final work will be the victory over all evil, including that sin which divides Christians from one another.

Like the rest of the gospel, Christian hope is a given that we must continue to explore and to discover. It is a corrective to all of the theological systems that imply that they have exhausted the truth of the Christian faith. Hope means that the pilgrimage is still an adventure, and there are always more discoveries to be made. This quality of life, this character of faith, this witness in the lives and actions of Christians demands an explanation. It must be "defended"; that is, we must speak about it to make plain what it is. It is easily misunderstandable. It can be taken for the crassest escapism from the realities of the world. It can be mistaken for drunkenness ("they are filled with new wine!"). It is almost impossible to understand the nature of Christian hope, as it is expressed in the lives and action of Christians, unless words express it. This is how the saying of the witness must necessarily emerge from being and doing the witness. It must be made plain, in response to the questions of a puzzled world, that our hope is the unavoidable consequence of the truth of the gospel. To know Christ and to be his servant is to be hopeful. To be called to the ministry of witness is to have one's life become imbued with a hope that bears one through the greatest suffering and hostility (see the context of 1 Pet. 3:15).

Evangelization, in this general sense, is the opportunity and necessity for every Christian to "defend" the gospel, to explain his or her faith as it is experienced in the world as an otherwise inexplicable hope. Every Christian can make this defense. In fact, Christians are spread throughout the land as light and salt in order to be the presence of that hope, and thus in order to be called upon to make this defense. Evangelization is, then, essentially an explanation of what is. It is putting into words what is already enfleshed in the lives and actions of Christians. It is not saying certain pat phrases or formulated testimonies. It is not imposing a Christian message when there is no readiness to hear it. Rather, it is the response of a Christian to one's desire to hear his or her witness (*martyria*) because of his or her impact as a witness (*martys*).

Every Christian is to "be prepared" to make this kind of defense. The apostle's injunction makes it clear that this kind of witness is a serious and often demanding undertaking. To make such a verbal defense, the Christian witness needs equipping. We spoke of this earlier, especially when we described the role of the church as the "equipping community" (6.3, pp. 105-11), which is the presupposition for every Christian to "be the witness." We shall discuss below (11.2, pp. 211-19) how this can be worked out in our understanding of the church's ministry. However, we should note here that, in the context of Peter's admonition, the witness will be able to make a defense when called upon because that witness has been prepared; and the church's major task in its inward life is to carry out that preparation.

Finally, the apostle states that this defense is to be made with gentleness and reverence. This important instruction strengthens the incarnational sense of evangelization. The way in which the defense is made is of great importance. We have already noted at several points that the way in which the community testifies to the reality of Christ's love in its midst is one of its most powerful forms of witness. The outward dimension of that love is the focus here. The context of the text reveals that this defense is probably to be made over against those who are attacking the Christian community, or suspicious of it. The presence of believers is calling forth questions and even opposition. Incarnational witness, as we define it, will do that—the presence of Christ is both attractive and threatening to a world whose entire system of values and customs is put into question by that presence. Therefore, the defense is to be done in such a way that those hearing it will know that they are loved by the witnesses. They are to experience Christians as people who are caring, gentle, concerned for the persons with whom they have to do, and even prepared to accept with honor and reverence the worldly orders to which they submit (see 1 Pet. 2:13-17).

The message the witnesses want to convey is really communicated properly only when the receivers sense that they are important to the witnesses. Incarnational witness is concerned that the message and its means of communication are congruent. Therefore, aggressive, manipulative, or arrogant communication will be impossible. The certainty with which Christians confess their faith is connected to the freedom to make that confession humbly, gently, persuasively, free of all rancor and judgmentalism. Jesus formulated the ultimate spirit of Christian witness at the cross when he said, "Father, forgive them, for they know not what they do." The injunction to "love your enemy" is central to evangelization as incarnational witness. Our words must be chosen and said in a spirit of concern for the welfare of the one with whom we are speaking. We may learn from Jesus how to look upon our neighbors with his compassion, through his eyes, and thus evangelize as an exercise of love, not of spiritual conquest.

The relational component of incarnational witness is important in this regard. The gentleness and reverence of incarnational evangelization will be difficult to express if our spoken witness is not surrounded by the preparation and continuation of relationships. It is the people whom we know, with whom we live and work, our "neighbors," who will most likely want our defense, and who should hear what we have to say. They will have experienced our hope in the course of these relationships. If they have not, then what we have to say will be weakened if not pointless—and they probably will not ask. If the relationships we have developed have already been channels of love and expressions of grace, then our words can be gracious and loving.

But if our words are in crass contrast to an otherwise general lack of care and concern for someone, then there is no gentleness and reverence, and probably no witness.

Part of the preparation of the Christian witnesses to make their defense will be to challenge them with the opportunities they already have to defend their faith. That is, the Christian community must learn to see the daily situations of its members' lives as the primary place for ministry. This is where we are to be, to do, and to say the witness. Too often, the church's formal instruction on how to witness emphasizes certain words, phrases, and propositions that one must present (frequently in a certain order), and even trains people to manipulate situations in order to make such conversations possible. How many opportunities for incarnational witness are missed while we try to "set up" the perfect opportunity for a testimony! The witness's most obvious concern should be for all the conversations and contacts in which "Christian talk" is not possible, but in which a Christian witness is evident in the life and actions of the witness. It would be a helpful ministry within the church to teach its members to think through their relationships, their daily opportunities for contact with other people, and to examine those relationships in terms of their effect as incarnational witness. The process is uncomfortable, but this is where most evangelization will start—in relationships of such an evangelical quality that the door for saying the witness will open.

We have been stressing the evangelization that every Christian individual does wherever he or she is each day. But we must also look again at the evangelization made possible by the kind of community that is the church. There is, in the inward dimension of the church, a strong outward dimension in which evangelization can and should happen. In our Western society in particular, where the church is still an institution that can and does have some appeal to the public and is a place where people can still come "to meet people," we should be aware that our life as community can afford opportunities to evangelize.

If the Christian community is intentionally becoming a healing community, if it can deal with the weaknesses and sinfulness of its members with loving support and biblical admonition, if faith is being nurtured and the responsibility of faith is being constantly focused for the members, then such a community can attract many people looking for help. Out of their search and the incarnational witness of the community, the opportunity to evangelize will arise.

Along a similar vein, the community exercises a witness in the ways in which it allows its traditions to be opportunities for evangelization in our secularized world. Although the process of secularization has moved further than many Christians will admit, it is still possible to see the traditional celebrations of faith and the "threshhold experiences" of life (birth, marriage, death, and in some traditions, confirmation) as opportunities for incarnational evangelization. Many people may enter a church only for a Christmas Eve or Easter service, or to attend a wedding or funeral. Rather than decry that as a lamentable deterioration of piety in our society, we must learn to accept gladly these opportunities for ministry. Everything we have emphasized about evangelization emerging out of the being and doing of the gospel needs to be rethought in relation to these functions of the institutional church. Certainly the gospel can be enfleshed in the form of premarital counseling, family ministry at a death, and even in baptismal counseling or instruction (which should be a requirement of all infant baptisms). Our churches are still perceived as places that provide needed services for our society. Even if the perception is a very diluted or distorted view of what the Christian faith is all about, it still is a point of contact and should be viewed by the Christian community as an opportunity for incarnational ministry, as well as for correction of secular misunderstandings of the gospel.

A family came to a church camp, and in the course of the weekend told us a remarkable story. The parents had separated and were in the process of getting a divorce. But they shared a desire to reconcile, if somehow they could. The wife had started bringing her children to our church—sensing, I think, that the friction at home needed some positive balance. The husband had begun to spend much more time at home and allowed himself to be persuaded to join the family at the family camp. He was there as a seeker, wanting help, and feeling that there was something in this community that would help him. Thus the community, which was already functioning as a witness in his experience, had the opportunity for saying the witness, for evangelization.

We may not neglect these powerful forms of ministry . . . nor should we see them as the only ways left to the church to evangelize. Every opportunity we have to enflesh the gospel is a gift of God that we must accept and exploit fully. But whether that evangelization happens inwardly or outwardly, it should take place as the consequence of our hope and its impact upon the unbelieving world. We may then be certain that the evangel which is the content of our evangelization is Christ and not our own spiritual achievement.

We will further enhance our readiness to make this defense as we learn to "read" our environment and understand candidly and realistically its opportunities and obstacles. To do incarnational witness, we have to understand the "flesh" to which the gospel is to be brought. We need, in particular, to sort out all the misunderstandings of the Christian faith that are given in our historical tradition. We have to learn what are the overriding spiritual concerns of the people with whom we live in relationships, not in order to make the gospel fit those concerns, but in order to establish functioning communication so we can proclaim the gospel understandably. There may be a "god-shaped vacuum" in the heart of man (Pascal), but there are not many people in the West today who know that, or who would recognize the godly shape of it. The road to evangelization is the being and doing of the witness that leads us to share the burdens of our neighbors, understand their lives and hopes, and confront them, "with gentleness and reverence," with the hope that God gives us in Christ. It is to that ministry that our churches send us, and for which our churches should equip and support us.

Finally, we have the wonderful and liberating assurance that Christ is accomplishing his work through the church as his Body. Since we understand the role of every Christian to be a witness who is enabled to say the gospel, we must emphasize the mutual interdependence of all the members of the Body. No Christian ever says all the gospel. No one single form of communication is an adequate expression of the gospel. Incarnational witness and evangelization are a work of the entire Body, each member doing his or her part to contribute to the comprehensive work of the Spirit. Evangelization is a work of faith: we do not need to know the results of our incarnational ministry, but we can be confident that God will use all that is happening through his Spirit and will complete his work faithfully. This is liberating because it frees the individual Christian from the guilt-producing sense that he or she must say everything in a particular testimony or else the individual addressed will be lost. That is ultimately evangelization out of fear, which is contrary to the gospel.

The marvelous fact is that God weaves together the various gifts and ministries of his servants into a work that is greater and more wondrous than our strategies could plan and our methods could produce. Our desire for perceptible results can endanger our own faith, as it tends to replace faith with sight, and it can even make our evangelization into a work that we interpret as a merit in God's eyes. In the equipping of the saints for their ministry in the world, we should insure that the gospel of grace and forgiveness does not produce guilt but rather freedom to serve and, especially, to defend the hope that is within us.

9.3 THE GIFT OF EVANGELISTS

Having emphasized that every Christian witness is called and equipped to evangelize, we now recognize that God does call and equip some members of the Body to carry out the specialized function of evangelist. We stated earlier that this term is used only three times in the New Testament (p. 136); the reference is to one who articulates the gospel, particularly to those who have not yet heard and responded. Generally speaking, the apostles are all to be regarded as evangelists, and in their church-founding ministry they firmly established the central definition of the church's mission as the continuation of that apostolic ministry. But not every Christian in the early church could stand on Mars Hill and formulate the gospel for that particular audience. Nor could every Christian be an itinerant evangelist, carrying the message from one town to the next.

Throughout the history of the church, God has given us men and women whose particular gift was evangelization—the saying of the witness in such a way that it called forth a response. These individuals have gone out from the church to new fields of missionary proclamation, and where they have gone, churches have arisen to continue the ministry of Christ. Within the church, God has given certain individuals the ability to restate the gospel for Christians so that their own process of faith would be deepened and nurtured. This is certainly an essential aspect of our understanding of ordered ministry in the church (see 11.1, pp. 204-11). This gift incorporates the ability to understand a particular culture in order to say the gospel in its terms, thus to formulate the gospel message understandably, and to establish communication in such a way that the Spirit works through the evangelist to create faith.

The specialized evangelist and evangelistic ministry are, therefore, a part of the Spirit's enabling of the church. They are not intended to replace the evangelization to be done by every Christian witness. They are, rather, a component part of the entire organic ministry of the church. Evangelistic ministry is not the sole definition of ministry, but it cannot be neglected in any biblical theology of ministry.

This specialized ministry takes place in a variety of ways within the church. It can be the missionary going into new territory and finding new words to express the gospel where it has never been heard. It can be the gifted preacher whose formulation of the gospel attracts the nonbeliever out of curiosity, and whose rhetorical skill is used by God to open hearts to belief. It can be the writer who presents the faith on paper in such a way that the nonbelieving reader can begin the process of response that will result in faith. It can be the teacher who, in a secular setting, can incorporate the Christian faith so that the student is enabled to examine the claims of the gospel in a new way. Many ecclesiastical structures have actually established the specialized function of "evangelist" as an order of ministry, recognizing these gifts and providing both identity and discipline for them. On the other hand, many orders of ministry have tended, in the modern age, to set aside this function and scarcely to give it attention in their definitions of ministry.

The historical process of secularization has called forth many new expressions of the office of evangelist. It is abundantly clear that the "Christian mission field" begins precisely in those areas where for centuries a form of Christianity was the strongest molding power in society—in Europe and the social and political world that resulted from European colonialization. In the early nineteenth century, the German churches realized that they had to combat secularization, and so began the ministry of "inner missions," which with time has combined the proclamation of the gospel for the nonbelieving public with the diaconic ministry, which presents the gospel to the world in the form of actions. Societies for the distribution of Christian literature, especially of Bibles, emerged to combat the growing ignorance of the Christian faith in the secularized West. In America, particularly, the nineteenth- and twentieth-century revival movements produced mass evangelists who have had a major impact upon society and upon the development of denominational structures.

But as the established churches began to neglect or even to reject the ministry of evangelization as a central focus of their work, other organizations emerged to take up this ministry. This has resulted in a plethora of specialized evangelistic ministries, which do not constitute themselves as traditional ecclesiastical ministries and are often highly critical of the traditional churches ("they don't preach the gospel"). These specialized evangelistic ministries frequently work from a theological base that stresses the benefits of salvation without any particular emphasis upon the responsibilities; they tend to solidify the benefits-mission dichotomy, although there are remarkable exceptions. A special feature of American Christianity has been the emergence of some denominations whose entire identity is, in effect, to be a continuing evangelistic crusade.

Secularization has contributed another factor in the emergence of these specialized evangelistic agencies. As our Western societies have secularized, they have produced new social groups and structures to which the traditional forms of the church have been unable to relate effectively. The forms and structures of the church are based on the past. Charlemagne divided Europe into parishes, a structure that has continued as the dominant form of ministry to this day. In America, the structure evolved further into the voluntaristic congregation, in which church membership, as the decision of the members, defined the outlines of ministry. Some of these parishes are geographical, although many are not. However, the needs and realities of these local congregations have usually dictated their understanding of ministry. But in our urban and secularized world, our neighborhoods are no longer the center of our community life. Rather, we associate with our professional groups, our interest groups, our ethnic groups, and, very often, our age groups. For example, our society has produced a youth culture that does not relate to traditional parish structures and has become a large and complex social reality that presents us with many challenges. There are other vast social groups like this youth culture that will not enter a church to hear the gospel. So there is a need to go out to these various groups since they will not come in—and no longer have the traditional cradle-to-grave identification with the Christian faith that was common in our society until the onset of secularization.

These specialized social groups call for specialized strategies and skills in ministry. The process of evangelization with youth will differ from that with other groups. The particular challenges of evangelization in the inner city may differ from those in suburbia, and similar contrasts will be found when we move from one socioeconomic group to another, or from one region of the country to another. The growing sociological complexity of Western society requires that the church diversify and specialize its ministry if it is to be a witness in all the world.

Perhaps the first challenge of this kind came about when Europe began to grapple with the fact that the world exploration that accompanied the onset of our modern age revealed whole cultures that had never heard the gospel. The result of that discovery was the modern mission movement. It is significant that, broadly speaking, that movement emerged outside the boundaries of traditional church structures—most of the missions societies of the eighteenth and nineteenth centuries were nonecclesiastical, although they founded churches in the countries to which they went. Gradually, the traditional church structures expanded to include this important ministry, so that independent missions societies became boards of foreign missions within the major denominations.

The analogous process in relationship to the newer organizations that have surfaced recently within our society has been more difficult. As the number of these organizations increased, the churches began to speak of them as *parachurch* organizations. This was an early attempt to provide some orderly understanding of what was, in fact, happening. But the term itself is theologically discriminatory. To be "parachurch" means to be "next to the church." The assumption is that those structures which are the traditional church are the "real" church, and those newer ministry forms which are "para" are not quite as much "church." One is reminded of the similar process in the early and high Middle Ages, when various specialized orders emerged in the Roman Catholic church in response to felt needs that the institutional church was not effectively addressing. They all had to struggle for their acceptance and identity within the church, but eventually the Roman church came to recognize and affirm a diversity of ministries and ministry forms within the church. Protestantism has had a harder time with this process and is caught today in a struggle with this diversification of ministries, which often appear to be both threatening and competitive—and often are theologically suspect.

Since I have devoted years of my own ministry to one such organization, Young Life, I would like to reflect at this point on the real nature of the challenge, in hopes that we may see some movement toward clarification and resolution of the problems (see also John Mackay, *Ecumenics: The Science of the Church Universal,* pp. 178-86). I observe the emergence of such movements as a constant process within the church, a means of renewal and refocusing of the church's ministry when its institutional forms begin to harden so much that the church is not responsive to its calling and the challenges of its society. That is not to say that the movements emerging on the margins of the church are always healthy and beneficial. In their divisiveness, judgmentalism, and certainly in their frequent reduction of the gospel to its benefits, they present serious problems. But their very presence is to be seen as an indication of a need for the institutional church to change.

Helmut Thielicke has said that heresies are a sign of a lack of vitamins in the body of the church. That is, I think, more often true than not: heretical movements often are an indicator of some component of the Christian faith that is being neglected by the church. The heretical movement overcompensates and goes beyond the boundaries of the acceptable. But the phenomenon is itself instructive. The so-called parachurch movements are not heretical, although they often are excessive in their reaction to a lack in the church. The primary deficiency that concerns me here is in the area of incarnational evangelization. It is fair to say, I believe, that the churches have needed correction in their understanding or practice of evangelization. The evangelistic movements addressing these needs outside traditional church structures are evidence of that, and the best possible resolution of the tension they cause is for them to cooperate with traditional churches, just as the foreign mission societies of earlier generations ultimately became highly respected parts of church structures.

The primary reason for my conviction on this point is theological, for the movements I have in mind are committed to the evangelistic task of the church. They tend to define the church's mission in terms of the proclamation of the gospel, and they look for conversion as the desired result of their ministry. Their views of how the Christian life is then to be lived vary, but they generally emphasize the need to be a part of a church in order to grow in the faith. They are all asserting, in one way or another, that there is, in fact, spiritual calling and gifting for evangelistic ministry, and their organizations assemble people who have sensed such a call and feel constrained to go about this ministry—yet often with the negative feeling that the traditional churches will not do it.

Even when they have tried, many have found little space or sympathy for this ministry within the churches. Some have reacted negatively to the idea that the goal of evangelistic ministry should be "making people into church members," when their understanding of faith is more in terms of a personal relationship with Christ and submission to his lordship in their lives. They generally see the church as instrumental to God's saving work, and not as an end in itself, but they can be very vague about the place of a theology of the church in their formulation of the Christian faith.

Those of this persuasion are often cavalier and uninformed about the churches' self-understanding and definition of ministry. There is a serious lack of communication between the traditional and the newer forms of ministry, and so both sides throw stereotypes at each other, which serves only to hurt the cause of Christ and to divide the Christian community even further. Theologically, I find that the movements I am describing are right in their emphasis upon witness as the focus of the church, but their definitions of the gospel, of witness, and thus of evangelization are often too narrow. The theological task, which is also an ecclesiastical one, is to retain the central commitment to the mission of the church as witness, while working toward a more fully biblical view of the gospel itself, the calling and function of the church, and the nature of incarnational witness.

For theological reasons, then, I prefer to call these movements "paraparochial." They have emerged outside of the "parochia," the parish, and are working in settings into which the parish structures have not entered successfully. In Young Life, the difference is described as one of direction: the traditional structures tend to be "come to us" ministries, whereas many see the new challenges of a secularized world calling us to become a "go out to them" ministry (there is an intriguing corollary here to Johannes Blauw's concept of centripetal movement in the Old Covenant, and the church's centrifugal movement since Pentecost; see pp. 37-38). Youth evangelization must then take place in the social settings where young people are found today, very often clustering around the high school or college campus. Evangelistic outreach to adult society can be done effectively through neighborhood groups, professional groups (teachers, lawyers, doctors, etc.), or through ministries that address problems such as divorce, drugs, single parenting, or even racial or economic discrimination. Traditional churches have begun to recognize these needs as opportunities for ministry, so that the distinctions between parochial and paraparochial ministry are beginning to blur, which is good.

There is, however, much work still to be done in our general understandings of ministry. It appears to me to be abundantly clear that the New Testament documents a diversity of ministries in the early churches. Even the titles we find (bishop, elder, deacon) appear to refer to various functions, although they often overlap. In the course of our history, we have restricted ministry to the clergy (creating the enormous problem of lay ministry and its underemphasis), and then to specific functions of clerical ministry. These are often defined in formal terms: liturgical, institutional, canonical. Theologically, they can be defined as "word and sacrament" ministry, and the terms become comprehensive and restrictive. Ultimately, the church's ministry is viewed as being done by only a few, in a special place and at special times. However the various traditions define it, ministry is restricted to a few, and in actual practice, ministry is reduced to one model. There is, in spite of much talk about "the priesthood of all believers," little diversity of ministries left.

In this way we reduce the whole emphasis upon evangelization developed in the last chapter and the first part of this one to a footnote to the work to be done by the professional minister. Evangelization can be either central or set aside, but as the church narrows its definition of ministry—and thus reduces the possibilities for ministry—it reduces its evangelistic impact upon the world. The paraparochial ministries present the churches with a challenge to their theologies of ministry, especially to this restriction of ministry to "word and sacrament in the local parish." Is not God, in fact, calling and gifting these movements to carry out the church's actual mission in places where the church is not working, and in ways that the church is neglecting? If the Salvation Army were not there, would all the other churches fill that gap? If Young Life were not reaching out to high school communities, would the local congregations carry out that specialized ministry?

It is particularly interesting that many of these movements have so strong a lay emphasis. There is within them, in my experience, an almost emotional need to resist any association with traditional churchly structures and especially with any of the forms of disciplined ministry that have evolved. At times, I sense that these movements are intentionally lay-centered in reaction to the church's inability to incorporate the laity meaningfully into its mission and ministry. In such movements, laypeople discover that they can in fact minister, evangelize, teach, proclaim—in short, do all of those things which appear to them to be reserved for the professional clergy in the established church structures. Thus, these paraparochial movements are reasserting the need for and capacity of the laity in ministry, and the churches can benefit from seeing this and working to expand both their definition and their practice of ministry to restore the laity to the center of our theology of the church.

A diversity of ministries is both biblical and historically well documented. Again and again, that diversity has expressed itself in the "gift of evangelists." This spiritual action is not easy for the church, for it almost always imposes upon the church the need to reexamine its understanding of the gospel and its practice of ministry. God uses the challenges presented by a changing world to reveal to the church dimensions of the gospel that it has not yet seen. As painful as that discovery process is, it is essential to the church's growth in its grasp of the Good News, and its maturing as the witnessing community.

Thus, the "evangelists" should be a fully integrated part of the church, however it is understood organizationally. "Parochial" and "paraparochial" forms of ministry are both acceptable and probably necessary. But we deny the significance of the church's unity for its witness if we allow these forms to be in conflict with each other. The evangelistic paraparochial ministries need the traditional structures of the church as much as the churches need them. If these movements confront the church with the spiritual fact that God is calling and gifting evangelists for the work of witness in the world, then the church should find ways to respond that will both support such ministry as well as hold it accountable to the church and draw it into responsible relationships with the whole Body of Christ.

9.4 THE PROPHETIC WITNESS

Although we have stressed evangelization as the presentation of the gospel to nonbelievers, so that their response may be called forth, we will be propagating the benefit-mission dichotomy if we do not immediately expand our understanding of evangelization to include the prophetic witness. "Prophecy" is understood biblically as the address of the Word of God directly to a specific situation in our historical experience. Prophetic proclamation moves the Word of God from the realm of the abstract and general to the very specific and experiential. For the Christian church, prophetic preaching is the saying of our witness in full view of the givens of our historical setting. In the course of prophetic preaching, the church presents the claims of Christ in such a way that their practical meaning becomes clear, thus revealing the revolutionary nature of the gospel.

The prophetic witness of the church will correct the narrow definitions of the benefits of salvation, which are so prevalent in the church, as well as help to rejoin the benefits and the mission, which tend to be divided in the church's theology and practice. Salvation, as we have so often pointed out, is both personal and universal in scope, and thus the benefits of God's work of salvation must be presented in all of its dimensions. Prophetic evangelization thus articulates what it means at every level of life that God is reconciling the world to himself in Christ. The effect of that healing work will be experienced in one's personal life, in families, in neighborhoods, but also in whole societies, nations, and races—and between them.

Prophetic evangelization cannot, then, be separated from the church's saying of its witness to God's salvation purposes. It is really too narrow an understanding of the benefits of salvation to restrict them to the personal experience of salvation, to the dimension of the individual's relationship with God. Salvation is cosmic: Christ came to save the world, not just Christians or "souls." When the church speaks prophetically, it must do so in terms of the whole gospel, which is both personal and corporate, both horizontal and vertical, both spiritual and physical (to make an unbiblical distinction).

If we are to overcome the benefit-mission dichotomy, then we shall find it necessary to evangelize prophetically. To do that is to state to the world that the coming of Christ and the proclamation of the kingdom of God spell the ultimate end of all orders of rebellion and judgment upon all sin, both individual and corporate. Again, we must emphasize that salvation is basically wholeness, restoration to the Creator's intention for his creation, and the process of salvation in history must include every aspect of that creation. Everything that we said when we discussed the gospel (5.2, pp. 78-88) applies to prophetic witness. The distortion of God's creation command and the resulting perversion of creation itself become themes that the prophetic evangelist must address, just as the church, in obedience to Christ, must translate the gospel into service (*diakonia*) as one central way of doing the witness.

It has been said that the Christian church was, in the first five centuries of its existence, the most radical movement for social reform that the world has ever seen. This is certainly true if we compare the social order of the Roman Empire with that of the emerging Christian states of the early Middle Ages. However, the early Christian church never set out to be an agent of social reform. There were no programs of political or social action that constituted the church's agenda. Rather, the changes that came in legal structures, in public ethics, and in the view of the value of human life were all an effect of the prophetic thrust of the church's witness. One could not be a Christian proclaiming that Christ died for all people and still permit the exposure of unwanted infants or the carnage of gladiatorial games. If the effect of the whole gospel is prophetic, then it is likely that it will go against the current of our society, as it constantly claims our obedience in every part of our lives, both private and public.

Many Christians are deeply disturbed when the church becomes political and addresses the issues on the world's agenda. They believe that the church should restrict its activity to the preaching of the gospel, meaning that the church should emphasize salvation and its benefits in the narrow and individual sense, but not explore the full meaning of that gospel as the witness to the kingdom of God, both coming and already present in the world. Such a division is difficult to reconcile with the ministry of Jesus himself, and it inhibits the incarnation of the witness in the world—which witness God calls us to be, to do, and then to say. Certainly we should be concerned that our prophetic witness not defeat itself by dividing the church—but at the same time we must submit to the biblical message, which in both the Old and the New Testaments will allow no restriction of God's work and word to the cultic or religious compartments of life, but sets out God's claim of total lordship over us. Thus, the prophetic evangelization of the church will be the risky task of saying what this gospel means in the world that does not want to know it, and may well reject it—and perhaps persecute the prophets in the process.

Prophetic evangelization is, we must emphasize, the saying of the whole gospel to the world with specific reference to the givens of history. When we emphasize prophetic evangelization, then we must also point out a danger that will immediately present itself. The church must be very careful not to permit this world to instruct the church as to the contents of that gospel and its practical application. There is a continuing debate as to whether or not the world sets the agenda for the church (the "Hartford Declaration" of several years ago was one attempt to address this problem). The broad-ranging effects of secularization have led many Christians to accept the view that the church's task is to serve the world where there is human need (see the discussion of *diakonia,* 3.4, pp. 48-54). Those who revise the church's mission in this way often link it with the view that it is intolerant to proclaim the Christian faith in a world of religious pluralism. We must reject this pattern of revision. The task of prophetic evangelization is defined by the gospel itself—but that gospel is world embracing and is bringing about the reconciliation of all creation to God. Therefore, our prophetic address cannot be a compromise with the world's current values and goals, but must always be the announcement of God's purposes for his world together with his judgment over all that rebels against the completion of his purposes.

When some Christians in the German church began to understand the cosmic dimensions of Hitler's National Socialist program, they clearly saw that the time had come for the prophetic statement of the gospel. These Christians gathered in Barmen in 1934 to formulate a confession that would state the meaning of the gospel over against the claims of that ideological political system. The Barmen Declaration, which is now one of the most significant confessions of faith in the Christian church, was a form of evangelization. It was a saying of Christian witness directly to a state system that was asserting for itself a lordship and supremacy that only Christ may have for the Christian church . . . and the world. Certainly it was understandable evangelization—the state understood it so well that it began the programmatic persecution of all those who adhered to that confession (the movement that became known as "The Confessing Church"). But there were Christians even then in Germany who rejected the Barmen Declaration, who said that the church had no business getting involved in politics. They claimed that the authorities of the world are always there at God's behest, and we must obey them. These familiar statements limit the gospel to a narrow slice of human life, and the resulting evangelization will always address only a part of human reality and obedience. It is a tragic heresy to reduce the lordship of Christ to the religious and spiritual side of life, when he clearly said that he had been given all authority in heaven and on earth. Because of that authority, prophetic evangelization is both necessary and possible.

If, however, prophetic witness is to reintegrate the wrongly divided emphases upon the benefits of salvation and the mission of the church, then we must confront honestly the difficulty of this challenge. Here is a place for incarnational witness between Christians! The tendency to divide and to judge on these issues is so very strong, as we have pointed out frequently. Theological suspicion within the church must be overcome and replaced by our common call to enflesh the gospel to each other and thus to the world. The concern for doctrinal purity (orthodoxy) must be linked with the concern for radical obedience to the gospel (orthopraxy), not as a cheap compromise, but as a maturing vision of the gospel, which is shaping and changing all of the groups within the church. As our sense of "the gospel before us" grows, as we learn to do our theology modestly, we will find God's Spirit enabling us to work zealously for a unity (Eph. 4:3) that serves rather than dilutes our evangelical witness. If our prophetic witness is to have credence in the world, we must submit to God's (perhaps chastising) guidance to enable us to accept and even glory in our diversity, while refusing to divide the Body of Christ.

Part Four

BECOMING THE CHURCH OF INCARNATIONAL WITNESS

"But grace was given to each of us according to the measure of Christ's gift. . . . And his gifts were that some should be apostles, some prophets, some evangelists, some pastors and teachers, for the equipment of the saints for the work of ministry, for building up the body of Christ, until we all attain to the unity of the faith and of the knowledge of the Son of God, to mature manhood, to the measure of the stature of the fulness of Christ."

—*Ephesians 4:7, 11–13*

Ten

CORRECTING
THE CHURCH'S COURSE

10.1 A CAUTIONARY APPROACH TO CRITICISM

There is no lack of criticism of the church today, ranging from the serious to the frivolous. Since it is so popular to criticize the church, I must clearly be very cautious in how I proceed at this point. There have been implied criticisms of the churchly reality throughout this book, but it has been my desire that the reader understand these critical judgments against my basic presupposition that the church is God's work in history. Thus, while criticizing, I am confident that God will complete what he has begun through this unlikely instrument, his called-out people. My critical remarks are born out of a deep commitment to the church's mission, a love for it as the Body of Christ, and a great excitement at what God is continuing to do through it. Its weaknesses are, in a sense, a part of its glory, for we constantly experience God working in and through its frailty. That is not, of course, a justification of churchly sin, but a cause to praise God's gracious willingness to complete his purposes through such surprising means as the Old and the New Israel.

The art of criticism, when directed toward the church, is a particularly appropriate example of how to deal with Christian diversity without permitting it to be divisive. We know that many of the divisions of the church have resulted from disagreement on very ecclesiastical questions, matters such as the theology and practice of the sacraments and of the priesthood. It has been my contention that we must, for the sake of the church's incarnational witness in the world, learn to work with our diversity, both theological and ecclesiastical, without permitting it to divide (or to continue to divide) the church. Just as we must do "modest theology," we must do "modest criticism." Parenthetically, I might add that this concern for diversity should be far more central in the ecumenical discussion today. Our discussion of unity needs to be conducted in combination with a theological evaluation of the fact of and even necessity for diversity in the church, so that we discover the biblical nature of unity, which includes diversity.

I submit my critique fully aware that it has its limitations, and I hope to experience those limitations in any responses this book might receive. Although I attempt to work beyond the "boxes" of my own background, race, theological and social conditioning, these factors, together with the sinfulness that is present in all humanly conducted theology, will always leave their imprint on my thinking. It will require the insight of others, coming from other "boxes," to correct and expand my vision. That does not lessen my wholehearted concern for the questions I am raising, but it does mean that I expect both my questions and my answers to be altered by others who are concerned, as I am, for the theology of the church's mission.

Modest criticism, as I hope that I am practicing it, should be a constructive contribution to the "emerging theological consensus," as Avery Dulles helpfully describes the process through which the church formulates and clarifies its thinking. This theological consensus is in a state of fluctuation and expansion with regard to our understanding of the church's mission today. I find the process stimulating and encouraging. There appears to me to be a greater willingness to listen to all sides, to expect God's guidance from any and all quarters of the church, and to move out where we have not been before in our ecclesiologies. Of course, that process is only a positive one if it, too, is conducted incarnationally; that is, if we criticize lovingly, with Christian compassion for those with whom we disagree, certain of our greater commonality in Christ.

In this spirit of cautionary criticism, I need now to address the corrections I see as necessary to the church's course, if in fact we are to be Christ's witnesses, to do the witness, and, then, to say the witness.

10.2 CHANGING HOW THE CHURCH VIEWS ITSELF

A few decades ago, when the theology of Bultmann was in vogue in Germany, several of us who were engaged in the translation of German theology into English debated the best translation of his fundamental concept, *Selbstverständnis*. The literal translation, which was most often used, was "self-understanding," which certainly will work. Bultmann's concept sought to convey his concern for the importance of the Christian's understanding of his or her life and future under the impact of the gospel. But I found another suggestion to be quite illuminating: the term could be more aptly translated "self-interpretation." This implies that the Christian does in fact interpret his or her existence as a believer, and that this self-interpretation needs reflection in terms of both its content as well as its process. Regardless of where one stands with regard to Bultmann, I think that it is very important for the church to examine its self-interpretation. What does the church believe it is for, and how does it go about carrying out that task? In particular, what do we learn from the possible (or even certain) discrepancies between the confessional definitions of the church's purpose and its experienceable reality?

If our understanding of the church's mission as the being, doing, and saying of incarnational witness is true, then the church's self-interpretation as it has evolved through the years must be revised. I look upon this revision as a process inherent in the church's reality as a people underway, or on pilgrimage. Thus, such a call for revision is not meant as an indictment of earlier generations of Christians, although a certain amount of critique is unavoidably implied in any statement one might make. To change the church's self-interpretation must mean that there are aspects of that interpretation, as it has been done in the past, that do not accord with our view of the church's mission now, although we are also the debtors of that very tradition we would revise. Thus we resemble young adults who love their parents and yet must learn to move beyond their parents' limitations, without diminishing either their love or their gratitude for what their parents did for them.

Our study of the church's history should acquaint us with all the influences and challenges with which the church had to cope, which molded its self-interpretation at any given time. This knowledge will make us cautious about overly harsh criticism. We do not live in the situations of the saints who have gone before us, and thus we really are not entitled to dismiss their decisions as though we would have done better or otherwise in their shoes. At the same time, our historical study will show us how our own situation has changed, which insight can enable us to make decisions other than those made by our predecessors. We can learn from these earlier generations, not to reproduce what they did, nor to condemn it, but to be responsible and more enlightened students of our own time and history so that we can enflesh the gospel understandably now.

A notable example of this process has taken place in the western and central European churches of the Reformation tradition in the last decades. After more than ten years of theological discussion, a joint commission of all these churches drafted an agreement that has been named the Leuenberg Agreement (or Concord), because the commission met and worked in the village of Leuenberg on the outskirts of Basel. This significant statement presented a theological basis for the establishment of the "fellowship of churches," meaning that all the signatory churches have agreed to respect and acknowledge each other's ministries, sacraments, and church membership. The agreement, which has since been signed by the vast majority of the churches deriving from the Reformation, has resulted in a new sense of unity that is not organizational (the churches are largely geographical entities anyway) but theological. For our purposes, it is helpful to see that the agreement specifically states that the reasons for division four centuries ago may have been valid then, but they are no longer relevant to the churches today. It is that sense of historical change, creating new opportunities for decision in the church, that should be nurtured, I believe, when we begin to criticize the church today and to advocate change.

Critique of the churchly reality today becomes an ever-growing necessity as our grasp of the meaning of Scripture grows. The results of critical scholarship in the last centuries, although resisted and even feared by many Christians, have in fact made it possible for the church today to understand Holy Scripture in terms of the authors' original meanings far more accurately than Christians did in the past. This has led to necessary corrections in many areas of theology. And it is leading us today to new insights about the biblical teaching on the church's mission and nature, which must necessarily result in corrections and a certain amount of modest criticism of the church as it has evolved.

There are, I think, three major areas of self-interpretation that require correction, if my understanding of the church's mission is accepted and translated into the church's life and ministry. These corrections have to do with the church's interpretation of its historical nature, of its role with regard to salvation, and of its organization for its task.

The Church in History: Temple versus Tabernacle

With regard to the church's interpretation of its role in history, I suggest that the church has developed, from early on, a "temple" interpretation of itself, whereas the biblical image of the church is more the "tabernacle" of the Old Covenant. The difference between these two images is profound. The temple is an unmovable building, a center for religious activity, even a headquarters for a religious elite or a group of religious professionals. It tends to be an end in itself, a massive building housing an organization whose commitment is to its continuation as it is. Temples often are walled compounds, separated from the world without, architecturally symbolizing a chasm between the so-called sacred and the secular. Temples can be places in which religion functions as an arcane discipline, reserved for the initiates. They are built to last forever, to resist change, to maintain their form and activity in as pure a fashion as possible.

Tabernacles, on the other hand, are a unique expression of a people's faith. The "tent-church" of the Old Covenant was not permanent but moved with the people whenever they followed God's leading into new territory. The furnishings of the tabernacle, and the acts of worship and community that took place there, constantly focused the people upon their God, his actions on their behalf, his presence in their midst, and his will and direction for their future. Israel symbolized and celebrated her faith in this tent-church. It carried both the history and the future hope of Israel's faith within it, and stood as a constant reminder of her identity as God's chosen people. At the same time, it was designed and equipped to be mobile, responsive to change, and to provide what the people needed spiritually as they continued their pilgrimage from bondage to the promised land.

Thus, the tabernacle maintained a dual function: it was clearly temporary, but at the same time it was the clear sign of God's enduring presence in the midst of the people, pointing to Israel's calling to be used by God for his purposes. Israel did not have to travel far to experience God in one holy place. He resided with them, and they were holy because he was there. The tabernacle was still a center for the practice of religion, but that religious activity was, by its very nature, intimately related to everything that was happening outside the tented walls of the building.

My contention is that the tabernacle is closer to the New Testament image of the church than is the temple. We have mentioned earlier that Peter refers to the Christian community as the *diaspora,* the aliens or pilgrims, when describing their situation in the world in his first epistle. The early church clearly had that sense about itself. Its first self-denomination was "the followers of the Way," which conveys the sense of movement and pilgrimage that we find in Peter and in the image of the tabernacle. The early use of the sailing ship as an artistic symbol of the church captures the same motif.

But very early in its history, the church began to adapt itself to the temple mentality. We see this in its architecture, once Christians began to build buildings or adapt other religious buildings to their use. Gradually, the accoutrements of temple worship crept into the church (we really cannot sort out how and when), so that within a few centuries we have altars, priestly orders, and many of the features of the temple-oriented religions that thrived in the Mediterranean world. This development went hand in hand with the evolution of the church's interpretation of its role in salvation, and of its organizational structure, as we shall shortly discuss.

As the Christian church became more and more woven into the fabric of society and government in the Western world, its temple self-interpretation expanded and hardened. The church became the central institution in the typical town or village, symbolized still today by the church steeple that dominates the skylines of Europe and America. The distinction between secular and sacred developed into a system according to which all of social life, even the practices of calendar keeping, was regulated. Rather than being understood as a pilgrim people, following God through history, the church was seen as a great unchangeable and permanent presence in the world, guaranteeing those central and sacred realities that the haphazard course of human history could not affect. In that position, the church exercised great power. But we must regard that power as a threat in many ways to the church's obedience to its primary calling. We shall return to that problem in the next section.

At this point, however, I would like to illustrate the temple self-interpretation, as it tangibly affects the ministry of the church, with two brief incidents from my experience as a minister on the staff of a large Presbyterian church in the 1960s.

The nation was in the midst of the youth revolt, and the main streets of our city thronged with young people "dropping out and turning on." Under the visionary leadership of the minister to students at our church, we began to develop an outreach ministry to this alienated youth culture before our doors. Among other things, an innovative and creative coffee-house ministry was established. As young men and women began to respond, we felt the need to conduct worship for them in a form in which they would feel more at home. This was not a criticism of the honored and beautiful worship at our church (in which I had grown up and which I loved), but the recognition that worshipers from that youth subculture simply could not relate initially to our traditions.

I was working in the Ministry of Christian Education and had to deal both with the design of that experimental worship as well as with the Christian nurture of the young people who had been raised in our church family. The young people in our own high-school group began to complain about the presence of all these "other kids" on our church campus. They said that they "had to be with those freaks at school all week and did not want to be with them on Sunday as well." I began to realize that, in our highly effective and disciplined system of Christian nurture, we had created a temple mentality—our young people looked upon the church as a fortress behind whose walls they could retreat from their world. The separation between sacred and secular was a comfortable one for them—but, of course, it meant a total reversal of the definition of the church's mission! While we could arouse their interest in missionary activity abroad, it was much harder to motivate them to mission with the members of their own culture to whom they found it difficult and distasteful to relate.

Similarly, when we began our experimental worship early on Sunday mornings, before the regular worship services, an unexpected reaction came from some (by no means all) of our members. Some worshipers began to complain that they did not want to see or pass by these unusual looking young people as they proceeded to their customary pews for worship at 9:30. It bothered them to share the room with these "others." We compromised by starting the youth service earlier, at 8:19 A.M. (we called it "the 8:19," making a problem into a virtue), and insured that it was over by 9:00, so that there would be a thirty-minute break to clear the room. But we felt that our compromise was in some ways foul, because it was conceding that for many, the church was to continue to protect its members from the evangelistic challenges of the world within which God had placed it. This, again, was temple mentality at work in the church.

The church as temple has thus interpreted itself in terms of its permanence and stability, its theological purity and rightness, and its faithfulness to its past. This self-interpretation has not meant that God has not been present, alive, and at work in the church through the ages. It would be both poor theology and poor history to assert that. But at this juncture in time, after centuries of secularization with the accompanying removal of the church from the center of society and public life, we must ask if God has not brought us to a rediscovery of our essential nature as a tabernacle church. Modern history may have forced the church to shift and even, apparently, to lose ground. But perhaps we can regard this process not as a lamentable step backward, but as an opportunity for the church to regain its mobility, its dynamic responsiveness to God's command, and thus become more obedient to its mission.

And yet, I see vast congregational establishments building impressive "plants" (a curious word to use for the church!) and developing activity programs that enlist virtually all the leisure time of all the members. At least, that often appears to be the goal of our most active (and, for church-growth specialists, most praised and studied) churches. Are not life-encompassing programs as effective a form of temple building as medieval cathedrals? Do they not effectively remove the Christian community from witness in the world? Do we not, in effect, create immature Christians and unusable witnesses if we provide an alternative social life for our congregations, so that they do not even have the time to be light and salt in the world in which they live?

Temples, especially modern ones, are expensive and complex institutions. Their development and maintenance must be the consuming passion of their leaders. Rather than using the Spirit's gifts for incarnational witness in the world, we find ourselves constantly planning and making strategies to increase our membership and especially our giving, in order to keep up with inflation. We call upon the most sophisticated technologies, be they in advertising, public relations, programming, or even in data processing, to maintain and expand the temple. The mission is to attract more people to the temple, and to make them members. The immediate problem is to provide enough activity in these churches to keep the people "involved." "Parish programming" becomes the overarching definition of ministry. The question is unavoidable: Are we working for the temple, or is the temple serving us? To be sure, the call of the gospel is a summons to become a part of the witnessing community, and membership in a congregation is the necessary tangible expression of that fact. But this membership is intended to be incorporation into a serving and witnessing community. The primary thrust of the church is its call to be, do, and say the witness in the world. The temple is a reductionist form of the church, since its evangelization often emphasizes "Come and join us," rather than "Come, join us, and be equipped to go back into the world with us."

Such criticism of the church today must, of course, be cushioned with understanding. We are, in fact, living in a threatening and rapidly changing world, and the psychological need to have the church "not change" is not hard to grasp (we shall return to the "psychological bondage of the church" below). However, if we properly understand the church as called to incarnational witness, then we must counter this tendency with biblical teaching and preaching that will center us on what God has called and equipped us to be, to do, and to say.

Certainly I am not denying the important ministries that are conducted by large churches with great resources. Such churches have very impressive capabilities for ministry. For example, the great music of the church can be performed in some churches, inspiring the whole community of Christ. In other words, such specialized ministries that would not otherwise take place can be carried out by large and complex congregations. It would certainly not serve the reality of the church to insist that congregations should not be larger than a certain specified size.

But those in such churches need to address very specifically the theological problems inherent in the temple mentality. Their own understanding of their mission must be scrutinized, and the conforming forces of budget, size, complex organization, and public relations should be confronted—they could well be the modern form of "the principalities and powers" that threaten the church's integrity.

It is not impossible for a vast modern "temple" to become a tabernacle church. Of course, the number and size of the church buildings is ultimately not the issue, but rather the definition of the church's mission and the actual way in which a congregation carries out incarnational witness in its setting. This could be determined in any given congregation only by an evaluation of the self-interpretation of the members and the staff. If the members did, in fact, understand themselves as commissioned for incarnational ministry and perceived their task to be an equipping community for that ministry in the world, then, regardless of size, the temple mentality would not be a problem. If, however, the membership interpreted itself more as "consumers" of the religious services provided by the professional staff, and thus the staff understood itself as the "real ministers," then there is probably a temple complex at work.

Even the medieval cathedral, as architecturally impressive as it is, has frequently proven itself to be an effective form of tabernacle ministry. This is being discovered again today as these large churches in the centers of European cities are finding ways to minister to the business community and to the street society. The Roman Catholic church has maintained the temple image of the church perhaps as much as any tradition. And yet it is undeniable today that the Catholic church, in particular in some of its most traditional and protected forms of ministry, is revealing a capacity for dynamic change and incarnational outreach that is inspiring. The issue really is one of theological self-interpretation. A church can be a tabernacle in a Gothic cathedral, and it can be a temple in a remodeled urban store or a tent.

As we study our past to learn from what God has done through the church, we can be thankful for the vast resources of experience that serve as the church's mentor today. But we must also recognize that there are chapters in our past to which we cannot and should not return. Where we find a temple mentality in the church today, we should be made cautious by that very history whose debtors we are. Those who resist change in the church today should begin to study and learn from the tabernacle nature of the New Testament church. There may well be other, nongospel reasons behind attempts to maintain or restore the temple church; this could be the expression of the various kinds of bondage that I will discuss below. The church of incarnational witness, however, will be a tent church, moving among the people and bringing God into their very midst. And such a church will never assume that it belongs entirely in its culture and historical setting, but will always know that its destination is beyond time, and thus it can sail without fear through the "ocean of time."

The Church and Salvation: Witness to Salvation rather than Dispenser of Salvation

Closely related to the correction of the church from temple to tabernacle is the question of the church's view of its role with regard to salvation. Here I need only to state briefly what I have been emphasizing throughout this book: When the church began to see itself as an institution that conveyed the benefits of salvation upon its members, it moved very far from its original calling. We cannot deny that, with this self-interpretation, the church itself has been the major source of the dichotomy between the benefits of salvation and the responsible mission of the witnessing community. The very theological structures of the church's faith have often maintained this distinction, reducing the Christian's discipleship to moral accomplishment, obedience to the church's rules and regulations, and participation in the rites of the church. To do these things was to gain assurance of one's own salvation, and this has been presented as the major purpose of the gospel and the calling of the church—to dispense the assurance of salvation.

When the church is seen as a depository of salvation, then both its mission and the biblical understanding of salvation are distorted, as we have shown. The market in indulgences in the early sixteenth century, which finally led to Luther's revolt, was an outgrowth of the concept of the church as the dispenser of salvation. The indulgence was the church's way of passing along to its members the alleged benefits of grace stored up in its spiritual treasuries, to compensate for these members' shortfall in grace, which would keep them (or their loved ones) in purgatory. Grace had become a thing that the church could possess and distribute. Luther raised the trenchant question, "If the church has the power to release all tortured souls from purgatory, then why does it not graciously do so?" If the church controls grace, why should it not dispense it freely? But grace is not a commodity to be dispensed, and salvation is not merely an individualized condition one seeks to attain and to keep (see the discussion of the three tenses of salvation, 5.2, pp. 78-88). We need to draw the benefits of salvation and the responsibility of the saved together in order to grasp again that the church is called out, set apart, and enabled to witness to the salvation that God intends and is completing for his entire creation.

To be freed of the role of a "dispenser of salvation" is to lift an enormous burden off of the church and to liberate it for that ministry to which it has been called. The Spirit's enabling of incarnational witness is effectively stifled when the church is made into the "dispenser of salvation." If the church sees itself as such a depository and dispenser of salvation, then it is going to have to concentrate upon itself. Its own perfection must ultimately be an overriding concern, if it is to be the credible and worthy agency that distributes the benefits of grace. But as the herald of grace, the witness to God's Good News, the church can point away from itself to Christ. Its credibility is not in its perfection but in its obedience, its willingness to be used by God, its growth toward the completion that God has promised. As the "dispenser of salvation," the church must concentrate upon itself. As the witness to salvation, the church concentrates upon Christ, and may with complete confidence leave the question of salvation in his gracious hands.

When the church corrects this error, many things change in the church's life, affecting both its theology and its practice. In its theology, the church is freed from the compulsion to develop systems that assure us of our salvation (or convict us of our damnation). Theology becomes again the study of the gospel, which equips us all for our ministry as the witnessing community. The organizational life of the church, to which we will shortly return, becomes oriented to the church's purpose of witness, and much that is not essential to or even contradicts its calling can be set aside. This correction of theological course is the primary step needed to move from the temple to the tabernacle.

Although it is no longer necessary for the church to develop either theological or organizational systems to determine who is saved and who is not, the church will still need internal disciplines to determine who will share in its ministry and who will not (more about that below)—but that is not a salvation question. All that the church needs to think about and work on is its faithful execution of its calling to be Christ's witness. That is such a massive and marvelous self-interpretation that the church can devote all of its energy and resources to it. When the church interprets itself in terms of witness, it can serve, it can love, it can evangelize, and it can change—with all of its confidence placed in God, who is faithful to complete what he has begun. It will focus its study of Scripture by the question: "How shall we be equipped to be, do, and say the witness?" Its worship will be reinterpreted as equipping for witness. It will not make a division between "word" and "deed" witness, because it will understand the organic nature of witness, calling upon the gifts of all its members and letting the Holy Spirit use them to accomplish God's gracious purposes.

The Church and Organization: People not Hierarchy

For this final correction in course, we return to the theme of Chapter Four, "Realism about the Church." What I presented there should be borne in mind now: the organizational or institutional structure of the church is a necessity of its incarnational reality. We make the church into a phantom and even Gnostic thing outside of history when we ignore the institutional reality of the church. However, as I also stressed in that chapter, we must insure that the institutional form of the church serves the church's calling, rather than replaces it with organizational maintenance and even survival.

The concept of incarnational witness emphasizes both the individual and corporate aspects of that witness, and it should be clear that we cannot separate these two dimensions of the church. The witness defines both the corporate life and activity of the church as well as the purpose of each Christian's life. Our theology of ministry must begin with the general ministry of all Christians, as we shall emphasize in the next chapter. But the tendency of the church has been to make a separation here where one should not be made. Linked with the temple image of the church, which requires its temple priesthood in order to function, and with the division between witness and dispenser of salvation, which reduces the membership of the church to being "consumers of salvation," is the separation between the hierarchy of the church, who do the ministry, and the believers themselves. We will turn now to the much-discussed problem of the clergy and the laity— or as some now see it, the clergy versus the laity.

The scriptural basis here is clear: there is only one "people of God" (*laos*) in the New Testament, and there is no specialized priesthood. The organizational leadership of the church (which is the topic of Chap. 11) is functional; that is, it is there to serve and equip the whole people for their ministry. We do not find any of the trappings of hierarchy in the early Christian churches. The authority of the apostles is not hierarchical but evangelical: they are the eyewitnesses to the gospel and thus its primary messengers. Their proclamation is authoritative not because of their "office" but because of their experience with Christ and his commission to them to be the initial witnesses out of whose ministry the church will emerge.

Hierarchy emerged as a social and political necessity of the church in the early centuries of its history. There is really no reason to fault that development, for reasons of the modest criticism I have already advanced. The pressures of those first decades of churchly existence were such that strong and centralized leadership was probably necessary. The problem arose (and continues) where this organizational necessity is transformed into a theological necessity. We must telescope centuries of historical development to make our point here, but it is still a valid one.

Some major theological traditions today have posited in their theologies that the church exists authentically only when it maintains certain organizational forms, offices, or historical successions. Thus, the essence of the church is sought in its organizational definition rather than in its mission. It demonstrates its true nature as the church only when it guarantees a certain hierarchical structure. The church has often linked this kind of definition with a system of spiritual estates, where its members regard as more spiritual those who have accepted the more stringent disciplines. Obviously, this kind of distinction makes the gap between clergy and laity even wider. For the purposes of church discipline, this approach has often meant that one was branded a heretic for refusing to submit to a certain organizational structure of the church, making that structure the primary theological definition of the church. When, however, we ultimately define the church in terms of various classes or levels of spirituality and of hierarchical structures, that is, when those who are in the spiritual hierarchy are considered in some sense "more Christian" than the general laity, then we must correct our course. The institution is then no longer serving the church's mission but is determining it.

We shall discuss the theology of ministry under the concept of incarnational witness in the next chapter, for at this point my concern is with our understanding of the laity, the people. A correction of course is called for in order to confront the people of God with their real calling. When we know that the church is more tabernacle than temple, and witness rather than salvation dispensary, then we must address the baptized community with its mission, which is to be, to do, and to say the incarnational witness to which we are called, in the world into which we have been placed (our dominant concern in all of Part Three). When any hierarchical structure establishes itself, it subtly—though in a very real way—removes the responsibility for mission from the laity. Almost invariably the Christian begins to feel that he or she needs only to insure that the "professional Christians" do their job, and then his or her Christian obligation is fulfilled. But if every Christian is to understand himself or herself as an evangelist, as an incarnational witness, then the church must correct the whole sense of its organization.

We need to invert the pyramidal organizational chart of the church so that the membership understands itself as the primary focus of the church's organization. That is, we need to envision the ordered ministry, in whatever form it is structured, "below" and not "above" the people. The laity need to understand that they are, in fact, the Christians on the front line, or, perhaps, between the fronts in no-man's-land. We will need to change the self-interpretation of the individual Christian as one who is a receiver of the church's benefits into a self-interpretation as servant, witness, enfleshment of this Good News in the world. This correction of course, obviously, would have to go hand in hand with the two I have already discussed. The organizational structures of the church, as its tangible reality, will require constant review and revision in order to insure that the "people of God" know who they are and what God has called them to do. (I am not being facetious when I suggest that there be "sunset laws" in the church's constitutional structures to insure regular reevaluation of the functional effectiveness of our organizations to carry out our mission.)

In a sense, we need to change our attitudes and expectations of the church. All of these corrections I am advocating intend such change. If this process of change is taking place (and I know that it will happen gradually), then the terms we use, even the emotions we have about the church will also change. Christians will begin to speak of the church as "we" rather than "they" when they interpret themselves in terms of incarnational witness. We will want to speak of the Holy Spirit more as the Teacher and Counselor than as the Comforter, when we translate *Parakletos* in John 14ff. We will read every "you" in the New Testament as applying to each of us and all of us together. Of course, we will not expect all Christians to be at the same place or level of understanding and growth—Scripture prepares us for differences of maturity. But we will know that all Christians, and not just some, are called to the "work of ministry," and are included in the "all" of Ephesians 4:13 who are intended to "attain to the unity of the faith and of the knowledge of the Son of God. . . . "

10.3 "*IN* BUT NOT *OF* THE WORLD"

In his High Priestly Prayer (John 17), our Lord prays for his disciples and those who will "believe in me through their word." He describes them as being "in the world," but they are "not of the world, even as I am not of the world" (vv. 11, 14, 16). Further, he defines their mission in relationship to the world: "As thou didst send me into the world, so I have sent them into thy world" (v. 18). The relationship between the two prepositions "in" and "of" captures much of the tension of Christian existence.

The witnessing community is being sent by its Lord into the world. But it enters into this world with its allegiance to the Lord to whom all power in heaven and earth has been given (Matt. 28:18). And so this community is in the world in Christ's service, which means that it will not fit neatly in this world. Although the vineyard of the world is the Lord's, its tenants do not respect that fact nor welcome his servants (Matt. 21:33ff.). This fundamental fact about the church in the world produces the tension that easily leads to compromises with the world. While "in" the world, the church is not to be absorbed by this world in such a way that it ends up being "of" the world after all.

From the beginning of Christian history, the church has been challenged by this aspect of its mission. How shall it go into the world and not end up being of the world? For the fact is that, to be obedient to its calling, the church must be deeply involved in the world. The gospel is to be translated into every tongue and culture. Christians will be called upon to serve as Christ's witnesses in every historical and social setting to be found upon the globe. There are to be no limits to the spread of this witness. But when we consider the universal scope of the gospel, then we must also deal with the fact that the gospel never enters into a cultural vacuum; rather, it is always going to be planted in soil that is already tilled and full of growth. The Christian church never establishes itself in an ideal situation, but always in confrontation or cooperation with what it already finds present as it follows its universal commission and goes out "to the end of the earth."

Thus, we read the New Testament documents as records of how the gospel was defined in the varying cultural settings in which the witness had begun. Nowhere does the apostle Paul define the ideal church. Rather, he shows how Christians in Ephesus may function in that culture with its givens, which may be different from those in Galatia or Rome. For a church called to incarnational witness, the challenge is always to enflesh the gospel in a particular place, within its particular givens. Language, history, tradition, customs, norms—in short, all the components of a culture—are to be vessels within which the gospel grows. That culture will be changed by the gospel, but the gospel must enter into it, and its witnesses must make this Good News understandable within each given culture.

The problem here is immediately obvious. The power of the Holy Spirit will, on the one hand, enable the church to make this witness in each given culture. But our sinful and rebellious natures must struggle with the strong temptation to allow the culture to begin to mold the gospel. The process goes both ways, usually simultaneously. As the gospel enters a culture, it begins to transform that culture. But at the same time, the culture can begin to dilute or distort the gospel. In the process of being "in" the world, the church finds itself very subtly becoming totally enmeshed and "of" the world.

Technically, the process of entrance and establishment within a culture is called "enculturation." It must take place. What we read in the New Testament is documentation of that process already happening, and we see the struggles it produces as the Christian church tries to understand its mission as a Jewish movement entering a Hellenistic world. Further, enculturation is usually accompanied by "assimilation," which is that more subtle process by which the Christian community accepts aspects of the culture it is entering, sometimes to the degree that the gospel itself is substantially changed. When the *kerygma* is translated into another language, it will find that its meaning is affected by the thought forms and grammar of that language. A particular culture's view of women, or children, or slaves will find itself accommodated within the gospel—even though these views are basically contrary to the gospel. Social patterns of authority and decision making will be incorporated into the church's theology until they appear to be biblically mandated and inseparable from the faith. The ethos of a particular political or economic system will be reexpressed in Christian terms and thereby sanctified, with the result that it can even be heretical to question such systems. Even scientific systems can be enshrined as dogma and protected by the church—we are reminded of the churchly endorsement of Aristotelian science and Ptolemaic astronomy in the Middle Ages, and the resulting struggle with the discoveries of Galileo (and perhaps some of this problem is present in the struggle some Christians have with the theory of evolution!).

Given the fact that enculturation is an absolute necessity if the church is to be obedient to its calling, and assimilation is a pervasive temptation with which the church must always struggle, it is no wonder that our Lord prays so passionately for the protection of the church as it is "in the world but not of the world." We can, I think, look back upon our history and recognize many ways in which we have assimilated too much, and where we need to be a repentant church, claiming the power of that High Priestly Prayer so that we can be freed for our ministry. I will describe some of these areas where we have become too much "of the world" as various forms of bondage. The scholarly study of cross-cultural communication and missiology in general deals with these themes more comprehensively than I will do here. The "bondages" with which I am concerned here are those which impede the church in its carrying out its mission of incarnational witness.

10.4 THE CULTURAL BONDAGE OF THE GOSPEL

In full view of the necessity for the gospel to "enculturate," to be implanted and find its means of expression in any and every human culture, we still must see the dangers to the church's calling that lurk in this process. We have already referred to the general problem of assimilation, which one might call "enculturation going too far." We are concerned with the way in which the church dilutes or distorts its call to be a witness as it proceeds to the "end of the earth." How does that happen—how does the church end up in bondage to a culture rather than being a witness to it?

Put in the most general terms, the gospel has become a cultural hostage when the culture into which it has entered is permitted to redefine the gospel. This can happen in a number of ways:

(a) The gospel can find itself being recast into the role of a "religion," fulfilling society's need for religious experience and expression. Certainly this is the most common form of cultural bondage. It is a complex and controversial theme. Karl Barth and Dietrich Bonhoeffer have spearheaded the twentieth-century critique of Christianity's degeneration into a "religion." In general, I agree with their thrust. Obviously, the basic question is one of definition: How do we define "religion"?

If we understand religion as one cultural component that addresses the human need for meaning, for a coherent system of value and life interpretations, and that provides a way to deal with the transcendent, whatever that is, then we certainly can see Christianity functioning that way. It is undeniable that Christianity often fulfills the social and cultural need for "religion" both institutionally and psychologically. In the process, the Christian faith ceases to be prophetic, ultimately ceases to be a witness to the lordship of Christ, and becomes a contributing factor to the stability of a particular society. The church's institutions and orders become integral parts of the social machinery, and its existence is guaranteed by society; in return, the church helps to guarantee society's existence. Frequently, then, the church becomes one of the "conservative" parts of society, devoted to "conserving" what has been.

(b) This cultural bondage can move from the role of "religion" to a more political and social role within cultural orders. In its most radical forms, this kind of bondage finds the church functioning as an agency of the state. There have been long periods of time in the Western world where this has been precisely the case: the centuries of state churches, and churches as major political forces in Western civilization. Even where the state church is no longer legally possible, the general expectation of the populace toward the church is that it will serve as a stabilizing factor in society, the "right hand of the government," as it were. Typical opinions one then hears about the church are these: "It is the church's job to teach us what we ought to do and ought not to do." "The church should help raise our children to know the difference between right and wrong." "The church should help us to be law-abiding citizens." "The church should not meddle in politics—its business is religion." In many instances, we see the church becoming an agency for "civil religion," providing a religious imprimatur on the affairs of state and society. Its presence conveys a sense of well-being and orderliness, together with a pleasing amount of ceremony and antiquity that are welcomed if not taken too seriously. In fact, the ethos that informs this kind of bondage was actually articulated by parents of students with whom I was once working in Germany. They were concerned that their teenage children were becoming too active in the church, although all these parents were baptized, confirmed, and church-tax-paying citizens. They said to me, "It is respectable to be a member of the church, but it is not respectable to take it too seriously!"

(c) This bondage can go so far that the church becomes the ideological partner of a secular ideology, remolding the gospel to conform to the tenets of that ideology. Christianity then becomes the partisan of political systems, the supplier of philosophical and even theological justifications for the dominant ideology, subverting the church entirely to purposes and programs that are foreign to the gospel. It blesses the weapons and sanctifies the political process, whether or not it is Christian. Perhaps the "brown" movement within the German Christian church in the Third Reich is the most blatant example of this kind of bondage: Protestant ministers blessed Storm Troopers and used the swastika as a religious symbol in worship and in church architecture, and some theologians even rewrote Christian theology to Aryanize it. But that crude example is not unique. In many ways, often quite subtle, we find the gospel being enslaved by our cultures. Our own American history demonstrates this: how often we have linked evangelical fervor with racism, anti-Semitism, party politics, and, especially today, with various forms of warmongering.

(d) We have addressed the more systemic kinds of cultural bondage in which the church finds itself: the political, social, economic, and ideological structures with which the church must cope but dares not compromise. There are other kinds of cultural bondage that weaken the church's incarnational witness as well. First is the bondage of aesthetic culture. In the Western world, society often looks upon the church as the curator of a marvelous and beautiful tradition, including its architecture, art, music, and liturgy (often understood as a form of religious theater), all of which must at all costs be maintained. This can easily become cultural bondage as well.

These truly wonderful parts of our tradition should be treasured and passed on. But they must be subservient to the church's mission and function within its incarnational witness. Certainly they can do so! Incarnational witness is not so narrow an understanding of the church's ministry that its expression cannot validly be in the oldest forms of Christian worship as well as in the most modern means of communication. We must be attentive to the motivation of our ministry: do we do what we do in the church to serve God's purposes by equipping the saints for the work of ministry? Or do we worship, sing, and build as we do because these things are "beautiful," or actually glorify their makers more than our Creator? Any reason other than obedience to the gospel is basically unallowable for the church of incarnational witness.

(e) We also see the church entangled in forms of psychological bondage. This is another way of talking about the effects of the benefits-mission dichotomy, and we have referred to this problem before. If one of society's goals is "self-fulfillment," "self-realization," or any of the other current terms that define our modern preoccupation with our inner health and gratification of our needs, then we find the gospel becoming a means to those ends. The wholeness of salvation does, in fact, restore the believer to psychological health, although it may be a slow process and might even require professional therapy. However, that restoration to health is not the purpose of the gospel in an exclusive sense—as we have seen, that benefit equips the believer for service. And yet, we find the gospel incessantly being offered as a way to meet one's personal needs, "get one's act together," find health, happiness, and even prosperity.

It is a theological task of the first order to free the church from these narrow and distorted reductions of the gospel. They are a bondage that keeps the church from carrying out its mission in the world.

Whenever we see the church bending its message to suit the cultural setting in which it is located, and tailoring its services to provide support and encouragement to the political and economic ideologies of the world at the cost of the gospel's own prophetic voice to those systems, we have cultural bondage. Whenever Christians link their religious identity with their national identity (Americans are Christians, Poles are Catholics, and so on), then we must suspect that cultural bondage is present to some degree. Whenever we find that biblical themes cannot be comfortably taught and preached in a certain setting (i.e., we will anger the members or jeopardize giving if we deal with certain doctrines in Scripture), cultural bondage may be at work.

The distinctions we are making are not easy ones. Since the church never works in an ideal setting, it is always struggling with its culture. As we said at the beginning of this section, the problem is in finding how to function as incarnational witness within a culture, articulating the gospel understandably, without distorting or diluting it. The church is not necessarily called upon to be a revolutionary force in every society. It is quite plain from the New Testament that neither Jesus nor the apostles sent the church out to revolutionize the social, economic, and political systems of that day—and those systems were by no means models of human justice and righteousness. But neither was the church merely to acquiesce to the systems of the world. The governing principle is faith in Christ: "Every spirit which confesses that Jesus Christ has come in the flesh is of God. . . . Whoever confesses that Jesus is the Son of God, God abides in him, and he in God" (1 John 4:2, 15). As believers, all Christians are to be Christ's witnesses, which is the overarching thrust of all New Testament teaching about Christian existence in the world. As far as possible, Christians should be a constructive part of the world in which they live, honoring authority, proving the gospel through the integrity, honesty, and goodness of their lives.

But when there is a conflict, Christians "must obey God rather than men" (Acts 5:29). The issue here has always been to identify the conflicts. In the process of cultural bondage, this equation has often been given: To obey God = to submit to this political system or that idology, to be a law-abiding citizen, to contribute to public order, to conform. If we reduce the gospel to the benefits of salvation, and reduce the church to being the dispensary of salvation, then it is not difficult to privatize Christianity, and to justify all of its compromises with the world. Cultural bondage does not appear then to be a problem. To be "in" the world has come to mean to be "of" the world, and there is no sense of tension or struggle left within the church. In this situation, much of the New Testament teaching becomes irrelevant, or must be reinterpreted to a compromised church in such a way that it does not challenge its bondage.

However, if the church understands the gospel as we have defined it, especially in terms of its wholeness, its focus upon reconciliation, its three tenses, and its dynamic discovery in history, then it will have to see this kind of cultural bondage as a threat to Christian truth and obedience. The benefit-mission dichotomy easily makes its peace with cultural bondage. But incarnational witness, understood as being, doing, and saying the whole gospel, will respond to cultural bondage with a firm No, and thus the church of incarnational witness will be a threat to the worldly systems in which it finds itself. It will also be a threat to the religious revision of Christianity, which has made the church so thoroughly a part of culture that it no longer senses the tension between the "in" and the "of." Outwardly, in that world, persecution may result. The church's witness may not be as "successful" by certain standards of measurement. Growth may not be as fast or as large as desired. A very difficult process of theological disagreement may well surface, one that threatens to divide the church (remembering that even the church in bondage is still the church of God's making). These things are all a part of the cost of being free of cultural bondage.

The effect of cultural bondage is theological. It changes the gospel. In effect, it domesticates and tames the gospel. By reducing it to a cooperative religious component in society, by making it a functional part of the cultural machinery, we deprive it of its prophetic thrust and fit it neatly into our systems. To reduce the gospel to systems of right and wrong, good and bad, to a schedule of religious celebrations that enhance our lives, to a philosophical rationale for our jurisprudence, to civil religion, may contribute to "a better life"—but these are only parts of the whole. Taken out of their context within the biblical message of salvation history, they become distorted and ultimately even replaceable. A "world come of age" (Bonhoeffer) discovers it does not need this God nor the trappings of this religion. And the dismissal of this domesticated, truncated, tamed Christianity is taken to be the dismissal of all that the Christian faith ever was and ever could be.

We domesticate the gospel whenever the church has lost its sense that "the gospel is always before us." Then the church is probably assuming that it has a comprehensive grasp of the gospel, that its dogmatic systems are an adequate summary of the truth, and that the way in which the church is carrying out its witness is also adequate. Such assumptions jeopardize the church's obedience to its calling. A tamed gospel, while containing truth, does not contain all the truth and is not open to discovering more of that truth. The gospel that we domesticate to fit our needs is ultimately a betrayal of the Lord whom we serve. It is at this point that we must set our priority in the church: to study and consider the gospel and our versions of it, in order to discover what we are leaving out, what we are bending to fit our situation, and what we are one-sidedly emphasizing to the point of distortion.

The final paradox is that this church in cultural bondage is still the church of God's making! The enculturation and assimilation process do not take place outside of his sovereignty. Even when our sinful reductions and domestications of the gospel take place, God is not banished from the scene. Although he does not forcefully overrule our rebellion and its effects in the church, he does not forsake his work, and he even makes our frailty serve his purposes. The cultural bondage of the church is wrong and must be corrected. But we are all Christians today who have received the gospel from a church that has been compromised in all of the ways described above and many more through the centuries. That imperfect instrument has still been used by God, which only affirms his graciousness but does not justify our human sinfulness as a church needing correction and continuing reformation. God surprises us with the ways he works in and through our very ambiguous history!

When the Enlightenment came over the European church, it led to radical dilution and reformulation of the faith. The traditional churches of Europe began to hear sermons from their pulpits that had little to do with the Christian faith. The texts were assigned and the themes were established by the liturgical year. Each Sunday received a specific text on which the minister had to preach. On Easter Sunday, there was an Easter text on which he had to preach. But the creativity of the enlightened mind was up to the task; we have records that illustrate how they solved this intellectual problem: they preached on the virtues of "taking walks early in the morning"! Obviously, resurrection was no longer a message for modern man! When he had preached the sermon, the minister then had to return to the altar and repeat the liturgy of the ancient tradition, including the prayers, the creeds, and the affirmations of faith that the dominant ideology of the day was criticizing and rejecting. The state church, with its conservatism and durability, insured that the gospel was still spoken at the altar, even when its denial was preached from the pulpit. In that cultural bondage, for both the altar and the pulpit were in bondage at that time, God still insured that his word was heard.

Thus, when we emphasize the cultural bondage of the church, we are addressing our problem as a called people who wander so easily away from our calling. But God has not ceased to be faithful, to issue the call, and to provide the Spirit to enable us to respond. The issue is one of our hearing and obeying. For the call to incarnational witness has not changed, the opportunities are certainly there, and the strength to do it is given.

Eleven

MINISTRY
FOR INCARNATIONAL WITNESS

11.1 GENERAL MINISTRY AND SPECIALIZED MINISTRY

The emerging "consensus" of the church regarding ministry today is that the entire church is called to the service of God, and out of that general call we then should develop our understanding of the function of "specialized ministers"—the clergy, the ordained, those who have official responsibilities in the church. This understanding of ministry accords with my definition of the church's mission as witness. Everything we have said about the nature of witness applies, clearly, to all Christians, just as it defines the very reason for the church's existence. The church's call to be Christ's witness could also be formulated in this way: the entire church is called to "the work of ministry" (Eph. 4:12), and the thrust of this book on incarnational witness could then be summarized as an exposition of Paul's injunction to "lead a life worthy of the calling to which you have been called" (Eph. 4:1). The doctrine of the church, then, is integrally related to the doctrine of Christian ethics—Christian behavior and Christian witness are inseparable realities that we should approach together in our theological work (see my appeal for a "Christian ethics of witness" in 7.4, pp. 128-32).

Language like this links us with the Reformation's emphasis upon the "priesthood of all believers," and the concern for the "theology of the laity," which has been so significant in the ecumenical movement since the end of World War II (I think here of the important work of Hendrik Kraemer on this theme). The "lay apostolate" has become a major theme of the Roman Catholic church since Vatican II, and we gratefully observe a broadening of the sense of shared ministry within the highly ordered structures of the Roman church. Lay movements have proliferated on the margins of the church, many of them called "parachurch" (see 9.3, pp. 167-74), and the numbers and vigor of these movements indicate a growing desire on the part of the Christian laity to be involved significantly in ministry. There appears to be a worldwide corrective process going on, which is revising the clergy/lay division of the church by actually changing the way in which ministry is being done. The laity is hearing again the general call to ministry, and is responding and acting.

I will not attempt here to analyze the century-long process of clericalization in the church. Rather, I will make my position clear and then discuss how this emergent sense of general ministry relates to the church of incarnational witness, and how, then, specialized ministry is to be understood within that set of presuppositions.

The entire struggle regarding ministry in the church's long history can be aptly summarized around the question of a strategic comma in Ephesians 4. Markus Barth, in his excellent commentary in the Anchor Bible, calls the first sixteen verses of this chapter "The Constitution of the Church." The chapter begins with the call to general ministry mentioned above, followed by the great statement on the oneness of that call and of the church. Much later in the course of the argument, in verse 11, the apostle presents the fact of "specialized ministers," to which we will return. But it is important for our understanding of ministry to go even farther in the text in order to examine the purposes given for these specialized ministers.

Verses 11-12 speak of the gift of apostles, prophets, evangelists, and pastor-teachers, whose purpose is "for the equipment of the saints, for the work of ministry. . . . " Our reading here is from an early edition of the RSV, which, along with other versions of the Bible, places a comma after "saints." This punctuation is an important interpretation made by translators or editors of the Bible, because the Greek original is not punctuated. Whenever that comma is inserted, the text is then being interpreted to read that the specialized ministers of verse 11 are given two tasks: "the equipment of the saints," and "the work of ministry." If the comma is left out, then the meaning is that the equipping of the saints is intended for the work of ministry that all of the saints have to do.

The effect, then, of inserting the comma is to state that the specialized ministers of the church are really the ones who do the work of ministry. And the result is the process of clericalization; that is, the remaking of the church into a divided body, with the clerics doing the actual ministry and the members receiving the benefits of that ministry. In terms of the benefits-mission dichotomy, this means that the select group of ministers or clergy carries out the mission, while the much larger general membership simply receives the benefits, which are normally channeled through the clergy.

If we truly believe that the "work of ministry" is the task and mandate of all the saints (i.e., all who are called and set apart to serve Christ as his ministers), the comma-less interpretation is the preferred one (Markus Barth gives a helpful survey of the history of interpretation). We can broadly understand this work of ministry if we consider the meaning of *diakonia,* the Greek term used here (see 3.4, pp. 48-54). *Diakonia* describes our work as serving Christ by continuing the incarnational ministry he both carried out and enables us to carry out as his disciples. The spirit of that work is that of a servant—that is built into the word used here in Greek. But it is a service ("ministry" means service) that Christ himself established for us as he taught his disciples to reject the world's models of authority and leadership and to chose to serve instead. It is a service that combines both the idea of "waiting at table" and carrying out "the ministry of the word" (the same word serves in both cases in the New Testament). There is nothing triumphalistic about Christian ministry: it is service in the imitation of Christ. That spirit must also permeate the evangelistic service of the church: it is not truly incarnational witness if it does not convey the humble, other-directed spirit of Christ's own ministry. His washing of the feet of the disciples was the final "picture lesson" for this fundamental concept of ministry—from that incident, we as the church are to learn how to carry on the apostolic tradition as those who do the work of ministry. This is what we are called to be, to do, and to say: to serve Christ by serving the creation under his lordship as his witnesses.

Thus, being, doing, and saying the witness can be restated as "doing the work of ministry," which defines the purpose for the calling of the church. Out of that general definition, we can then develop our understanding of specialized ministry. I am persuaded that the biblical theology of the church does, in fact, include the specialized ministry. We will not properly resolve the justified concern that we not divide the church into two classes, the clergy and the laity, or the more spiritual and the less spiritual, if we seek to remove all distinctions between clergy and laity. We need to understand this specialized ministry as it relates to the general call of the church; we need to see that the specialized ministers are a part of the *laos,* the people of God, and have their identity and their particular function in relationship to that *laos.*

When we work out our concept of specialized ministry in terms of incarnational witness, then, we will immediately recognize that this ministry is not to be seen as a mediator between the people and God, and certainly not as a spiritual hierarchy placed over the people of God (we criticized that view in 10.2). I have suggested that the organizational chart of the church be an inverted pyramid, with the broadest section at the top, representing all the people. Beneath it on the chart I would place the specialized ministers, who are best described as the "servants of the servants of God" (an expression used for the pope, which John XXIII revived in his unique ministry).

Having emphasized that there should be a specialized ministry, but that it must be seen in its servant role toward the general ministry of the whole church, we can then define its function in terms of Ephesians 4. The basic idea, beginning in verse 7, is that Christ gives himself graciously to the church in the form of specialized ministers, who are described here as apostles, prophets, evangelists, and pastor-teachers. It is helpful to work with a scholarly commentary on this text, such as Markus Barth's Anchor Bible commentary on Ephesians, because the translation of the original language presents difficulties. The thought of Christ's gift out of grace, initiated in verse 7, is interrupted by a parenthesis in verses 8-10, dealing with the theme of ascent and descent. Then it resumes in verse 11, where it is more helpful to read, "And his gift was that some should be. . . . " Then follows this particular list of people who are the expression of Christ's gracious gift of himself. (This is certainly an incarnational understanding of ministry as the continuation of the work of Christ in the church!) We should not regard this as an exclusive list of the specialized ministers, however. Other functions of ministry are found in the New Testament literature, and we should derive our understanding of these functions from all of the relevant passages. What is important in this particular text is the emphasis upon the gracious gift of Christ in the form of persons who have particular functions in the church.

This emphasis, to restate our main point, ties in with the central thrust that all ministry, both general and specialized, is a continuation of the work of Christ. There is no ordering of higher and lower ministry; rather, there is a distinction of interdependent functions. The "offices" listed in verse 11 are such functions, and they will, in fact, overlap.

The apostolic function can be said to be foundational for all other expressions of specialized ministry: the apostles are those sent out by Christ to carry out his mission in the world, and the entire church is built upon their message and their work. It is questionable, however, whether the apostolic office, as the foundation of the church, should evolve into a hierarchy of superior and inferior offices. Rather, the apostolic office defines *all* ministry, and is expressed in the broad diversity of ministry both in the early church and throughout the history of the church. The church is "apostolic" (as we confess in the Nicene Creed) when it faithfully continues to carry out the apostolic witness in its entire life and work.

Prophets are those, as we have said before (9.4), who address the Word of God to specific historical situations. Evangelists (9.3) proclaim the gospel to nonbelievers, calling forth faith and founding churches. Pastor-teachers (I agree with the translation of the last "office" as one function, best described with the hyphenated form "pastor-teacher" or "teaching-pastor"; see Markus Barth) combine the functions of teaching the faith with the shepherding care of the congregation. The latter function has become the primary definition of formal ministry, with the other forms frequently finding their expression in more unconventional ways (e.g., the missionary movement can be said to be an expression of "evangelism" that developed when the established European churches had largely lost sight of the importance of this particular specialized ministry).

It is important that Christ's gracious gift of himself to the church takes place incarnationally, that is, through persons. In distinction from other passages in the New Testament dealing with the gifts of the Spirit, this teaching on the gift of Christ stresses that *people* are an expression of Christ's self-giving to the church. This refers to their entire life: they do not *have* an apostolic gift or a teaching gift; rather, they *are* apostles and teachers. Out of that understanding of the way in which Christ is preparing his church for its work, we have developed all of our "orders" of ministry, seeking to provide a disciplined structure for the acknowledgment of these gifts of people, as well as for the exercise of their ministry.

All of these "offices," however, are drawn together in Paul's central definition of their purpose: "to equip the saints for the work of ministry." If the general call of all Christians is to "the work of ministry," then the task of these specialized servants is to equip all of the saints for that work. The saints are, as we have said, all those who are Christians, who are called to Christ's service as witnesses. The work to which they are called is not easy. We have seen, I believe, that under-standing and carrying out incarnational witness is not a simple task, but rather a life-embracing commitment. To do that, the saints require preparation. We have already emphasized, when discussing the "being of the witness," that it is the task of the Christian community to equip each witness for his or her ministry, and we developed this concept as a "model of the church," using the method advanced by Avery Dulles (6.3, pp. 105-11). Now we are adding to that concept a more refined understanding of the role of the specialized minister within the equip-ping community. The entire community is to equip all of the witnesses for incarnational witness, for being, doing, and saying the witness. Those who are Christ's gifts to the church as specialized ministers are especially commissioned to serve the entire body as their equippers.

In particular, these ministers are to be servants of the Word of God, whose specific gifts in regard to that Word provide the nurture and guidance that all of the saints need in order to do the work of ministry. It is significant that in this passage all of those listed in verse 11 are ministers of the Word. That is their common element: they are students and proclaimers of the Word of God. Out of that spiritual source, the Christian church is to be prepared for its work.

This view of specialized ministry both expands and narrows our common understandings of ministry. It is clear that there is a diversity of ministries here (we discussed this concept in 9.3, pp. 167-74). Nowhere in the New Testament do we find one clearly defined role that will always serve as the proper model for the specialized minister. Just as there are many spiritual gifts, there are many different functions through which Christ gives himself to the church. Our narrowing of the definitions and the practice of specialized ministry to "word and sacrament" within the local congregation is a reduction of the biblical spectrum of specialized ministries, and we impoverish the church through this restriction. Thus, we need to expand our concept of specialized ministry so that we can respond to the challenges of incarnational witness placed before the church at any time and place in history with disciplines of ministry that will equip the church for its task. We have the freedom, as the church called forth and empowered by the Holy Spirit, to organize ourselves however we need to do so, as long as we are obediently going about the mission for which we exist.

At the same time, we must remember that Paul narrowly defines all functions of specialized ministry as preparing the saints "for the work of ministry." There appears to be no place for any definition of specialized ministry that is not focused on the preparation of the saints (this, I think, can be said in general of all New Testament teaching on specialized ministry). As we have said, hierarchical functions are not foreseen, nor are priestly and mediatorial roles, nor any other specialization that would replace the work of the saints rather than prepare the saints for the work. However our churchly constitutions define episcopacy, presbyterate, or diaconate (to use the three major ecclesiastical terms for specialized ministers in the New Testament), their function in the church must always be basically one of preparation of the laity for the incarnational witness that is the church's commission.

Paul emphasizes this in a second goal for the equipping of the saints for the work of ministry: it is "for building up the body of Christ until we all attain to the unity of the faith and of the knowledge of the Son of God . . . " (vv. 12-13). There is an important spiritual promise in this passage: those who are, in fact, Christ's gift of himself to the church for equipping ministry will guide the saints toward the unity of the faith and of the knowledge of the Son of God. Neither the unity of the faith nor the knowledge of the Son of God are understood here (or elsewhere) as easy and immediate results of the Christian response to the gospel. Just as we must work hard "to maintain the unity of the Spirit" that is already given to us (v. 3), we must recognize that the Christian growth process is a difficult and demanding one, and specialized ministers are given to equip us all to mature in our faith. Mature faith will be marked by unity, and by ever-expanding knowledge of Christ (remembering that "knowledge" must be understood as a relationship, as the personal experience of Christ linked with the growing understanding of what that experience means).

If asked whether I regard specialized ministry as essential for the church or merely beneficial (the classic question of the *esse* or the *bene esse* of the ordained ministry), I would answer on the basis of this text that it is essential. But it is "of the essence" of the church because that is the way God has chosen to provide for the equipping of the saints. There is no sense in which we can directly link the issue of salvation with this understanding of ministry. When the church is no longer regarded as the "dispenser of salvation" but rather as the "witness to salvation," then the specialized, ordained ministry no longer functions as the actual dispenser of salvation benefits, but as the equipper of the heralds.

There is spiritual calling to this office, and there is spiritual gifting for the exercise of these equipping functions. It is incumbent upon the church to develop orders of ministry that will examine such calling and gifting, provide discipline for the determination of their authenticity, and then set up structures—with accountability—for their exercise; that is really what the disciplines of candidacy and ordination for ministry are for. And what the church has done throughout history by developing such disciplines is basically correct. The ordination theologies and practices err when they are taken to mean that those who are ordained are somehow spiritually special people who have a kind of salvation or a relationship with God that normal Christians do not have. This is where we must apply the concept of equipping ministry for the equipping community in order to correct our church practices and move closer to the concept of incarnational witness as the mission of the church.

Some important traditions of the Reformation are especially helpful in this regard. I believe that the church today should explore carefully the Reformed tradition, and in particular that understanding of the church's essence and ministry developed in Geneva. There is much to be learned there about the functional nature of equipping ministry, the diversity of ministry, the general ministry of all Christians, and especially about the central role of the teaching ministry.

The equipping ministry of the church must center upon the Word—we cannot tire of emphasizing that. But we should be careful not to restrict our understanding of the ministry of the Word to the "preached word." Its teaching, its study in a variety of settings and with many methods, and its translation into the daily existence of all the witnesses must be equally stressed in the life of the church. It would be helpful if our theological seminaries would examine their concept of the educated minister: Do they, in fact, envision that minister as an equipper of the community of witnesses? Are their theological curricula and their education in the practical skills regarded as necessary for ministry defined by the overarching concept of witness (i.e., of every Christian in service as an incarnational witness to Christ), and therefore are they constantly equipping their students for that ministry in the church? The popular image of both the "preacher" and the "priest" might well change if the equipping definition of ministry were translated into the practice of ministry.

11.2 EQUIPPING THE EQUIPPING COMMUNITY

How do the specialized ministers go about the task of equipping the saints for the work of ministry? The answer is deceptively simple: much of what they should do is what ministers have traditionally done, but their purpose and vision in doing so may need correcting. They will continue to administer the sacraments, to lead worship, to preach and teach the Word, to care for the members of the church, to provide spiritual counsel and guidance. But in the process, their understanding of themselves, together with their understanding of those whom they serve, their members, and their common goals, will be grounded upon the concept of incarnational witness as the primary definition of the church's mission. With this understanding, they will not do some things they have done, they will change the way they do many of their traditional activities, and they will undoubtedly do some things they have not done. And they will struggle with the patterns and under-standings of ministry that they have inherited and that call for correc-tion, but are by no means easy to change.

We can examine what this might mean by considering the tradi-tional activities of specialized ministry from the perspective of incar-national witness and equipping for it. We begin with the ancient concept of the "means of grace." Although variously interpreted in the church traditions, the "means of grace" are understood as opportuni-ties Christ gives to his church, which are rendered spiritually powerful by the work of the Holy Spirit, through which the Christian's concept and appropriation of grace are strengthened. These means of grace have included (in various listings) prayer, the sacraments, worship, preaching of the Word, as well as many of the spiritual exercises developed in the tradition of "spiritual formation." The church has closely identified the ordained ministry with the exercise of these means, often giving them the sole responsibility for their administra-tion. What happens to the "means of grace" and to the role of the ordained ministry in relation to them, when we understand the church as incarnational witness?

The first major change will come at the very beginning, at the point of our understanding of the purpose and effect of the means of grace. The church that is characterized by the separation of the bene-fits of salvation from the mission for which we are being saved primar-ily focuses the means of grace upon the issue of salvation. They are ways to guarantee our salvation, to regain it if lost (by sin), to deepen our understanding of our salvation, and, in some theologies, to convey to us our salvation. When we overcome this dichotomy, the means of grace become the means of equipping for our incarnational witness. If we know that our salvation is entirely in God's hands, and that our certainty of salvation is intended to liberate us to serve him and his purposes, then the means of grace become the wonderful source of strength for us as we seek to be, to do, and to say the witness. When we hoard the benefits of salvation with no sense of our mission, then the means of grace flow Jordan-like into our egoistic Dead Seas, accumulating more and more quantities of "grace" (for grace is easily misunderstood as a quantifiable thing in the benefits-mission dichotomy), and moving us dangerously close to the Pharisee in Jesus' parable who thanked God that he was not like other men (Luke 18:9-14). This Pharisee enumerates all the things he does, all the "means of grace" he carefully makes use of, which satisfy him that he is truly in possession of the state of righteousness and thus "saved." This is the attitude with regard to the means of grace that we must totally replace, as we experience them and their ministers as God-given resources to equip all the saints for the work of ministry.

Although it would be the subject of another book to examine in detail the actual meaning of this understanding of incarnational witness and the means of grace, we can point out briefly some of the important ways in which our traditional concepts will change.

(a) We will understand baptism differently. As the celebration of the individual Christian's engrafting into Christ's body, it will be understood as the first and central outward confession of the fact that every Christian, including the one being baptized, is being called and set apart by God to serve him. As part of that calling, the baptized ones are made certain of their salvation. They receive the Holy Spirit as the "guarantee of their inheritance until they acquire possession of it" (Eph. 1:14). Their baptism makes them into servants and witnesses of Christ, to whose saving purposes they are to witness and in whose saving work they now are enlisted.

Thus, baptism is the churchly celebration of our common call to ministry. It is the foundation of our understanding of our corporate identity as the incarnational witness to Christ. Those who administer baptism will do so then in the awareness that they are carrying out a significant part of the equipping of the saints for their work of ministry. For we derive our sainthood solely from our calling, from God's Yes to us with its enabled Yes in response. That is what we are celebrating when we baptize. We are testifying that we gratefully recognize the work of God in the life of the individual believer, whether it is by virtue of the fact that this believer has been given to Christian parents and will be raised in the faith, or by the fact that this person has come to faith as an adult and now confesses that faith while submitting to baptism and joining the company of witnesses. As many are emphasizing in the church today, baptism is the general ordination of all Christians to our common calling.

As the baptized, we are all ministers, servants of Christ. We all have to grow up into the fuller understanding of what that means. The church's equipping ministry to us is to make that growth possible, to lead us, guide us, correct us, nurture us, and then to send us out to our particular form of ministry as a witness to Christ. Thus, the theological foundation for the educational ministry of the church with its children is the sacrament of infant baptism (in those traditions that celebrate it).

(b) Confirmation, or admission to the communicant membership of the church, builds on baptism as an equipping event in the church. Here again, the focus should be upon our ministry, our service of Christ as the incarnational witness in the world. As we grow in the faith, we come to the point where we assume responsibility within the community of witnesses for both its life and leadership. That has become, since very early in the church, a step associated with admission to the Lord's Table. If we understand the Lord's Table as the supreme form of equipping, a theme to which we will shortly return, then this is a beneficial association. Thus, we should not set aside so much as revive and expand its meaning for the entire church. We need to move from some almost superstitious understandings of confirmation and communicant membership to a functional understanding: the Christian person who is "confirmed" or is now a "communicant member" of the church is one who has personally appropriated and affirmed by his or her Yes (also an enabled Yes) the calling to be a witness to Christ and a part of the witnessing community. In addition, the church should be affirming each individual witness at this point by helping that person grasp more fully his or her calling, and especially his or her gifts for ministry.

If we divorce confirmation from the narrow idea that one's eternal salvation, once sealed in baptism, is now being publicly affirmed, and expand it into the full ordination of each Christian to ministry, then it can become a tradition that is not dead, but vital and central in the life of the church. But the way in which we go about it will undoubtedly change. It appears to me that confirmation should become a central point in the equipping ministry of the church. It should not be locked into set ages and based upon social and familial traditions. The Christian man and woman who are growing in the faith should be confronted, in the context of the witnessing community, with the meaning of his or her calling to be a witness and then helped to identify his or her obedient response to that call. Whenever that spiritual realization comes, the church should celebrate it by confirming that calling and committing itself to continue its necessary ministry of equipping for every Christian in its midst. The role of the specialized ministers in this process is thus greatly expanded, for it becomes their teaching/ pastoral responsibility to lead the members of the church to these events with full understanding of what they mean, and to insure that their observance will serve the equipping of all the saints.

Confirmation, then, can help to equip the saints for the work of ministry by making each Christian's call to incarnational witness quite specific and concrete, and by knitting each Christian's part of the church's total ministry into the fabric of the church's life. It should be a celebration of calling given and received, gifts bestowed and ac- knowledged, responsibility assigned and accepted. It is, then, a signifi- cant step in the maturing process of faith.

(c) The same emphasis upon equipping for ministry will apply to our concept and practice of worship, especially of the Lord's Supper and of preaching ("word and sacrament"). We return to our early theme of the place of the church in salvation history (Chap. 1), in order to emphasize that the church is carrying out its work in the tension between the fulfillment of salvation and its consummation. It lives in the "already" and the "not yet" of the gospel, and in that realistic tension the church carries out its incarnational mission. In that context, we understand the worship of the church, and especially its celebration of the Lord's Supper, as a foretaste of the heavenly jubilee and the eternal bridal banquet. We break bread and drink wine, proclaiming "the Lord's death until he comes" (1 Cor. 11:26). Thus, our worship now is not an end in itself, but is oriented toward its own consummation when it will no longer be one day in seven, but the unending Sabbath rest. In our current position in salvation history, we gather for worship and the sacrament in order to be together in the presence of God, to present ourselves as living sacrifices to him as our spiritual worship (Rom. 12:1), to present to him our thanksgiving and praise, not only for ourselves but on behalf of the entire creation for which Christ died—and then to be reequipped to return to the world for the work of ministry. It would be too narrow a view of "work of ministry" to define it as what happens inside church buildings during worship services. The work of ministry is the total work of the church as Christ's witnesses in the world. Our assembly for worship is our preparation for that ministry.

For some, this functional view of worship and the sacrament is not "high" enough. There is a desire to elevate worship to an end in itself and, in fact, to the highest end of man. Certainly, it is man's chief end to know and to worship God, as the Westminster Catechism teaches. But we must remember that this formulation is properly understood eschatologically. That is, it is the chief end of all humanity to know God and worship him. We are still in the period of witness, the epoch of the church, obediently carrying out the Great Commission. It would be spiritual arrogance for us to assume that we are already fulfilling that definition of the "chief end of man" by reducing the word "man" to "Christians."

It is important that we do go into the church one day in seven to worship. We are not yet in the Sabbath rest. There is still the work of incarnational witness to be done. The church's worship dare not become a retreat from our calling, nor dare we assume that the church can already claim the ultimate and final celebration of salvation, which will come "when the Lord comes." We experience that glorious celebration only in the form of anticipation of it, as a foretaste of heaven, and that is a source of great joy. But we are still the Body of Christ looking forward to the bridal banquet at which he will "present the church to himself in splendor . . . " (Eph. 5:27).

It is, then, quite essential that we understand our formal worship and our celebration of the Lord's Supper as central means of grace through which we are equipped for the work of ministry. The proclamation of the Word is, therefore, of much significance. Augustine emphasized that the "visible word" must be accompanied by the "audible word." That spoken word, the means of grace of proclamation, is obviously the central and major form of equipping that takes place within Christian worship, for the Word is spoken in its most direct form here. Without even attempting to address the classic discussion of the alleged distinctiveness of preaching over against teaching, I would still insist that our understanding of the goal and the method of Christian proclamation within the witnessing community should be defined as "equipping the saints for the work of ministry." This will include the "ongoing evangelization" of the community, which we have already discussed (8.4, pp. 148-52). Where there is a tendency to treat preaching primarily in terms of its communicative methodologies and skills, and to neglect its theologically defined purpose, we need a reorientation. There is a real problem in theological education when the discipline of homiletics and communications is separated from the doctrinal understanding of the church and its mission. We must focus upon the purpose and the content of preaching, and out of that emphasis then develop our science of the methodology of preaching.

And in that process, the equipping of the saints will necessarily be the operative presupposition for the church of incarnational witness.

Every corporate expression of faith in formal worship should be experienced as equipping. It is not a lessening of our view of worship to place the emphasis upon equipping. We can understand and experience our liturgy, our music, our prayer, our preaching, and our celebration as true channels of God's equipping power, preparing us to depart from our assemblies into the actual world of the church's work. We can expect God to encounter us in our corporate worship in such a way that we are enabled to do what Christ is sending us into the world to do: to be, to do, and to say the witness.

The Lord's Supper is, supremely, such an experience of equipping. Its very symbolism is that of nurture, of feeding and providing strength. Christ gives himself to us so that we can be his bearers into the world and give him to the world. Christ gives himself in his healing lordship in bread and wine, so that we may incarnate him in our frail but faithful witness to him wherever we are. The confession of our sins and the affirmation of our pardon that are sealed in the Eucharist are essential forms of equipping for our ministry, for through this experience of grace we are again liberated from those burdens which keep us from serving Christ totally. The confession of faith we make as we come to the Lord's Table is a way in which our faith is renewed for the ongoing work of witness to that faith.

And then, those who are the specialized ministers within the church, those who lead in worship and interpret the sacraments through the spoken word, are by doing so carrying out the equipping of the saints in its most sublime form. For in their ministrations they are themselves the channels for Christ's self-giving to the witnesses. In these experiences of mediated grace, where Calvin speaks of the spiritual and thus real presence of Christ, the individual Pentecostal flames on every Christian are renewed, so that the Pentecostal mission may go on. Certainly there is nothing about this equipping understanding of the means of grace, of ministry, and especially of worship and communion, that dilutes their spiritual significance. To say that these experiences of God's real and tangible preparation of his church for its work are functional to his saving purposes is to assign to them the highest possible theological significance. We do not come to these assemblies of the faithful dependent upon our own spiritual energies to make them meaningful. We come depleted, to be filled and renewed for our work. That is their role and their promise, and that is why the disciplined and regular participation in the assemblies of the faithful is so important.

We may broaden this interpretation of equipping for ministry even further. There is much interest today in the valuable heritage of spiritual formation that has continued to flourish within the Roman Catholic, the Orthodox, and the Anglican traditions. We are finding that these spiritual exercises, as interpreted to us by Thomas Merton, Henri Nouwen, Richard Foster, and many others, are of great benefit to all Christians, even if they are somewhat foreign to many. Spiritual retreats and exercises, liturgical prayer, disciplined meditation, the varieties of prayer that come down to us through a rich spectrum of traditions, and even the counsels of poverty, celibacy, and obedience are all contributing importantly to our sense of the Spirit's work in our lives.

But the danger is also present that these spiritual riches will be taken as a means to their own ends, or as ends in themselves. The benefit-mission dichotomy can creep subtly into the whole discipline of spiritual formation and divert it—if not distort it. We should not define too narrowly the purpose of these means of grace as the spiritual welfare and maturing of the individual who practices such exercises and benefits from them. That is to dwell on the benefit at the exclusion of the responsiblity for mission. The great resources of the traditions of spiritual formation must be claimed for the mission of Christ's church in the world. To experience the reality of Christ personally in a more intensive and life-embracing way is to be better equipped to serve him as incarnational witness.

Of course, this is known and has often been stressed in the history of spirituality. Mother Theresa represents, in a challenging and humbling way, the integration of benefits and mission in her life and ministry. But we may tend to think that such remarkable examples are exceptions to a more general rule of what I must call "self-centered spirituality." Here we must insist on the functional nature of every valid means of spiritual formation. Going back to Pentecost itself, we must be reminded constantly that the Spirit entered and continues to enter the church so that we may be witnesses. To stop short of that, to cut the flow of the Spirit through us and divert it into the dead-end of our own personal spiritual edification, is to prevent that work to be done which is the very reason for the gift of the Spirit to the church.

There is no limit to the resources of the Spirit. And thus there is no limit to the possibilities for our equipping for our ministry. The ways in which the Spirit can work in us will constantly surprise us. But there will always be the temptation to follow Peter on the Mount of

Transfiguration: we, too, will easily seek to build crude human huts in order to preserve a spiritual experience the real purpose of which was to challenge us and enable us to go down from the mountain to the world that needs to encounter Christ through his witnesses. The resources of spiritual formation, like the spiritual resources of the charismatic movement today, must be understood in their evangelical purpose, that is, as God's direct equipping of us for our ministry. The Spirit does not point to itself but to Christ, and it leads us to Christ in order to make us into vessels who take Christ into the world.

My appeal, then, is that we not look upon only some of the activities of the church, such as the clearly educational programs we develop, as equipping ministries. Rather, let us define our entire life as a formal and visible community in terms of the equipping mandate of the church. And then let us define specialized ministry under that purpose, so that the saints will be equipped for the work of ministry. The leadership of any congregation should constantly be reviewing the life and ministry of that body of believers, asking the questions, "How are we equipping each other for our ministry in the world? How does our worship equip us? How do our study and small-group life equip us? How does our fellowship equip us? How does our recreation equip us? How does our administration of the sacraments equip us? How does our prayer equip us?"

Clearly, when we establish the priority of equipping, then the ministry of the Word in its richness will be made central. We are equipped for ministry as we are "transformed by the renewing of [our] mind" (Rom. 12:2), which is the function of the Word of God at the center of our corporate life. For that purpose, we need Christ's gift of ministers of the Word, but we must insure that they are equipping us, and not doing our work of ministry for us. We are all witnesses, and God's Spirit provides all the resources needed to equip us all so that we can lead lives worthy of the calling that we have received.

11.3 THE AUTHORITY OF MINISTRY

In the previous section, I presented some general theses on ways in which specialized ministry could function as the "equipping of the saints" in the practice of the "means of grace." In this final section I would like to examine the role of specialized ministry from another perspective. When we have defined the specific task of ministry as equipping, the danger still results that it can be exercised in a hierarchical fashion, and that the equipping ministry will still not produce the equipping community. I have purposely delayed the discussion of equipping ministry for this late point in this book, while addressing the equipping community quite early in our discussion. The larger and more important issue is the community: at Pentecost, God called forth a people, not a hierarchy and a people. If the equipping community is not both our goal and also the emerging result of our specialized ministry, then the equipping of the saints is not happening as it should.

Yet there are more than enough examples of that very breakdown in the process. How often do we see in the past and present reality of the church a form of ministry that is very "educational," with exciting teaching and preaching, stimulation of minds, and even statistical growth and people responding to the personality and gifts of a truly talented preacher . . . and yet, frequently, there is no equipping community and little sense of incarnational ministry flowing out of such churches! Great biblical expositors do not necessarily equip the church to become an equipping community with a sense of shared call and responsibility for incarnational ministry in the world.

It often appears that certain kinds of "equipping ministry" produce undue dependence upon the preacher or teacher, in some instances resulting in various questionable forms of a personality cult. It is not enough to say that the specialized ministry must equip the saints for the general work of ministry, which is our mission, and that ministry should actually be happening as a result of such equipping. It is possible for an "equipping" ministry to exist within the benefits-mission dichotomy, for instance. This is true, for example, if the teaching in the church focuses on salvation and its benefits for its members, or upon the maintenance of that salvation, or on the kind of separation from the world that must be exercised to guarantee that salvation. Although teaching and learning are happening, the incarnational community we have been discussing is not going to emerge. Even though "equipping" is going on, there is a subtle reversal of the pyramid, and the clergy are again at its pinnacle and the people are again underneath. And the benefit-mission dichotomy is creeping back into the actual reality of the church.

For specialized ministry to equip the saints in such a way that the whole community understands itself and functions as the equipping community, and moves into the world as incarnational witness, the specialized ministry must change its self-understanding. I suggest that the problem we are confronting here has to do with divergent understandings of authority. We may have rejected traditional understandings of hierarchy, which we Protestants often claim (with some pride) that we have done. But we still maintain a kind of spiritual hierarchy where some Christians (the preachers) are made into authorities upon whom all the rest of the church membership depend for their Christian identity. I suspect that there is often even a sense that one's salvation is somehow related to the figure of the charismatic preacher. Thus, even though the theologies represented would disclaim this, there is a salvific sense about the authority that many Protestant clergy lay claim to and exercise. Where that happens, we cannot expect equipping community or incarnational witness to result.

But the concept of authority here is, as I said, questionable. The root meaning of the term *authority* is found in the Latin verb *augere,* which means "to increase, to make grow" (our verb *to augment* still has this sense). Building on that idea, the *auctor* is "one that gives increase," "an originator, causer, doer," and *auctoritas,* which is the root of our English word *authority,* means "giving of increase, respon-sibility, support," and, in that context, "power." An author, then, is someone who increases our knowledge by what he or she originates or contributes. But the person who exercises this kind of authority is not properly understood in a static sense as one who has power, who by virtue of office has certain prerogatives and rights. Rather, this kind of authority is oriented toward what it accomplishes, what it brings about, what it stimulates in other people. It is relational and functional in nature, not static and rigid. (We can see how far we have come from this basic meaning when we consider the connotations of words like "authoritarian" and "the authorities"!)

The German educational philosopher Erich Geissler has helpfully built upon this fundamental meaning of authority in developing his concept of pedagogical authority (his book is *Erziehungsmittel* [Bad Heilbrunn/Obb.: J. Klinkhardt, 1973]). His concept of authority, which he conceives with regard to the work of the educator in a secular sense, can be applied admirably to the concept of equipping ministry that I am advocating.

Geissler defines "pedagogical authority" by use of a triad made up of three important factors in the learning process. There is, at the top of the triad, the so-called superior entity, by which he means that content to be learned in a particular field of endeavor, the insights to be passed on, the laws or norms to be learned. In our setting, the "superior entity" would be the content of the faith, the scriptural witness, the means of grace, ultimately "the knowledge of Christ" into which we are all to grow. What the specialized minister has to say, as

DIAGRAM OF GEISSLER'S CONCEPT OF PEDAGOGICAL AUTHORITY

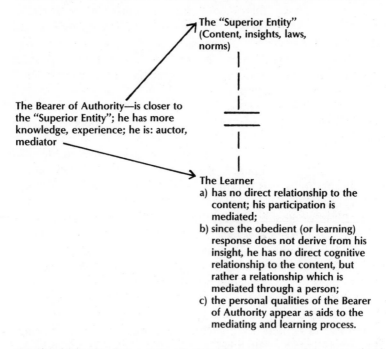

The "Superior Entity"
(Content, insights, laws,
norms)

The Bearer of Authority—is closer to
the "Superior Entity"; he has more
knowledge, experience; he is: auctor,
mediator

The Learner
a) has no direct relationship to the
   content; his participation is
   mediated;
b) since the obedient (or learning)
   response does not derive from his
   insight, he has no direct cognitive
   relationship to the content, but
   rather a relationship which is
   mediated through a person;
c) the personal qualities of the Bearer
   of Authority appear as aids to the
   mediating and learning process.

(Translated from the diagram on p. 65 of Geissler's volume cited above: used with
the kind permission of the publisher.)

a minister of the Word, so that the saints will be equipped for the work
of ministry, is the "superior entity." The lower point of the triad is the
learner, the one who hears and responds, the student (in a pedagogical
setting). There is a dotted line between the learner and the superior
entity, which is broken off in the middle—this learner does not have a
direct relationship to the content of the superior entity, but is growing
toward mastery of that content. And the agent of that growth is the
third point in the triad, off to one side. This third factor is the "pedagogical authority" (or, for our purposes, the "equipping minister").
This equipping minister is connected to the superior entity by an
unbroken line, and to the learner by a similar unbroken line.

The dynamics of this theoretical image are fascinating. What it
says about the nature of authority is this: The authority is the person
who has a more or less unbroken relationship to the content to be
learned, and also has a relationship with the learner that makes it
possible for the authority to be the mediator of that content to the

learner. The authority is closer to the content than is the learner. He or she has had more experience with it. He or she can be an *auctor,* can increase the knowledge and exposure of someone else to this superior entity.

Applied to the concept of specialized ministry, this means that the equipping minister has a grasp of the content of the Christian faith, knows the Bible and can expound it, and is gifted by God to equip the Christian community for the mission of the church. This relationship of the minister to the content and reality of the faith does not mean that this person is a "better" Christian in some absolute spiritual sense, but, rather, that this person has the gifts, the call, and the opportunity to carry out the function of equipping minister within the community.

The other line of the triad is of particular importance, however. Not only does this equipping minister have the closer relationship to the content of the faith, but this person also can establish a line of communication, trust, and mutual openness with the learner, so that the equipping process can take place. The learner, that is, the church member who is growing in his or her faith, must be able to place confidence in the equipping ministry of the "authority," must be able to rely upon him or her to mediate the content so that the learning process will be spiritually sound and lead to authentic maturity. The quality of this interpersonal relationship is, therefore, of equal importance to the qualifications of the authority in a technical or academic sense.

The authority figure, the equipping minister, mediates this knowledge to the learner, so that the learner will move closer to the superior entity, that is, will master the content, and will develop the same kind of relationship to it that the authority has. The authority functions as a "channel for the increase of spiritual growth," and, in that process, will make himself or herself progressively less needed. If the work of the authority figure in this model is effective, then there will be constant change . . . and the learner could even end up becoming the authority figure for his or her equipping minister! This is why this model will not permit a hierarchical structure. The authority position and relationships change as actual spiritual growth happens.

Geissler introduces a second theoretical model that elucidates even further this dynamic understanding of the learning relationship. He speaks of the "legitimation" and the "constitution" of authority; and, again, I find these concepts useful in defining the equipping ministry. The pedagogical authority, or, in our case, the equipping minister, must be both "legitimated" and "constituted." Legitimation

GEISSLER'S DIAGRAM ON LEGITIMATION AND
CONSTITUTION OF AUTHORITY

LEGITIMATION ———————│AUTHORITY│——————— CONSTITUTION
through law, norms,   through spontaneous
content, education   or induced willing
                                         obedience and response

There are legally   There are
qualified persons who   charismatic leaders
cannot gain a following.   who are not legitimated.

(Translated from the diagram on p. 66; used with permission.)

is the formal process of providing for the education of the equipper, that attainment of certain standards of knowledge and experience, the passing of examinations and the certification of an individual as a minister or teacher. The disciplined aspect of authority is regulated in the churches in the various orders of candidacy and education for ministry. But completing a series of studies and passing a set of examinations alone do not make a person into an equipping minister (or into a teacher). The constituting process must also take place. In a general sense, this refers to the willingness of those who are to be taught to submit to the teaching authority of the legitimized teacher. Without that acknowledgment of authority, the most highly educated person could not function as an actual teacher. For the equipping ministry, the same will be true. The gifts and call of the equipping minister must be confirmed and acknowledged by the church at large, and, more specifically, a particular congregation of Christians must be willing to accept the authority of the equipping minister by submitting to it. Apart from that submission, the legitimate authority has no ministry. But without the legitimation, the alleged authority figure might well be a demagogue, a heretic, or a charismatic figure who can command the allegiance of people but is really not qualified to serve them as an equipping minister. It is certainly true that both of these functions must be fulfilled in order for equipping ministry to happen.

This understanding of authority accords well with our concept of general and specialized ministry, because it emphasizes both the needed competence of the equipping ministry, and the relational skills of that person, so that the Christian community will be willing to learn from him or her. The authority here is not an end in itself; it is not a rigid and unchangeable thing; rather, it is a serving function of the whole community, making it possible for all of the members of the church to grow toward the maturity of faith that is our common goal. Again, the church itself must participate in the process of recognizing and acknowledging such authority—it must constitute that authority. The call and gifts of the equipping minister are fully established only when the church affirms them in a disciplined and constitutional process.

This concept of authority precludes the establishment of a person or an office as a necessity for salvation. The church does not commit itself to one structure of specialized ministry and then rigidly identify itself with that structure in order to remain the true church. The necessary dynamic of responsive change is built into the concept. What remains unchanged is the "superior entity"—the gospel, the mission of the church, ultimately the person and work of Christ. It is a dangerous error to identify the structures of the church's ministry with the unchangeable gospel. We serve the gospel as the incarnational witness to it, and to do so we must respond to the historical pilgrimage we are on by changing our forms of ministry when needed. Our guiding principle remains the Pauline definition of ministry: that the saints be equipped for the work of ministry. For this to happen, the equipping ministers must also be Christians who are, do, and say the witness to the gospel, whom God then uses to assist and support the entire community as it grows into the fullness of its calling to incarnate the gospel in the world.

Twelve

ON NOT SEPARATING
THE INSEPARABLE

12.1 AN APPEAL FOR THEOLOGICAL UNITY

When Paul defines the purpose of ministry in Ephesians 4:11ff., he stresses that the work of ministry is to lead to the unity of the church. The Body of Christ is to be built up as the equipped saints do the work of ministry, "until we all attain to the unity of the faith and of the knowledge of the Son of God . . . " (4:13a). This passage, together with many others in the New Testament, addresses the visible and experiential unity of the church in submission to the person and for the purpose of carrying out the work of Christ. For the apostles, the unity of the church is not an abstraction. It is a real and tangible component of Christian obedience.

We must see this unity, then, as a central theological concern as we are defining the church's mission. But, given the enormous theological diversity within the church, how can we talk realistically about theological unity? Let me hasten to say that I am not advocating theological uniformity, any more than I would establish ecclesiastical uniformity as the proper definition of the unity of the church. The New Testament church was very diverse . . . in terms of organization and community life, as well as in terms of theological approach. The various theological traditions within the New Testament give impressive evidence of the rich diversity with which the early church taught and understood the gospel. In their writings, the apostles urged these early Christians toward a unity that would not squelch that diversity but would, instead, incorporate such diversity fruitfully into the church's life and work.

Paul defines this unity that incorporates diversity in slightly different terms in Philippians: " . . . complete my joy by being of the same mind, having the same love, being in full accord and of one mind" (2:2). We could describe the unity at stake here as the bringing together of all the expressions and meanings of the gospel into an emerging comprehensive understanding of the "whole gospel." It is a unity of purpose, of common commitment, of experienced call and mission. It is a unity that emerges out of our common submission to Christ, not out of our uniform formulations of one official theology.

However, we have allowed this beneficial diversity to become divisive. We have set up our various theological traditions as absolute definitions of the faith, excluding all other approaches to the fullness of the gospel. We tend to divide the gospel, emphasizing the themes that comfort and please us, and often neglecting the dimensions of the gospel that challenge us. The "cultural bondage" we have discussed has often led us, theologically, to espouse one way of thinking and explaining the faith and rejecting every other possible way. Thus, we separate the components of the gospel that should not be separated, and divide the church into theological camps. Often we find that our own logical limitations lead us to impose on the gospel rational confines that ultimately are irrelevant to God the Creator and Redeemer.

Remembering that the "gospel is always before us," it should be the goal of all theological work to help the church grow toward that unity of the faith in which we experience more and more of the meaning of the gospel in all its diversity and fullness. This means that we must be prepared to contribute our view of the gospel to the emerging consensus of the whole church, and, in the process, work zealously to join together what we have separated in our doctrine and practice.

This is definitely a theological task. We are struggling here with the fullness of the gospel, with its cosmic meaning, with the meaning of the fourfold "all" in the Great Commission and of the "world" in John 3:16 and 2 Corinthians 5:19, and with the meaning of "in heaven and on earth and under the earth" in Philippians 2:10 (to name only a few of the texts that challenge us with the universal scope of the gospel). If we, as the church, are to attain to the unity of the faith, then we will have to work hard in our theology to draw together "one body and one Spirit, . . . one hope . . . , one Lord, one faith, one baptism, one God and Father of us all . . . " (Eph. 4:4ff.).

It will take a combination of great modesty and great vision to do a theology of the church that accords with the vast dimensions of the gospel. It will require from the outset the humble awareness that our theologies all tend to divide and conquer, and that it is our calling to move beyond our theological boundaries and categories in order to discover more of the fullness of the gospel.

For "divide and conquer" is certainly the watchword of our theological systems as they limit our vision of the gospel. In today's world, the sheer size of the world of knowledge, theological and otherwise, compels us to reduce our expectations over against the challenge to do a theology that unifies us. One can no longer be an expert in all of the themes and subdivisions of theology. There is no longer a "body of knowledge" that any scholar can be said to have mastered. We all are confronted with our individual limitations, and our response is often to divide the gospel into sections and then concentrate on one part of it, as something we can cope with. Thus we lose sight of the goal that we should contribute to the unity of the faith.

In the early church, the struggle to understand the nature of Christ as perfect man and Son of God dominated theological development, and other significant parts of the gospel were neglected. The Reformation focused upon justification by faith through grace alone, correcting the works righteousness of medieval theology. But at times that emphasis lost sight of the reality of Christian witness in the world, and underemphasized the significance of Christian ethics. The orthodoxy of the next Reformation period stressed correct dogmatic systems and propositional clarity, but lost the experiential excitement of the faith, both individually and corporately. Pietism turned away from the orthodox concern for correct doctrine and upheld the centrality of Christian experience, and lost its moorings in the process.

In the contemporary world, the evangelical movements often react to the excesses in liberal and more critical theologies with an anti-intellectualism and a reduction of the gospel to the personal and private, which becomes as problematic as that which they are criticizing. On the other side of the spectrum, liberation theologies raise valid and urgent concerns about the bondage of Christian thought to outmoded and irrelevant Western thought systems, and challenge us with their insistence that the gospel speaks centrally to the issues of oppression, injustice, and poverty, yet they appear at times to "sell out" to thought systems that are at their roots in opposition to the gospel.

Our theological movement tends to be like a pendulum, swinging from one side to another. And the extremes at both sides are narrow understandings of the gospel, bent on separating the unseparable, not the broad and comprehensive middle road that draws all of these important emphases together into a consensus on the whole gospel. Such consensus would be marked by a fundamental accord as well as by a diversity of method and expression that the whole church experiences as enriching. Understandable as this pendulumlike tendency is, we must learn in our theological work to view what we do as a part of a much larger whole. We must view our particular work as a contribution to the understanding of a much bigger gospel. We must be very careful that we are not, again, taming and domesticating the gospel by reducing it to the manageable limits of a particular theological approach or system, or a particular cultural, social, or political interest.

The church, we said, has always separated what was inseparable in the gospel. This is a humanly understandable reaction to the revolutionary meaning of salvation as brought about by Christ: restoration to wholeness, new creation, ultimate victory over all the divisive results of our sin. This Good News is also threatening news to sinful humanity, calling forth resistance as well as acceptance. Where sin has divided every dimension of existence, the gospel heals and draws together, which means that it "turns the world upside down," rearranges fundamentally the orders of existence and the values by which we live. We can only respond to the gospel as we are prepared to confront the fact that we are sinners. We begin our pilgrimage of faith as believers who are now walking in a new direction, but who still must contend with the dividedness of our sin, which we bring with us as the "conformity to the world" out of which we come to Christ.

We keep trying, then, to fit the gospel into these old and sinful divisions, reducing it to our fragmented reality, seeking to blunt its prophetic edge and cushion its revolutionary impact. But it is the power and force of the gospel that it builds bridges over the chasms of division in our reality and draws together what we could not rejoin. Thus, the gospel of Christ, who is the Prince of Peace, creates a peace that is solely of divine origin but can and will transform our human existence, even this side of the completion of the work of salvation and the "day of the Lord." To have a vision of the church that is characterized by less than that kind of unity is to have too small a vision and to compromise with the little faith that does not really expect God to complete what he has begun.

Thus, on one hand I am appealing to the theological guild consciously to turn its diverse efforts to the goal of the unity of our faith, which means to do the hard and often detailed work of theology with a view toward our common growth to unity. The theological guild must help the entire church by showing how the great and overarching themes of Scripture draw together the various emphases of our faith, which we so easily deal with in isolation from each other. Scholarship must make us uneasy about our too facile concessions to the sinfully narrow views that we develop of the gospel, to keep that Good News from having its revolutionary impact upon our lives and world. Our separations of the inseparable are not easy to overcome—yet we should not be complacent about them, but rather be "eager to maintain the unity of the Spirit in the bond of peace" (Eph. 4:3).

On the other hand, I am appealing to the churches to work consciously and humbly toward this same unity. Here, much prayer and fasting will be needed. Our reductions of and separations within the gospel are deeply entrenched in our various traditions, and we now feel a great deal of pressure to defend them. The power of God's Spirit will have to work in us and through us to enable us to move beyond our self-imposed walls of separation, to each other, as well as to rejoin within our ministries what we have long separated for the sake of convenience and comfort. We must recognize that the various versions of the gospel that we proclaim are only partial, are all filtered by our "ecclesiastical defense mechanisms" so that we can live and work comfortably with them. Like the church in Acts struggling with the fact that the gospel was intended for the Gentiles as well as the Jews, we continue to resist the powerful thrust of the gospel toward drawing all things together in Christ.

This entire book has been about our separating the inseparable. I have been calling for a vision and practice of ministry that is congruent, that coheres, that reflects the fullness of the gospel and claims the powers granted to the church through the Holy Spirit since Pentecost. I have not been so arrogant as to assert that my particular version of the gospel is, in fact, that broad and comprehensive consensus to which all should come. The gospel is still before us, but I firmly believe that we will discover more of what it is and what it demands of us if we will turn our energy to overcoming the present separations of the inseparable. Therefore, as a concluding summary, I would like to survey these separations again, very briefly, as a final appeal for intentional work within the church toward their restoration to wholeness, so that we might attain to the unity of the faith.

12.2 THE INSEPARABLE IN OUR CONCEPT OF SALVATION

If salvation is in fact wholeness, healing, the work of God reconciling his creation to himself and thus to itself, then we must examine and correct all of our theological definitions of salvation in terms of that wholeness. Here, unallowable separations are rampant. We must work to overcome the unbiblical separations between the past, present, and future tenses of salvation. In addition, while theological distinctions among justification, sanctification, and glorification may be helpful for the purposes of theological analysis, they separate the inseparable when our theology does not draw them together around the central biblical theme of the faithfulness of God and the certainty that he will complete the work he has begun.

If we choose to neglect the open-endedness of God's work of salvation, we willfully ignore authoritative scriptural teaching. Thus, when we do theologies of salvation that draw lines between the saved and the unsaved, that sort out the elect and rejected, and in effect do God's judging for him, we separate the future tense out of our gospel. For there is still a "day of the Lord" coming, and it is still in the future that we obtain "the outcome of our faith, the salvation of our souls" (1 Pet. 1:9).

Of course, Christ, in his person and work, has done all that is necessary for our salvation. We cannot violate the closing admonition of the Bible: "I warn every one who hears the words of the prophecy of this book: if any one adds to them, God will add to him the plagues described in this book, and if any one takes away from the words of the book of this prophecy, God will take away his share in the tree of life and in the holy city, which are described in this book" (Rev. 22:18-19). But that admonition is surrounded by the prayer, "Come, Lord Jesus!" There is a difference between working for the wholeness of what is already in the gospel, and inventing a gospel that purports to go beyond Christ. Our call is to rejoin what we have separated, sometimes in order to understand our salvation better, and often to make our gospel more palatable in our various cultural settings, or even to our own sinful minds.

We have divided and subdivided grace in our theologies so that the graciousness of God becomes a limited characteristic of the divine. The effect has often been to set the mercy of God at odds with the justice of God. That separation was overcome on the cross of Christ, but we have often not managed to uphold that unity in our theologies. Thus, as Eberhard Jüngel has pointed out, we have done our theology of God the Father in virtually total isolation from the fact that he did, in fact, become flesh in his Son, who did in fact die for us. Our doctrines of Christ and of salvation have tended to be worked out on one page of our dogmatic textbooks, and our doctrine of God, with his grace, mercy, and justice, on another page. And we seldom relate them to each other.

The gospel of reconciliation is particularly difficult for our theologies and our churches in their various cultural settings. The reconciled wholeness that is God's intent flies in the face of our sinful insistence that our racial differences, our ethnic distinctives, and our historical traditions are to be upheld as more important and more powerful than the peace-making power of God in Christ. Thus, we bless wars and justify racial and historical divisions in the church. These are separations of the inseparable that can only call forth the cry of the biblical prophet to the church: "Repent!" For we need to approach God as penitents and to be healed of our sinful divisiveness, which has led us again and again to obstruct the healing work of the gospel.

Thus, our greatest priority, particularly in our theologies of salvation, should be to rejoin the benefits of salvation with the responsibilities and call to the saved to enter into God's mission in the world.

We have emphasized that salvation is the definition of God's intent for all of his creation, and that we are to understand the whole sweep of salvation history from that intention, as its beginning and its ultimate ending. God called Israel to receive the blessing of salvation in order to be the agent of that salvation within the world. When the people diluted that election to service into election as a special privilege of the nation, then they obstructed God's purposes. But that is the tendency over and over again in our history: to reduce God's call and action to our personal salvation, and to set aside the call to serve him. We become salvation egotists and gospel individualists. We are concerned about our own salvation, and about who is saved and who is not.

The church, to look ahead to the next section, becomes primarily an institution that conveys and administers salvation. But the Bible makes it plain that salvation is God's business, and our calling is to witness and to obedient service. That is our mission: to be used by God for the accomplishment of his salvation purposes.

Certainly this separation is the most widespread dilution of the biblical gospel in our churches, and therefore overcoming it will be most difficult. But it is the unavoidable demand of the gospel of Jesus Christ that we understand that we are saved in order to serve, blessed in order to be a blessing. We must leave behind all of our refined and sophisticated forms of "cheap grace," and proclaim the whole gospel, and more: we must do that whole gospel. This will require us to review constantly our concept of salvation from the perspective of biblical teaching, both Old and New Testaments, so that we can see our self-imposed reductions and correct them. As we do so, we will find ourselves better equipped to address the separations of the inseparable within our theology of the church and the practice of its ministry.

12.3 THE INSEPARABLE IN OUR CONCEPT OF THE CHURCH

Our struggle to overcome the separation between the benefits and the mission of the gospel prepares us to deal with the separations of the inseparable within the church. This has been the major thrust of this book. We have been concerned about the separation of the message of the gospel from the messenger. We need to grasp that the witness to which we are called is an all-encompassing definition of Christian existence. That witness is something that we are, then that we do, and, finally, that we say. The only way in which the gospel can be made known in the world is through its ambassadors, those sent out by Christ to make it known. The mission given to that apostolic community defines our reason for being as well as our way of being.

We have then seen that it is necessary to rejoin the inward and outward dimensions of the church in order to carry out our mission. We must see that it is our call to serve God in the world that constitutes our priority, and that thus our inward life should serve us for that calling by equipping us, by drawing on all the resources of the means of grace so that we can effectively be incarnational witnesses in the world. False separations of the church from the world render us ineffective, and are usually the result of an erroneous concentration upon our salvation and its maintenance while ignoring the reason that we are saved.

When we grasp this fact, we must then rejoin further separations, especially the wrong distinctions between clergy and laity. We will look upon our general call to ministry, to the service of God as witnesses to Christ, as the common ground of all ministry. Upon that basis we then learn to make the proper functional distinctions, accepting the wonderful fact that God does provide the people and the resources so that we can obediently carry out our calling. Among those he provides are the specialized ministers whose task it is to equip the saints for the work of ministry. Rather than being separated, we are then joined in our mutual dependence, our organic bonds that enable the entire community to carry out its mission.

In the practice of ministry, we will recognize that there must be congruence between what we are, what we do, and what we say. We will become conscious of the wrong separation of the gospel into word and deed, distinct from each other. We will recognize the danger of allowing the gospel to become a disembodied word that is not supported by the reality of its power in the community that proclaims it. We will work on our ethics as an essential and potent form of witness in the world. We will learn to say what we have earned the right to say in the world. We will learn to risk a life as community that conveys the truth of the gospel, out of which our evangelization will emerge. We will be candid about our failings as the church of Christ, and we will not claim more for ourselves than we can, knowing that our salvation is the gracious work of God and not the result of our meritorious actions.

In our education for ministry, we will work to overcome the false distinctions between clergy and laity as well. The people of God will come to understand themselves not as consumers of religious services, but as partners in ministry, whose function and place in the work of God cannot be occupied by the clergy, and who therefore are absolutely essential where they are, carrying Christ into all the world. The professional image of the specialized minister will move from that of a member of a separate spiritual caste to that of a servant of the servants of God. That minister will come to see herself or himself as a genuine authority, as one through whom God increases the spiritual preparedness of the people of God for their common ministry.

Thus, we will join together the various expressions of Christian ministry in community, which are so often distinctive and unrelated to each other. We will experience and proclaim the sacraments as equipping means of grace. We will understand the music and discipline of worship as the supreme form of preparation for the work of ministry outside the walls of the church. Preaching will become the powerful Word of God equipping, challenging, correcting, and commissioning the people for their incarnational witness in the world.

And as the church begins to attain the unity of the faith, it will discover that the world will respond with wonder, with curiosity, and with rejection. We will begin to read the prison Epistles, 1 and 2 Peter, Jude, and the Book of Revelation in their true relevance to the church in the world. For we are to expect the world to react with hostility to the gospel of grace, when it is witnessed to in all its fullness, with the power of the Holy Spirit. We need not seek that resistance. In true obedience to Christ, which will result in the risk of becoming incarnational community and doing incarnational witness, we can expect it to happen. But we know that, in Christ, we are liberated from fear, and that we can continue in obedience, even when it results in suffering. For his faithfulness will prove itself conclusively, precisely in that moment of testing.

We can and we must become a church of sowers, who are willing to sow that seed everywhere, in every kind of soil. Our task is clearly defined for us in the parables of the kingdom in Matthew 13 (and parallels). We are to sow liberally, constantly, obediently. We are not to be surprised at the various kinds of growth and lack of growth we experience. Our Lord prepared us for that reality. Our task is to make sure that we are sowing the right seed, all of the Word, the entire message of the kingdom. As we do so, we discover more about the seed we are sowing. And we find ourselves also becoming a part of the soil, in which the sown seed grows. But we find that the soil varies even within the church. And in another parable, Jesus tells us that there will be weedy growth in the church, which looks so much like good wheat that it cannot be separated out without endangering the entire harvest. And yet, even when we face those kinds of disillusionments in the church, we continue to sow. Obedient sowing is our task: "You shall be my witnesses."

But the harvest that God will bring about will overwhelm us. It will be far greater than our sowing would ever merit. The size of God's harvest is ultimately not dependent upon our sowing, but upon his grace. He can transform our frail and often stumbling ministry, our inadequate witness, into a harvest of faith that is attributable only to his grace. It is in that confidence that we are witnesses, called and equipped by God to be his instruments in a pilgrimage of service, discovering more of the gospel before us as we follow Christ. We look forward to God's completion of the work he has begun, and we set our "hope fully upon the grace that is coming to [us] at the revelation of Jesus Christ" (1 Pet. 1:13).

BIBLIOGRAPHY

The following list of books makes no pretense to being a comprehensive bibliography for my subject. Rather, this is a list of the books that have most influenced me in my study of the church's mission and in the preparation of this book.

Barth, Markus. *Ephesians.* The Anchor Bible. 2 vols. Garden City, NY: Doubleday, 1974.

Blauw, Johannes. *The Missionary Nature of the Church: A Survey of the Biblical Theology of Mission.* New York: McGraw-Hill, 1962.

Cullmann, Oscar. *Christ and Time: The Primitive Christian Conception of Time and History.* Translated by F. Filson. Philadelphia: Westminster, 1950.

Dulles, Avery, S.J. *Models of the Church.* Garden City, NY: Doubleday, Image Books, 1978.

——. *The Resilient Church: The Necessity and Limits of Adaptation.* Garden City, NY: Doubleday, 1977.

Forsyth, P. T. *The Church and the Sacraments.* London: Independent Press, 1964.

Glen, J. Stanley. *Recovery of the Teaching Ministry.* Philadelphia: Westminster Press, 1960.

Glenn, C. Leslie. *A Scornful Wonder: What's Right with the Church.* New York: David McKay, 1977.

Griffin, Emory. *The Mind Changers: The Art of Christian Persuasion.* Wheaton: Tyndale, 1976.

Küng, Hans. *The Church.* London: Search Press, 1973.

Ladd, George Eldon. *The Presence of the Future: The Eschatology of Biblical Realism.* Grand Rapids: Wm. B. Eerdmans, 1974.

Mackay, John A. *Ecumenics: The Science of the Church Universal.* Englewood Cliffs, NJ: Prentice-Hall, 1964.

Newbigin, Lesslie. *The Open Secret: Sketches for a Missionary Theology.* Grand Rapids: Wm. B. Eerdmans, 1978.

——. *Sign of the Kingdom.* Grand Rapids: Wm. B. Eerdmans, 1980.

Paul, Robert S. *The Church in Search of Itself.* Grand Rapids: Wm. B. Eerdmans, 1972.

——. *Ministry.* Grand Rapids: Wm. B. Eerdmans, 1965.

Schillebeeckx, Edward. *Ministry: Leadership in the Community of Jesus Christ.* New York: Crossroad, 1981.

Selwyn, E. G. *The First Epistle of St. Peter.* London: Macmillan & Co., 1958.

Snyder, Howard A. *The Community of the King.* Downers Grove, IL: Inter-Varsity Press, 1977.

——. *The Problem of Wineskins: Church Structure in a Technological Age.* Downers Grove, IL: InterVarsity Press, 1975.

Weber, Otto. *Foundations of Dogmatics.* Translated by Darrell L. Guder. 2 vols. Grand Rapids: Wm. B. Eerdmans, 1981-83.

7233

DATE DUE

DEC 2 '87			